DISCRIMINATION AS STIGMA

This book reconceptualises discrimination law as fundamentally concerned with stigma. Using sociological and socio-psychological theories of stigma, the author presents an 'antistigma principle', promoting it as a method to determine the scope of legal protection from discrimination. The anti-stigma principle recognises the role of institutional and individual action in the perpetuation of discrimination. Setting discrimination law within the field of public health, it frames positive action and intersectional discrimination as the norm in this field of law rather than the exception. In developing and applying this new theory for antidiscrimination law, the book draws upon case law from jurisdictions including the UK, Australia, New Zealand, the USA and Canada, as well as European law.

Discrimination as Stigma

A Theory of Anti-discrimination Law

Iyiola Solanke

•HART•
OXFORD • LONDON • NEW YORK • NEW DELHI • SYDNEY

HART PUBLISHING
Bloomsbury Publishing Plc
Kemp House, Chawley Park, Cumnor Hill, Oxford, OX2 9PH, UK

HART PUBLISHING, the Hart/Stag logo, BLOOMSBURY and the Diana logo are trademarks of Bloomsbury Publishing Plc

First published in hardback, 2017
Paperback edition, 2019

A catalogue record for this book is available from the British Library.

Library of Congress Cataloging-in-Publication Data

Names: Solanke, Iyiola, author.

Title: Discrimination as stigma : a theory of anti-discrimination law / Iyiola Solanke.

Description: Oxford ; Portland, Oregon : Hart Publishing, an imprint of Bloomsbury Publishing Plc, 2017. | Includes bibliographical references and index.

Identifiers: LCCN 2016037919 (print) | LCCN 2016038126 (ebook) | ISBN 9781849467384 (hardback) | ISBN 9781782256380 (Epub)

Subjects: LCSH: Discrimination—Law and legislation—Social aspects. | Equality. | Stigma (Social psychology) | Discrimination—Law and legislation—Great Britain. | Discrimination—Law and legislation—United States.

Classification: LCC K3242 .S657 2017 (print) | LCC K3242 (ebook) | DDC 342.08/701—dc23

LC record available at https://lccn.loc.gov/2016037919

ISBN: HB: 978-1-84946-738-4
PB: 978-1-50992-982-5
ePDF: 978-1-78225-637-3
ePub: 978-1-78225-638-0

Typeset by Compuscript Ltd, Shannon

PREFACE

On 8 November 2016, just before this book went to press, Donald Trump, a billionaire businessman with no experience of public office at any level, was elected 45th President of the United States of America. During his campaign, he was heard boasting about sexual harassment of women, promised to ban all Muslims from entering the USA and described Mexican immigrants as drug dealers and rapists. His victory despite overt sexism and racism confirms that there remain deep, dark wells of social hatred and hostility towards women and minority groups; and not only in the USA but—as made clear by the UK Referendum on 'Brexit'—also in the UK. It is almost as if the last 50 years of anti-discrimination law did not happen; and there is good reason to expect rapid reversal of the progress that has been made. The need for effective legal protection from and prevention of discrimination remains. Yet how to secure this? The aim of this book is to contribute to this important task.

Like most monographs, it progressed through workshops, conferences and seminars before becoming a book proposal—in many ways it is the culmination of a line of enquiry that began in 2007 at University of Michigan School of Law, where I was a Jean Monnet Fellow working on EU law. During my time there, engagement with the issue of intersectional discrimination and the search for its legal form brought me to question the role of immutability in anti-discrimination law and to wonder about the relationship between stigma and discrimination. Some of these musings have already been published and the theory set out in the current book is therefore a continuation of this previous work.

There are many to thank for the privilege of being able to commit time to write a theory of anti-discrimination law. I am indebted to numerous people for helping me to access the necessary resources. These include Nicola Lacey, Rosa Greaves, colleagues at Wake Forest School of Law and those at the School of Law in the University of Leeds—especially Clive Walker, Louise Ellison, Julie Wallbank, Shirley Tate and Ian Law. Thanks in particular to Colleen Sheppard, Catherine Barnard and Belinda Smith, I was able to spend many productive hours working in the world-class libraries at the University of McGill, the University of Cambridge and the University of Sydney, reading and talking about stigma, human rights and anti-discrimination law. It was in the McGill Law School library that I first encountered the diaries of John Humphries. A special mention must also go to members of the Interdisciplinary Research Network on Discrimination and Inclusion at the McGill Centre for Human Rights and Legal Pluralism for taking an interest in this work. The generous support of these institutions—especially the Parsons Fellowship at the University of Sydney—is gratefully acknowledged.

I would also like to take this opportunity to thank the team at Hart Publishing—Commissioning Editor Bill Asquith for seeing the potential in the book proposal; Production Editors Alan Worth, John Hort and Anne Flegel; as well as Emma Platt and Annie Mirza—I am indebted to you all for your patience, assistance and guidance.

Emotional support is an equally essential resource for the completion of academic work. Such an ambitious project would not have been possible without the fellowship, friendship and ongoing encouragement of many people. Heartfelt appreciation goes to those who spurred me on when I needed it most, including Flo and Rudy Dixon, PJ and Blake Morant, Donovan and Lauren MacGrath.

Last but not least, I pay tribute to my adventurous parents, my inspirational siblings and the coming generation—Tobias, Kamikun, Asher and Rere: I dedicate this book to you.

Iyiola Solanke

CONTENTS

TABLE OF CASES

Australia

Canada

European Court of Human Rights

European Union

India

Ireland

New Zealand

South Africa

Sweden

United Kingdom

United States

TABLE OF LEGISLATION

Australia

Canada

Croatia

Czech Republic

European Union

Hungary

International

Ireland

New Zealand

Russia

South Africa

United Kingdom

United States

Introduction

This book is about the use of anti-discrimination law to pursue equality. The focus is on discrimination because, as explained by Sayce, 'discrimination' highlights the 'producers of rejection and exclusion—those who do the discriminating'[1] rather than those who are the recipients of such rejection behaviours. In this book, I suggest that the producers of discrimination are not only individuals acting alone but also society as a whole. To speak of discrimination is therefore to focus on the individuals and society as collectively responsible for the problem and to identify specific prescriptions for action.

Anti-discrimination law has a dual mandate: it protects and prevents. However, what determines when individuals or groups with a particular trait, attribute or condition will be protected by anti-discrimination law, or when law will prevent persons without that trait, attribute or condition from discriminating against those possessing it? This is the question that is at the heart of this book. It focuses on the question of when law should be used to remedy discrimination: when should a distinction be unlawful discrimination? Not all distinctions are unlawful discrimination, so how should this be determined? What logic should guide legislators as they make anti-discrimination law?

In 1976—the year of the second Race Relations Act and the first Sex Discrimination Act in Britain—Brest described the anti-discrimination principle as 'the general principle disfavouring classifications and other decisions and practices that depend upon the race (or ethnic origin) of the parties affected'.[2] The anti-discrimination principle is not limited to race—it also applies to a range of other attributes which may or may not be biological. In most jurisdictions where it is recognised, it applies at a minimum to age, disability, political belief, religion, gender and sexual orientation but it can also encompass genetic make-up[3] and even publication of enforcement details regarding fines.[4]

Post describes this principle as the 'simple but powerful logic' that informs American anti-discrimination law and 'underwrites the important trope of "blindness" that dominates antidiscrimination law'. Blindness, he writes, 'renders

[1] L Sayce, 'Stigma, Discrimination and Social Exclusion: What's in a Word' (1998) 7 *Journal of Mental Health* 4, 331.

[2] P Brest, 'In Defense of the Anti-Discrimination Principle' (1976) 90 *Harvard Law Review* 1, 1.

[3] Title II of the Genetic Information Nondiscrimination Act (GINA) was introduced in the USA in 2008. It applies to the sphere of employment only.

[4] The Equal Opportunity Act 1984 (WA) Part IVC prohibits 'discrimination on ground of publication of relevant details of persons on Fines Enforcement Registrar's website'.

forbidden characteristics invisible; it requires employers to base their judgements instead upon the deeper and more fundamental ground of "individual merit" or "intrinsic worth"'. Thus the logic behind American anti-discrimination law 'requires employers to regard their employees as though they did not display socially powerful and salient attributes, because these attributes may induce irrational and prejudiced judgments. Each time the law adds another proscribed category of discrimination, it renders yet another attribute of employees invisible to their employers'.[5]

The anti-discrimination principle is traditionally activated via categories, which are used to mark the boundaries of who is guaranteed protection by law and in which circumstances. These categories have different names—they are called 'protected characteristics' in British anti-discrimination law,[6] 'grounds' in Canadian and Australian legislation and 'suspect classifications' in American equality jurisprudence. Once protected by law, a characteristic, ground or classification may not form the basis of any disadvantageous decision by a public or private decision-maker across a range of fields of activity. Where this is found, it constitutes direct discrimination, which in most jurisdictions can never be justified unless the distinction is protected because it is genuinely essential to the job or role[7] concerned or is related to age.[8] In most cases, only indirect discrimination may be justified by a non-discriminatory reason. Indirect discrimination, or 'disparate impact' arises where a 'general policy or measure that has a disproportionately prejudicial effects on a particular group may be considered discriminatory notwithstanding that it is not specifically aimed at that group'.[9]

Decision-makers can choose to include additional categories that are not set out in the legal instruments—for example, in the recent consultation on university-level teaching, the Secretary of State included 'lower income groups' in the scope of the impact assessment under the public sector equality duty.[10] In *EAD*, it was decided that anti-discrimination law protects legal as well as natural persons.[11] However in *Tirkey*[12] it was confirmed that although 'caste' is an autonomous concept, it is not a specific protected characteristic under the Equality Act 2010. This does not mean that the Equality Act provides no remedy for caste discrimination as some of the factors relevant to caste may fall within

[5] R Post, 'Brennan Center Symposium Lecture: Prejudicial Appearances: The Logic of American Antidiscrimination Law' (2000) 88 *Calif Law Rev* 1, 11.

[6] Section 4 of Equality Act 2010 lists nine protected characteristics—Race, Sex, Disability, Age, Sexual Orientation, Religion or Belief, Gender Reassignment, Marriage and Civil Partnership, Pregnancy and Maternity.

[7] The 'genuine' or 'bona fide' occupational requirement is a common feature in anti-discrimination law.

[8] See EU Equal Treatment (Employment) Directive 2000/78, Art 6.

[9] *DH v Czech Republic* (2008) 47 EHRR 3 [175].

[10] Section 159 of the Equality Act 2010 sets out the 'Public Sector Equality Duty' (PSED) which applies to all protected characteristics. See Secretary of State for Business, Communities and Skills, 'Fulfilling Our Potential: Teaching Excellence, Social Mobility and Student Choice', November 2015, para 39.

[11] *EAD Solicitors LLP & Ors v Abrams* [2015] UKEAT 0054_15_0506.

[12] *Chandok v Tirkey* [2014] UKEAT 1090_14_1912.

'ethnic origins' in s 9(1)(c) of the Act. 'Ethnic origins' has a broad and flexible ambit, including characteristics determined by 'descent'.

Attention regularly focuses on the interpretation of these categories: who is included, who is excluded, and in relation to which activities and forms of behaviour? However, there is a more fundamental question to be answered: how do we decide which categories are to be regarded as—to use the American term—'suspect'? When should we worry about the use of personal attributes, characteristics or conditions as ratio? And more to the point for this book, when should legal protection be introduced to prevent and protect against this?

This is an increasingly important question because the categories that enjoy this legal protection have expanded over time, albeit at a different pace in different places. The selection of categories is usually a reflection of a context-specific collective recognition that individuals with the trait form a group that has a legitimate need for legal protection. This recognition is often preceded by various forms of social action such as lobbying.[13] What has become increasingly blurred is the explanation of why anti-discrimination law may provide that protection to individuals with trait A (for example, a religious belief) but not individuals with trait B (for example, obesity). Is it just a matter of the existence of a strong enough lobby with sufficient resources for campaigning? This is the question at the centre of this book. It asks 'When is discrimination wrong?'

This question is not posed in a moral[14] sense, in other words, it is not an enquiry into why some forms of discrimination are seen to be so bad that they require legal regulation. Hellman explains this moral question thus:

> A sign that says 'men only' looks very different on a courtroom door than on a bathroom door … the problem with the courthouse prohibition is that it distinguishes between men and women in a way that *demeans* women whereas the bathroom prohibition does not.

It is the infringement of dignity that makes this form of discrimination wrong. In this book, the question takes on a more sociological hue so as to generate consideration of which targets of demeaning or disadvantageous treatment should be protected using anti-discrimination law in particular. Any person or group of people can suffer damage and distortion if the people or society around them show them a demeaning or contemptible picture of themselves.[15] Why then does anti-discrimination law only protect some groups of people and not others? This is not just a question of the content of our categories, but the logic that informs that content.

The question also suggests that there is a singular logic that can explain why discrimination is wrong. The feasibility of a unified theory of discrimination law

[13] I Solanke, *Making Anti-Racial Discrimination Law* (Abingdon, Routledge, 2009).

[14] D Hellman and A Moreau (eds), *Philosophical Foundations of Discrimination Law* (Oxford, Oxford University Press, 2013).

[15] C Taylor, *Sources of the Self* (Cambridge, Massachusetts, Harvard University Press, 1989).

is keenly debated. Some authors, such as Shin[16] argue this is not possible. I agree with Khaitan[17] that it *is* possible, although our purposes differ. While he seeks to clarify the purpose of discrimination law, my goal is to clarify the mechanics of that law. Thus he argues that discrimination law is 'grounded not in the value of equality but autonomy—its purpose to provide people with a free choice between valuable options. It presents discrimination law as a distinctively liberal social programme.' I would argue that this brings us no closer to the practical question of whose free choice—the individual's or the group's—should benefit from legal protection offered by discrimination law.

This question also has relevance in the context of criminal law and hate crime. Hate crime laws provide additional protection for selected victim groups but how is it to be decided when this extra layer of protection will be available? Should it depend upon which group has the resources to campaign?[18] Should paedophiles benefit from it? Mason asks whether the 'targeted victimization of adults who sexually assault children should be recognized as a form of hate crime under the criminal law?'[19] Should therefore the murder of Bijan Ebrahimi[20]—killed because he was mistakenly identified as a paedophile by his neighbours—be treated as a hate crime as well as murder?

This book therefore seeks to offer a possible solution as to how we can identify those who should benefit by legal protection from discrimination. In so doing it challenges the rhetoric of 'blindness': is this really a 'timeless liberal virtue that inherently produces fairness and equality'?[21] Must society pretend that differences do not exist in order to prevent and protect its members from discrimination? Does blindness to difference ameliorate or perpetuate discrimination? To what extent does it help, for example, a disabled person if society is blind to the difficulties experienced as a result of that person's particular affliction or condition?

While blindness may have inspired the movements that campaigned for civil rights in the 1960s and 1970s, Harris and Lieberman observe that its 'meaning and valence have changed dramatically in recent decades, from liberal aspiration in the era of Jim Crow segregation to a conservative rhetorical device frequently mobilised to evade collective responsibility for the persistence of racial inequality and

[16] P Shin, 'Is There a Unitary Concept of Discrimination?' in Hellman and Moreau (eds), *Philosophical Foundations* (n 14).

[17] T Khaitan, *A Theory of Discrimination Law* (Oxford, Oxford University Press, 2015).

[18] For example, the fight for gay rights: see K Eleved, *Don't Tell Me to Wait: How the Fight for Gay Rights Changed America and Transformed Obama's Presidency* (Basic Books, 2015), which tells the story of the struggle for gay rights under Obama's presidency.

[19] G Mason, 'Victim Attributes In Hate Crime Law: Difference and the Politics of Justice' (2014) 54(2) *British Journal of Criminology* 161.

[20] S Morris, 'Police officers jailed over Bijan Ebrahimi murder case' (*The Guardian*, 9 February 2016).

[21] FC Harris and RC Lieberman (eds), *Beyond Discrimination: Racist Equality in a Postracist Era* (Russell Sage Foundation, 2013) 13.

to oppose policies such as affirmative action, designed to tackle racial inequality head on'.[22] It is unclear that it continues to play a progressive role in the ongoing struggle for equality. Arguably, it has, on the contrary, been 'appropriated by an antigovernment, premarket conservative culture that is at best indifferent (and at worst hostile) to demands for racial equality'[23] and results in the paradoxical sociological phenomenon of 'racism without racists'.[24]

In fact, it is accepted that in order to effectively tackle disability discrimination, it is sometimes necessary to see the disability and make adjustments to help the individual manage the resulting difficulties. There are different ways of 'seeing' disability: according to the 'medical model' of disability, disability is a 'personal tragedy' intrinsic to the individual—it is part of their body. The focus is therefore on 'fixing' or 'curing' the broken body and, where this is impossible, hiding the individual away from society in hospitals and institutions. The medical model therefore underpins institutionalisation of the disabled and their segregation from mainstream society. By contrast, the 'social model' of disability—created by disabled persons themselves to characterise their experiences of disability—sees disabled persons as victims of an uncaring society.[25] It locates the key problem in *structure*—social and institutional organisation—that actively *disables* individuals, rather than individual impairment. This can include external obstacles within the environment, for example the provision of stairs rather than a ramp to access a building or the use of small type text instead of braille to present information. Ignorance, stereotype and prejudice are also problems under the social model—obstacles to equality frequently reside in prevailing ideologies. Under this model the focus thus falls upon changes required in society and institutions to remove barriers that disable the individual. The purpose of their removal is to enable disabled people to live equal, independent and autonomous lives.[26]

Discrimination law can be inspired by the way of seeing which is used in the social model of disability. This social approach can replace the notion of blindness with a social vision wherein the characteristic is seen in its context. My premise is that anti-discrimination law should not aim to be blind, for to take this stance is to make the same mistake as the medical model—to see the problem as inherent in the individual. Blindness is not the solution because the individual attribute *per se* is not the problem. It is the social meaning given to the attribute that is the problem, thus it is this social meaning that should be the focus of anti-discrimination law. In other words, anti-discrimination law needs to tackle social stigma not individual sight. This is the vision of anti-discrimination law under the anti-stigma

[22] Harris and Lieberman, *Beyond Discrimination* (n 21) 13.
[23] Harris and Lieberman, *Beyond Discrimination* (n 21), 13–14.
[24] E Bonilla-Silva, *Racism without Racists: Color-blind Racism and the Persistence of Racial Inequality in the United States* (Maryland, Rowman and Littlefield Publishers, 2006).
[25] M Oliver, *The Politics of Disablement* (Basingstoke, Macmillan, 1990); M Fine and A Asch, 'Disability Beyond Stigma: Social Interaction, Discrimination, and Activism' (1998) 44(3) *Journal of Social Issues* 22.
[26] S Carr, *Personalisation: A Rough Guide* (London, SCIE, 2009).

principle developed in this book. If to destigmatise is to change society rather than individuals,[27] then the goal of anti-discrimination law under the anti-stigma principle is not only to protect and prevent individuals, but also to change society. From the perspective of the anti-stigma principle, blindness contributes to the continuation of discrimination because it leaves intact the social stigma that is the source of discrimination.

The anti-stigma principle begins from a similar place as the social approach promoted by Post[28] but moves in a different direction. In particular, it does not encourage a retreat from legal intervention in discrimination cases. I do agree with Post that anti-discrimination law should have a socially educative role and that it should focus on 'transforming' social practices. Like him, I also think that social norms are a major problem that anti-discrimination law should tackle, but so are the actions of individual people—it is both the behaviour of people and the social norms from which their behaviour is drawn that should be the target of law. Thus, under the anti-stigma principle, individual employers would be punished for behaving in ways that conform to prevailing social norms. For example where, as in *Jespersen*[29] an employer fires a woman who refuses to wear make-up, the problem is both the employer's decision and the social norm according to which women are expected to wear make-up. Anti-discrimination law under the anti-stigma principle would seek to change the way society thinks and acts as well as the way employers behave.

The anti-stigma principle moves anti-discrimination law away from its socio-biological basis. Like the 'vulnerabilities'[30] approach, it recognises that there are an increasing number of groups who experience risk in everyday society, many of whom—for example, young people leaving care or the homeless—are not protected by the legal frameworks that emerged from the era of civil rights and social movements. Unlike the vulnerabilities approach, however, it does not argue for a framework based on capabilities[31] or functioning.[32] The groups may be created

[27] R Harre, *Social Being: A Theory for Social Psychology* (Oxford, Basil Blackwell, 1979) 315.

[28] RC Post, *Prejudicial Appearances—The Logic of American Antidiscrimination Law* (Durham, Duke University Press, 2001) 22.

[29] *Jespersen v Harrah's Operating Company* 444 F.3d 1104, No 03-15045 (9th Cir. 2006) (en banc). For comment on this case see D Carbado, M Gulati and G Ramachandran, 'The Jespersen Story: Makeup and Women at Work' in JW Friedman (ed), *Employment Discrimination Stories* (Foundation Press, 2006) and in general CL Fisk, 'Privacy, Power, and Humiliation at Work: Re-Examining Appearance Regulation as an Invasion of Privacy' (2006) 66 *Louisiana Law Review* 44.

[30] M Fineman and A Grear, *Vulnerability: Reflections on a New Ethical Foundation for Law and Politics* (Ashgate Publishing, 2013).

[31] A Sen, 'Human Rights and Capabilities' (2005) 6(2) *Journal of Human Development* 151; M Nussbaum, *Creating Capabilities: The Human Development Approach* (Cambridge, Harvard University Press, 2011).

[32] Wolf and de Shalit define 'disadvantage' as a 'lack of genuine opportunities for secure functioning' (p 84) where there are six categories of functioning: life; bodily health; bodily integrity; affiliation (belonging); control over one's environment and sense; and imagination and thought (p 106). The least disadvantaged groups lack all or some of these. J Wolf and A de Shalit, *Disadvantage* (Oxford, Oxford University Press, 2007).

as a result of shared attributes, statuses or conditions. I propose the anti-stigma principle as a lens through which to determine in a systematic, robust and consistent manner where legal protection from discrimination is warranted and where it is not. As awareness of and respect for equality grows it becomes even more important to clarify to the general public why, for example, people with a religious belief are protected from discrimination but people with tattoos are not.

The anti-stigma principle is more than an anti-stereotyping approach as suggested by Morris and Timmer, although stereotypes are recognised as a mechanism of discrimination. Anti-stereotyping approaches can be seen in early cases of sex discrimination. Supreme Court Justice Ruth Bader Ginsburg used this route to challenge gender roles assigned to both men and women. Ginsburg argued that the 'state could not act in ways that reflected or reinforced traditional conceptions of men's and women's roles'.[33] Her approach was not to challenge stereotyping *per se* but to focus in particular on those practices and institutions that led to sex inequality. As Franklin notes, this limited application had little success. Morris proposed a broader role for the anti-stereotyping principle. She suggested it be used to deal with cases involving a mixture of protected and unprotected characteristics, such as gender and weight. She argued for a 'stereotypic transformation of a non-suspect'[34] characteristic when combined with a suspect characteristic so that it gains an 'honorary' protected status in anti-discrimination law. Timmer goes further still, suggesting that courts adopt an anti-stereotyping analysis that includes two phases: a 'naming' and 'contesting' of stereotypes.[35]

The anti-stigma principle proposed in this book goes beyond anti-stereotyping. It shares the targeted vision of Ruth Bader Ginsburg. It also incorporates both stereotypes and a procedural analysis, as suggested by Morris and Timmer. However unlike stereotyping, it explicitly identifies the role of power and its application involves more phases. The anti-stigma principle is also activated in the creation of categories of protection, not just the determination of discrimination. It proposes a process through which the state can recognise which stigmas should be within the scope of anti-discrimination law and which should not be. Finally, by drawing upon models of stigma it also offers a useful and novel connection between anti-discrimination law and public health: anti-discrimination law as public health offers a range of different actions to tackle discrimination including 'early intervention' as well as protection and prevention.

[33] See C Franklin, 'The Anti-Stereotyping Principle in Constitutional Sex Discrimination Law' (2010) 20 *New York University Law Review* 101, 106.

[34] M Morris, 'Stereotypic Alchemy: Transformative Stereotypes and Anti-Discrimination Law' (1989) 7 *Yale Law & Policy Review* 251.

[35] A Timmer, 'Toward an Anti-Stereotyping Approach for the European Court of Human Rights' (2011) 11(4) *Human Rights Law Review* 707.

I. Construction of the Anti-stigma Principle

Chapter 1 establishes the conceptual origins of the anti-stigma principle. The intellectual heritage of the anti-stigma principle lies in the work of classical and critical scholars of stigma, as well as scholars in public health. The most famous work on stigma was written by Erving Goffman in 1963.[36] His studies, however, should now perhaps be seen as a starting point for an understanding of stigma. The concept has since been used and developed by social psychologists, sociologists, criminologists, psychiatrists, medical scholars, management specialists, urban planners, development scholars and public health experts who, as explained below, have conducted a more critical analysis of stigma, linking it to social power.

Goffman belongs to a tradition of social psychology that centres upon the individual and her behaviour. His work is an example of cognitive social psychology that may recognise but pays scant analytical attention to the social relationships surrounding individuals; it can be described as 'micro-sociological'[37] and apolitical. In his work, cognition and conation[38]—behavioural intentions or reactions to stigmatised persons—are strictly 'face-to-face' phenomena. The key task of critical social psychology has been to redress this narrow focus by explicitly directing 'attention to the social and cultural contexts within which individuals find themselves'.[39]

Critical social psychology replaces the isolated individual with an individual connected to a social world, where the social is comprised of two levels: an *interpersonal* level of interactions and individual relationships as well as a *societal* level of broader social norms and practices. Both levels 'surround and penetrate the individual, impacting on personal identity and public practices'.[40] The two levels interact: the language that is used to communicate at an interpersonal level draws upon assumptions and 'common sense' provided by the surrounding culture. Critical social psychology emphasises that there is no escape from this: 'no individual is separate from social relations and systems of difference which serve to position people in various, often inequitable ways'.[41] Thus as Harre states: 'all our actions are carried out against a structured background'[42] where individuals as actors contribute to the construction of that background through their actions. The key factor determining the level of influence on both the interaction and the construction of that background is power.

[36] *Notes on a Spoiled Identity* (London, Penguin 1990 [1963]).

[37] Harre describes Goffman's work as 'micro-sociology'. Harre, *Social Being* (n 27), 124.

[38] J Gottlieb and BW Gottlieb, 'Stereotypic Attitudes and Behavioural Intentions Towards Handicapped Children' (1977) 82(1) *American Journal of Mental Deficiency* 65.

[39] B Gough and M McFadden, *Critical Social Psychology—An Introduction* (Basingstoke, Palgrave, 2001).

[40] Gough and McFadden, *Critical Social Psychology* (n 39) 11.

[41] Gough and McFadden, *Critical Social Psychology* (n 39), 13.

[42] Harre, *Social Being* (n 27) 192.

Power is a key theme in critical social psychology. There are different ways to depict power. Foucault depicts power as being manifested at numerous points and through a web-like matrix, with individuals at different points in a spectrum of exercising and undergoing power. In this formulation of power it is imaginable that some will be more regularly at the former and others most frequently at the latter end of the spectrum. Bachrach and Baratz identify two faces of power in relation to the exercise of power—the power to take action as well as the power to prevent something from happening.[43] Other scholars such as Gaventa have posited power as a three-dimensional cube with one dimension focusing on levels (global, national, local) a second on spaces (closed, invited, claimed) and the third on forms (visible, invisible, hidden).[44]

According to critical social psychology, power influences cognition. Loury uses the idea of 'social bias cognition' to highlight the interaction between social power, cognition and stigma. Under the theory of 'social bias cognition', cognition is an individual action but is not an independent process. Loury argues that cognition is set within a cultural and historical context where individuals undergo the process of learning the meanings of things in their context, just as in Nina Simone's song 'Turning Point' which is discussed in Chapter 1, a little girl learns the meaning of brown skin in her world from her mother. Cognition, according to his theory, is therefore informed by a subtle performance of social practices. He attributes the perpetuation of racial stigma and enduring racial inequality in the USA to socially biased cognition. He argues that in relation to racial stigma, cognition is automatically negatively biased. This negative cognitive response informs the conative response, or how we choose to behave with the stigmatised person: will we punish them by withholding access to resources? Will we associate with them, befriend them or avoid association with them?[45] More significantly, this negative cognitive response determines our willingness to use public resources to address racism and racial disparities.

Consideration of power is important to understand the role it plays in stigma. It is the social power behind stigma that differentiates it from stereotype and prejudice. A stereotype is a categorisation that can be either negative or positive; a prejudice is an endorsement of these categorical stereotypes. Thus although any individual can encounter stereotypes and prejudice—even, as has been reported, young, white British men[46]—this does not always result in the social opprobrium that is stigmatisation. They may suffer negative stereotypes but are neither tainted

[43] P Bachrach and MS Baratz 'Two Faces of Power' (1962) 56 *The American Political Science Review* 4, 947.

[44] J Gaventa, 'Finding the Spaces for Change: A Power Analysis' (2006) 37(6) *Institute of Development Studies Bulletin* 23.

[45] Gottlieb and Gotttlieb, 'Stereotypic Attitudes' (n 38).

[46] 'Young, white British men are the least popular group in the country, according to a poll that shows the public think that they drink too much, are lazy, promiscuous and rude.' R Bennett, 'Young, white British males really do have a bad name' *The Times* (17 December 2015), available at http://www.thetimes.co.uk/tto/news/uk/article4643023.ece.

for life nor subjected as a result to discrimination, that is, a 'behavioral response based on prejudice' that is likely to harm the members of that group.[47] Despite the data on educational attainment, young, white British men remain the most likely to go to university and to obtain the most important senior leadership positions in every branch of politics and sector of industry in this country. By contrast, young black British men remain over-represented in the criminal justice[48] and prison system, and the least likely of all demographic groups to go to university. This suggests that skin colour is inescapable unlike being Irish.[49]

Critical social psychology therefore embeds stigma in social relations and social context. From this perspective stigmatisation is characterised as a process that is contingent on access to social, economic and political power.[50] Stigma is the consequence of a continuum of disempowerment, that results in the experience of discrimination. It is this critical psychological understanding of stigma that underpins the anti-stigma principle.

The purpose of Chapter 2 is to provide an overview of current approaches in law to protection from discrimination. The chapter sketches a historical review of the development of the anti-discrimination principle in international law, beginning with the use of Aristotelian ideas in Ancient Greece. Aristotle's ideas on equality are frequently used as a starting point for understanding what this idea means. However, his morality has been described as 'a morality of the privileged, a morality … that requires the services of women and other Others to maintain its integrity'.[51] Indeed, his vision of equality was not at all inclusive: it was limited only to those who were equal as a functional necessity to secure political stability and the status quo. During the later period of the Enlightenment inequality took on two forms: natural and political. Only the latter was seen as the avoidable consequence of human behaviour to reserve power and privilege for the few at the expense of the many. Yet Enlightenment philosophers such as Rousseau offered few suggestions to address this. Later Romantics such as Herder and Hegel saw no need to address this—the natural distribution of talents was the source of uniqueness and individuality. Toleration of inequality was the price to be paid for individual brilliance.

Tolerance and celebration of 'natural' difference was arguably the basis for the pseudo-science of eugenics which imparted intellectual credence to racist systems such as slavery, colonialism, apartheid and national socialism. It was this thinking that had to be overcome using international norms. Chapter 2 discusses

[47] P Corrigan, FE Markowitz, A Watson, D Rowan and MA Kubiak, 'An Attribution Model of Public Discrimination towards Persons with Mental Illness' (2003) 44 *Journal of Health and Social Behavior* 162, 163.

[48] Home office figures for 2010 to 2015 show that black men were three times more likely to be tasered than white men. See 'Black people "three times more likely" to be Tasered', BBC News, 13 October 2015, available at http://www.bbc.co.uk/news/uk-34511532.

[49] N Ignatiev, *How the Irish Became White* (New York, Routledge, 1995).

[50] BG Link and JC Phelan, 'Conceptualizing Stigma' (2001) 27 *Annual Review of Sociology* 363.

[51] SL Hoagland, 'Engaged Moral Agency' (1999) 4 *Ethics and the Environment* 91, 93.

the development of the UN Declaration of Human Rights (UNDHR) and the International Convention on the Elimination of All Forms of Racial Discrimination (ICERD). Drawing upon material from the diaries of John Humphries,[52] the chapter identifies some of the religious and political tensions underlying the UNDHR in its ambitious goal of creating a 'new universal society'. The diaries also show the difficulties at the time in understanding the relationship between prejudice and discrimination.

Humphries, a professor of law at McGill University in Canada, became the Director of the Human Rights Division in the UN Commission of Human Rights tasked with preparation of the International Bill of Rights that would provide a new baseline for international morality. He negotiated every provision. History has proved him correct in his assessment of the importance of the UNDHR but wrong in relation to the ICERD: he foresaw that the political and moral function of the Declaration would be its most important function, but underestimated the value of the work of the Sub-Commission on Discrimination, which prepared the groundwork for the ICERD. As this chapter shows, the ICERD has also exerted significant moral and political authority in the legal entrenchment of the anti-discrimination principle. I provide examples of the different ways in which this has been done. Some countries, for example Britain, the USA and Australia, carefully iterate in closed lists every group that will enjoy legal protection, while others, including Canada and South Africa, provide examples and leave scope for other grounds to be included (open lists). The chapter ends with discussion of the concepts of dignity and immutability, and their use in international and national anti-discrimination law by way of preparation for consideration of stigma in Chapter 3.

Chapter 3 opens the exploration of the role of stigma in law. It has a very simple objective—to provide an overview of where this idea appears in litigation. It will be seen that stigma is used by judges, albeit in an ad hoc and general way, across a range of cases from criminal to family law. The idea has also appeared in discussion on cases concerning discrimination, for example, *Hoffman* in South Africa, *Law* in Canada and *CHEZ* in the European Union. This leads into the introduction in Chapter 4 of the anti-stigma principle, drawing upon the concept as developed by critical stigma scholars discussed in Chapter 1. Chapter 4 also presents different models of stigma created by psychologists and public health researchers. Elements are adopted from these models to create a multi-level dynanic anti-stigma principle that will guide the creation of categories and action in anti-discrimination law. In this chapter I also explain the scope and priorities of an anti-discrimination law informed by the anti-stigma principle. It will be seen that the anti-stigma principle can change the priorities in anti-discrimination law. First, it makes social action to tackle discrimination the norm rather than the exception; second, it embraces complexity rather than shunning it; and, finally, it opens discrimination law to additional protected characteristics that are not immutable.

[52] AJ Hobbins, *On the Edge of Greatness: The Diaries of John Humphrey, First Director of the United Nations Division of Human Rights* (Montreal, McGill University Libraries, 1996).

The key contribution of the anti-stigma principle is that it creates a new lens through which to view the current tools of anti-discrimination law. Highlighting social responsibility in anti-discrimination law throws up a different question. In relation to individual responsibility, the question asked is one of explanation ('Why did A do X?'); in relation to social responsibility, the relevant question is one of enablement ('Why could A do X?'). Attention does not therefore fall on the individual perpetrator alone but also on the context within which their action is set: Why could young girls in Rochdale be groomed by adult men? Why could 200 schoolgirls in Nigeria be kidnapped by Boko Haram? How were these young women ejected from the realm of the right to regard in the minds of their abusers and captors? Why could a disabled man be killed by his neighbours? Why can young black men be shot dead with impunity? What feeds such contempt in individual minds? Arguably, public stigma made these things possible thus there is social as well as individual responsibility.

Recognition of the social role in discrimination creates the potential for more socially focused remedies in anti-discrimination law, strengthening and even going beyond positive action and public sector equality duties. Thus stigma can modernise the vision of anti-discrimination law: it can improve what, how and who anti-discrimination law 'sees'. In terms of 'what', it includes the social as well as the individual level; in relation to 'how' it accomodates intersectional and single dimension discrimination and in respect of 'who' it broadens the personal scope to groups defined by, for example, weight. A model of 'ecological anti-discrimination law' can replace the prevailing single-dimension version. In the ecological version, the priority moves from individual attributes and behavioural deficits to social meanings and discourses, such as the stigma of obesity and the representation of fat in the media.[53] These specific contributions of the anti-stigma principle will be discussed in the final chapters of the book, which focus on the application of the anti-stigma principle.

II. Application of the Anti-stigma Principle

Chapter 5 takes up the first of these contributions. Pursuing the link with public health, it posits discrimination as a virus that can be tackled using public health tools. It is interesting to consider what becomes possible when discrimination is re-imagined as a public virus. I suggest that depicting discrimination as a virus, or non-communicable disease (NCD) has analytical and practical advantages. First, this requires consideration of how the discrimination virus is transmitted as well as how it looks, sounds and feels. Second, this creates an opportunity to apply methods used in the field of public health to tackle discrimination: if it is

[53] K Holland, RW Blood, SL Thomas and S Lewis 'Challenging Stereotypes and Legitimating Fat: An Analysis of Obese People's Views on News Media Reporting Guidelines and Promoting Body Diversity', 51 *Journal of Sociology* 431-45.

regarded as a virus, discrimination has to be addressed not only at the interpersonal and structural levels, but also at the public and individual level. Public action to combat discrimination is therefore as important as individual remedies.

Tackling discrimination as a virus also makes its eradication everybody's business. As with other NCD's, public action becomes a norm. Thinking of discrimination as an NCD draws attention to the role of the public in addressing this risk: public action, including but not limited to education, is required to stem its progress. Thus to think of discrimination as a virus highlights its effect on the environment, not only the impact of discrimination on the public but also the role of public action in containing its spread—public action can be both cause and cure. The discussion moves away from solely focusing on individual or institutional behavioural change and emphasises the role of social action in both perpetuation and resolution of discrimination.

As mentioned above, this approach is similar to the social model of disability which focuses on the characteristics of the environment that make everyday activities and interactions difficult for persons with physical or sensory limitations. The anti-stigma principle makes this social approach the norm for anti-discrimination law in general rather than disability discrimination alone. However, the anti-stigma principle adds the idea of power to the social model and identifies multiple levels for intervention.

Chapter 5 presents the argument that if the public level is the source of stigma then anti-discrimination law must acknowledge and address the role of the environment or context within which discriminatory behaviour occurs. With this acknowledgement comes acceptance that individual perpetrators take the cue for their behaviour from public norms and narratives—these act as a resource for discriminatory ideas and create a backdrop for face-to-face discriminatory behaviour. Arguably, persons who discriminate do so with some consciousness of a public norm that will sanction their behaviour unless—and sometimes even if—they are caught. Nadeem Saddique, a firearms officer who once guarded Tony Blair, wrote in his complaint about an inspector who had described him as a 'black c***' and 'just a P***', it is the environment that supports or excludes discriminatory behaviour. His words below make the point with poignant simplicity:

> I wonder why they feel so confident in the work environment to make such comments and display robust racism? One has to come to the conclusion that this is an environment where they feel so comfortable as no one challenges it and in most cases it is positively encouraged.[54]

[54] 'Firearms officer wins case against Cleveland police over racism' *The Guardian* (25 November 2015) available at https://www.theguardian.com/uk-news/2015/nov/25/nadeem-saddique-firearms-officer-cleveland-police-racism. Nadeem Saddique had joined the police force in 1991, just before the murder of Stephen Lawrence, and so should have been the beneficiary of the new spirit with the police under the Race Equality Duty. This was not so, and Cleveland Police continued to allow the type of sentiment and culture to flourish that contributed to the death of Lawrence. For example, Saddique told the tribunal that a firearms colleague displayed an English Defence League sticker on the holster of his weapon. The badge made reference to Muslims and a crusade, the tribunal found.

Silencing the social aspect of discrimination leads to responses that in effect tackle symptoms but overlook the key source of discrimination. The anti-stigma principle therefore does not ignore the social: it highlights social power and enables analysis of discrimination in the environment. In order to illustrate how discrimination can be tackled as an NCD, this chapter draws upon the experience of tackling a major medical epidemic such as ebola. For example, one of the key tasks in tackling a public health virus is identification of modes of transmission. I therefore consider the media as one of the key mechanisms for transmission of stigma at the social level.

Chapter 5 also considers the practical tools in the Equality Act 2010 that could be of use, such as the provisions for positive action and the public sector equality duty. I suggest that neither tool is rigorous enough: positive action is confusing and voluntary, while the public sector equality duty although obligatory imposes only a superficial duty. What is required is a tool that directly addresses 'common sense' and actively challenges individuals in particular and society as a whole on a regular basis to confront stigmas and take responsibility for them. I therefore suggest an alternative in the form of education and training at the workplace. This tool would be presented and promoted as integral to workplace health and well-being agendas, which would help it to avoid the controversy that sometimes arises in relation to positive action and the public sector equality duty.

From 'what' in Chapter 5, Chapter 6 discusses *how* anti-discrimination law 'sees'. Traditionally, this field of law has used a single dimension vision, seeing each attribute separately and forcing complainants to choose just one ground under which to bring their claim, for example either gender, race or religion.[55] The theory of intersectional discrimination, however, argues that there are times when such a choice is impossible due to the interaction of the attributes. As put by Scales-Trent, employers, landlords and institutions do not discriminate in neat categories.[56] If perpetrators do not pick grounds, why must victims? Intersectionality theory therefore promotes a disruption of the categories of anti-discrimination law to address its structural blindness. The aim thereby is to enable anti-discrimination law to more effectively tackle structural discrimination.

It is important to clarify what is meant by 'social structure'.[57] The social structure can be thought of as two-dimensional: the first dimension is the *relational*:– 'systemic relationships between individuals in their social roles', for example at work. The second dimension is the *institutional*: the formal and informal institutions and networks mediating those relationships.[58] From a structural perspective, discrimination is not the consequence of actions by any 'perceiver' but the result

[55] PK Chew, 'Freeing Racial Harassment from the Sexual Harassment Model' (2007) *University of Pittsburgh School of Law Working Paper Series*, No 54.

[56] J Scales-Trent, 'Black Women in the Constitution: Finding Our Place and Asserting Our Rights' (1989) 24 *Harvard Civil Rights-Civil Liberties Law Review* 16.

[57] J Lopez and J Scott, *Social Structure* (Buckingham, Open University Press, 2000).

[58] J Turner, 'American Individualism and Structural Injustice: Tocqueville, Gender, and Race' (2008) 40 *Polity* 197.

of accepted habits, rules, practices and procedures, such as the seniority system at General Motors within the context of 'Jim Crow'[59] that caused black women workers to be the 'last in and first out'.

As will be seen, the theory of intersectional discrimination has ambitious substantive goals that require more than can be achieved using current provisions for indirect and institutional discrimination. Although provisions on 'indirect' discrimination can be used to address structural discrimination, they are limited as, ultimately, indirect discrimination can be justified if the discrimination arises in pursuit of a legitimate aim and the means are seen to be proportionate. The chapter considers the challenges arising from the attempt to provide a legal remedy for direct intersectional discrimination. It discusses the various responses to intersectionality, for example the concern that the 'sex-plus' approach treated black women as a departure from a white norm, as if 'being a woman or being black were like icing on a cake' rather than an 'integrated, undifferentiated, complete whole' consciousness.[60] I suggest the anti-stigma principle avoids these problems by enabling anti-discrimination law to see differently.

Chapters 7 and 8 then consider who anti-discrimination law 'sees'. Chapter 7 discusses how the anti-stigma principle can enable anti-discrimination law to extend its scope of protection, without losing its sense of boundaries. Chapter 8 does the opposite, showing how the anti-stigma principle helps anti-discrimination law retain its boundaries. Chapter 7 focuses on 'fattism'. Discrimination against the overweight or obese is a growing problem. According to Roehling, 'weight discrimination in the American workplace is a widespread phenomenon that has a significant negative impact on the lives of untold individuals',[61] and being 'slightly overweight, extremely overweight, or obese are all generally viewed in various employment contexts as less desirable than being average or thin'.[62] Weight discrimination is evident at every phase of the employment cycle including career counselling, selection, placement, compensation, promotion, discipline and dismissal.[63] Researchers have also found that 'if hired, persons who are obese are often assigned to non-visible jobs, receive more disciplinary actions, have their performance evaluated more negatively and earn less when compared to non-obese employees'.[64]

There is some evidence that the social approach intrinsic in the anti-stigma principle is being recognised in strategies to tackle obesity. In recognition of the

[59] M Alexander, *The New Jim Crow: Mass Incarceration in the Age of Colorblindness* (New York, The New Press, 2010).

[60] R Austin, 'Sapphire Bound!' (1989) 3 *Wisconsin Law Review* 539.

[61] MV Roehling, 'Weight Discrimination in the Workplace: Ethical Issues and Analysis' (2002) 40 *Journal of Business Ethics* 177, 187.

[62] MP Bell, ME McLaughlin and JM Sequeira, 'Age, Disability and Obesity: Similarities, Differences and Common Threads' in MS Stockdale and FJ Crosby (eds), '*The Psychology and Management of Workplace Diversity* (Malden: Blackwell Publishing, 2003) 210.

[63] MV Roehling, 'Weight Discrimination in the Workplace' (n 61).

[64] Bell et al, 'Age, Disability and Obesity' (n 62).

obesogenic environment in which we live, the All Party Parliamentary Group on Obesity calls for an ecological approach to obesity to be taken. As suggested in Chapter 4, they recommend an approach applied at a population level, rather than at the individual level, to shift the emphasis away from current unsuccessful strategies that view obesity as a personal disorder requiring treatment. Their approach 'regards obesity as a normal response to an abnormal environment, rather than vice versa'.[65]

The anti-stigma principle would not be useful if it did not also provide a systematic method to determine what should not be brought within the scope of anti-discrimination law. Its effectiveness in this task is shown in Chapter 8, in the context of tattoos. A tattoo is a modern day form of voluntary branding, now linked with 'coming of age' and freedom of expression rather than deviant behaviour, such as criminal activities or violence. However, persons with tattoos are not protected from discrimination—discrimination in employment may help to explain why tattoo removal has increased 440% in the last 10 years.[66] Should such individuals be protected? If yes, why, and if not, why not? Tattooing has a lengthy and interesting cultural history and there are a wide variety of tattooing practices with different origins and objectives across cultures. There is also a diversity of opinion among people of all ages as to whether tattoos are a 'positive, negative or neutral' presence in the workplace. Opinion is often informed by the type and location of the workplace, its mode of business and clientele, and the individuals who work there. There is no single approach taken by an employer—some are tattoo friendly, others are 'tattoo phobic'—and in the absence of a clear policy it can depend upon the individual manager. The more traditional or conservative the workspace, the more negative the attitude to tattoos is likely to be. Should the state take a position on this, forcing all employers to be tattoo friendly? Chapter 8 illustrates how legislators would apply the anti-stigma principle to decide this.

The book concludes with some thoughts on how regulation of discrimination can be holistic even if legal protection from discrimination is not universal. The 'anti-stigma principle' is a way to create an equality law that is neither *per se* inclusive nor exclusive. The anti-stigma principle allows anti-discrimination law to adopt a more flexible approach, which would allow this law to protect more groups that currently stand outside the law. This is important because as Theran points out, it enables 'a much closer relationship between the law (especially legislators) and the social sciences, since, in many cases, what the law considers a "new" or as yet untouched problem has actually been the subject of research for many years'.[67]

[65] All-Party Parliamentary Group on Obesity, 'Carrot and Stick: The Behavioural and Psychological Aspects of Obesity Management' (Meeting 5 Report, 9 July 2003).

[66] 'Ink blots', The Economist (2 August 20140, available at http://www.economist.com/news/united-states/21610334-body-art-growing-more-popular-though-few-employers-are-keen-ink-blots.

[67] EE Theran, 'Free to Be Arbitrary and ... Capricious: Weight-Based Discrimination and the Logic of American Antidiscrimination Law' (2001) 11 *Cornell Journal of Law and Public Policy* 113.

1

Stigma

'Turning Point'[1] is a song recorded by the singer, composer and pianist Nina Simone, an African American woman born in Jim Crow America who trained as a classical pianist and had a long celebrated career as a composer and musician. She was also an outspoken civil rights advocate, writing music to accompany the freedom campaigns of the 1960s. This action marked her career with controversy and she did not achieve the full acclaim that her talent warranted.

She wrote a song called 'Turning Point' in 1967. The song, sung as if an innocent playground rhyme, is all about stigma. It tells the tragic story of how children are taught to differentiate, stigmatise and to segregate, if not at school then at home. The story-teller is a little white girl—let's call her Wendy. Wendy is happily telling her 'Mom' about the relationship developing between her and a girl new to the class, whom we can call Beatrice. Wendy has clearly taken to Beatrice and wants to be friends. Wendy has noted that Beatrice has 'brown' skin, describing her as looking 'just like chocolate', but this means nothing to her: there is no negative cognitive response attached to this fact. Wendy also has a positive conative[2] response—she likes Beatrice, who can sing prettily. The two girls sit next to each other in class and protect each other against playground bullies. Wendy now wants to take their friendship further and asks her mother if Beatrice can come home to 'play dolls'.

Wendy's positive cognitive and conative responses are thrown amok when she asks for permission to have Beatrice over on a play-date. First, her mother refuses, thus informing Wendy that her conative response is wrong—she is not allowed to associate with Beatrice. When she sadly asks 'Why not?', she discovers that her cognitive response was also wrong: she overlooked that 'chocolate skin' has meaning. Wendy's Mom teaches her that Beatrice is 'different' because of her skin colour and furthermore this skin colour makes Beatrice an unsuitable friend.

Thus Wendy learns three lessons: first, that brown skin has a meaning; second, that brown skin has a negative meaning; and, third, that due to this negative meaning people with brown skin are not to be associated with. Prior to this lesson, Wendy sees colour but does not link it to prejudiced ideas or stereotypes; her conative response is therefore positive—she is keen to befriend Beatrice. Her

[1] Nina Simone, 'Turning Point', 1967.

[2] J Gottlieb and BW Gottlieb, 'Stereotypic Attitudes and Behavioural Intentions Towards Handicapped Children' (1977) 82 *American Journal of Mental Deficiency* 65.

mother's response is the opposite: negative cognitive and conative response. Thus despite her own positive response, due to stigma Wendy must also express a negative cognitive and conative response. To manage this disjuncture she adopts an emotion common to stigma—ambivalence.

This is the turning point for Wendy: it is to be assumed that from then on she will have a negative cognitive and conative response to brown skin. Brown skin is stigmatised. Wendy learns that while she and Beatrice may interact in the public space of the school—and even that is now questionable—they may not do so in the private space of her home. Yet it is hard to believe that Wendy actually understands why she should think badly of Beatrice and also not play with her. Simone highlights Wendy's confused compliance in the final line: in a voice full of hesitation, Wendy says to her Mom, 'Oh … I … see'. On the contrary, the faltering response suggests that she does not understand at all but decides to act as if she does. Simone cleverly uses the voice of a child in this final line to express both the ambiguity and ambivalence which accompanys stigma. Stigmatisation does not feel good for Wendy yet she will comply. It will feel as bad for Beatrice.

This short and unassuming song tells an important tale of stigma and highlights the process of stigmatisation. It also highlights the themes of arbitrary difference, social attribution of meaning and discrimination that are at the centre of this book. Stigma is fed by compliance, borne of confused and uncomfortable ambivalence. This may be why Pinker describes stigma as 'the commonest form of violence used in democratic societies' and an effective form of social control:

> Stigmatisation is low, unobtrusive and genteel in its effect, so much so, that when the stigmatized hit back physically in Londonderry or Chicago they can technically be accused of being the first to resort to force. Stigmatisation is a highly sophisticated form of violence in so far as it is rarely associated with physical threats or attack. It can best be compared to those forms of psychological torture in which the victim is broken psychically and physically but left to all outward appearances unmarked.[3]

I. Defining Stigma

It has been 50 years since Erwin Goffman wrote his seminal book on stigma. However the idea predates Goffman. Stigma is an ancient social construct. In its essence, a stigma is a mark. Taken literally, the word refers to a permanent visible mark made by a painful process involving a hot branding iron or pointed instrument. The word is derived from the Greek word meaning 'to stick', as in to pierce or tattoo.[4] Unlike tattoos in the twenty-first century, these marks are not made for

[3] RA Pinker, *Social Theory and Social Policy* (London: Heinemann 1971) 175.

[4] GM Herek, 'Thinking About AIDS and Stigma—A Psychologists Perspective' (2002) 30 *Journal of Law, Medicine and Ethics* 594.

pleasure. They 'were cut or burnt into the body' for a specific purpose: to denigrate the bearer. They were used to publicly advertise that 'the bearer was ... a blemished person, ritually polluted, to be avoided, especially in public places'.[5] The original stigmatas were social outcasts: runaway slaves with a mark burned into their skin as a sign of disgrace. Ancient Greeks would also use knives and branding irons to 'slice and burn criminals and traitors to denote their immorality or lack of fitness for regular society'.[6] Persons bearing such 'stigma' were discredited, scorned and avoided. A later more positive meaning referred to religious stigma, such as blemishes on the hands. Branding was also used to identify persons devoted to religious duties.[7] This gave rise to the notion of positive stigma.

However, it is the negative Greek meaning that remains dominant. Current definitions continue to link the idea of stigma with a blemish and negative connotations. In the natural sciences, writers and editors are informed that 'stigma (*pl.* stigmas; preferred to stigmata)' are either 'the receptive surface of a carpel' or 'an eyespot'.[8] Medical students are told that 'Stigma *n.* (*pl.* stigmata)' refers to either 'a mark that characterizes a particular disease, such as the café au lait spots characteristic of neurofibromatosis' or 'any spot or lesion on the skin'.[9] In the social sciences, the definitions are more extensive. Social workers are informed that 'stigma' is:

> Severe condemnation of someone because of what are regarded as negative characteristics that distinguish them from others. ... Social workers meet many service users who have been stigmatized and the fact that they are seeing a social worker may add to their stigmatization in their own estimation and that of others.[10]

The Oxford thesaurus lists synonyms as 'shame, disgrace, dishonour, ignominy, opprobrium, humiliation'.[11]

Stigma should not be confused with deviance, stereotype or prejudice. As both stigma and deviance refer to a departure from a putative standard or norm, some authors use the terms interchangeably.[12] However deviance is usually applied to rule-breaking behaviour, such as criminality, which is not essential for stigma. In addition, deviance is not necessarily linked to an arbitrary attribute (a 'mark') but to specific behaviour. Nonetheless, a deviant behaviour such as theft can be and is often stigmatised, usually for purposes of social control.

[5] E Goffman, *Stigma: Notes on a Spoiled Identity* (London, Penguin, 1990) 1.

[6] S Neuberg, DM Smith and T Asher, 'Why People Stigmatise—Towards a Biocultural Framework' in T Heatherton, RE Kleck, MR Hebl and JG Hull (eds), *The Social Psychology of Stigma* (New York, Guildford Press, 2000) 31 argue that those who threaten group functioning are stigmatised.

[7] L Osborne, 'Beyond Stigma Theory' (1974) 9 *Issues in Criminology* 71.

[8] E Martin, *The New Oxford Dictionary for Scientific Writers and Editors*, 2nd edn (Oxford, Oxford University Press, 2009).

[9] *Concise Medical Dictionary*, 8th edn (Oxford, Oxford University Press, 2010).

[10] J Harris and V White, *A Dictionary of Social Work and Social Care* (Oxford, Oxford University Press, 2013).

[11] M Waite (ed), *Oxford Paperback Thesaurus*, 4th edn (Oxford, Oxford University Press, 2012).

[12] Page uses 'stigma' and 'deviance' interchangeably. R Page, *Stigma* (London, Routledge, 1984).

Stigma is broader than deviance: it relates to what people 'are' as well as what they do. This difference produces what may be the clearest distinction between stigmatisation and deviance: the possibility of repair. As there is no distinction between the stigma and the stigmatised, the mark takes total control:

> social control may turn to stigmatization when a deviant condition is increasingly perceived and responded to as a defining or essential attribute of the 'whole' person or social group, or of the person's group's reputation, character or identity.

Non-deviant attributes of the individual or group are thereby over-shadowed making the person 'essentially' bad and withholding the second chance (repair) afforded to those seen as 'deviant'.[13] Harre links stigma to 'fatefulness', since there is nothing that the stigmatised can do to remove the stigma and they cannot help but acquire it: 'someone born into a despised ethnic group cannot by his own actions clough off that ethnicity'.[14] The ethnicity is 'marked' as is the person bearing it—the stigmatised person thus becomes engulfed by an attribute, status or condition to the extent that that she becomes it. There is no separation between the mark and the person: the possibility of rehabilitation linked to deviance does not exist in relation to stigma. Even authors who place stigma as a method of social control alongside deviance avoid full conflation.[15]

Stereotyping is a different form of categorisation. According to psychologists, human beings categorise as an efficient means of processing large amounts of information. When we stereotype, we generally ascribe negative beliefs to those in our categories. For example, young black men are stereotyped as criminal delinquents—the number of such young people who have lost their lives while standing on the street illustrate how dangerous stereotypes can be. In an experiment inspired by the killing of Amadou Diallo—shot 41 times by New York police officers—a black or white face was flashed on a computer screen followed by an image of a gun or a wrench. Upon seeing the black face participants resorted to stereotypes: they were not only faster to decide that any object was a gun, but also that a wrench was a gun.[16] In addition, stereotyping is a cognitive response that does not always result in the conative response of stigmatisation: a refusal to associate or avoidance of association is integral to stigma but not stereotyping.[17]

Likewise, stigma is distinct from, but linked to, prejudice. A stigma is described as a 'condition that engenders prejudice and discrimination',[18] and stigmatised persons are always the target of prejudice. It is also argued that stigma and prejudice

[13] A Dijker and W Koomen, *Stigmatisation, Tolerance and Repair* (Cambridge, Cambridge University Press, 2007) 7.

[14] R Harre, *Social Being: A Theory for Social Psychology* (Oxford, Basil Blackwell, 1979) 315.

[15] Dijker and Koomen, *Stigmatisation, Tolerance and Repair* (n 14) 9–13.

[16] M Gladwell, *Blink—The Power of Thinking Without Thinking* (London, Penguin, 2006) 233.

[17] Gottlieb and Gottlieb, 'Stereotypic Attitudes' (n 2).

[18] BA Pescosolido, J Martin, A Lang and S Olafsdottir, 'Rethinking Theoretical Approaches to Stigma: A Framework Integrating Normative Influences on Stigma (FINIS)' (2008) *Social Science & Medicine* 67, 431.

occur at different 'levels': stigma 'resides in the structure and relations of society but prejudice resides in the minds of individuals'.[19] Social support—or power—distinguishes prejudice from stigma. Prejudice refers to a negative generalised attitude towards members of a majority or minority social group for any reason that appears reasonable in the mind of the prejudiced person. This reason does not have to be supported by society. Social engagement is, however, integral to stigma—indeed, this is the purpose of the 'mark': to spread a generalised negative message about the group in society. Thus, if HIV/AIDs sufferers are stigmatised as a result of their illness, they will also be subjected to prejudice. Health researchers also argue that 'much HIV- and AIDS-related stigma builds on and reinforces earlier prejudices' that characterise sufferers as addicts and prostitutes.[20] Prejudice can also be differentiated from discrimination. The former is attitudinal bias—'an avertive or hostile attitude towards a person who belongs to a group, simply because he [or she] belongs to that group'—while the latter is behavioural, including 'practices and actions of dominant race-ethnic groups that have a differential and negative impact on subordinate race-ethnic groups'.[21]

Stigma seems to emerge from nowhere yet exists everywhere. Once in the 'social imaginary'[22] stigmas entrench themselves there. As their origin and transmission remains obscure, ridding society of stigmas is very difficult, if not impossible. However, given their role in socialisation, it might be worth making the effort to try to identify their origins as well as how to change them. Socialisation[23] is a process that refers to the acquisition of norms and conceptions. It can be described as the 'inculcation of morality in the individual especially through his or her sharing a sense of honour, and informal control, as exerted in various degrees by the communities and social groups'.[24] Socialisation focuses on the processes of education at home, in the playground and beyond. According to sociologists and psychologists, we begin to learn them at a young age. In one sense, learning about stigma is integral to socialisation—they create a frame for navigation of the known and unknown risks of everyday life. It is a process of preparation with some manipulation 'whereby the individual becomes a participating member of a society of human adults'.[25] It can be active or passive—in the case of Wendy, it is active. She is therefore learning life-lessons.

[19] Herek, 'Thinking About AIDS and Stigma' (n 4) 595.

[20] M Maluwa, P Aggleton and R Parker (2002) 'Health HIV- and AIDS-Related Stigma, Discrimination, and Human Rights: A Critical Overview' 6 *Health and Human Rights*, 1.

[21] SE Zemore, KJ Karriker-Jaffe, S Keithly and N Mulia, 'Racial Prejudice and Unfair Treatment: Interactive Effects with Poverty and Foreign Nativity on Problem Drinking' (2011) *Journal of Studies on Alcohol and Drugs* 361.

[22] C Taylor, *Modern Social Imaginaries* (Durham, Duke University Press, 2003).

[23] K Danziger, *Socialisation* (London, Penguin Press, 1971).

[24] S Segre, 'A Simmelian Theory of Marginality, Deviance and Social Control' in F Doerr-Backes and L Nieder (eds), *Georg Simmel: Between Modernity and Post Modernity* (Wuerzburg, Koenigshausen & Neumann, 1995) 143.

[25] Danziger, *Socialisation* (n 23) 17.

Socialisation covers almost every aspect of life. For example, we are socialised in how to react to mental illness:

> people develop conceptions of mental illness early in life as part of socialization into our culture. Once in place, people's conceptions become a lay theory about what it means to have a mental illness. People form expectations as to whether most people will reject an individual with mental illness as a friend, employee, neighbor, or intimate partner and whether most people will devalue a person with mental illness as less trustworthy, intelligent, and competent.[26]

Once we have acquired these ideas through socialisation, they become a 'lay theory' or basic foundation for social interaction. Courtesy of her mother, Wendy now has a 'lay theory' to guide future meetings with people who look like Beatrice. Socialisation is therefore a dual process of social inclusion and exclusion: it sets patterns for social interaction and sorts those who may partake in social interaction from those who may not. Those who may not are marginalised through the use of stigma, and they may be shunned socially (like Beatrice), culturally and institutionally.

According to Simmel, socialisation secures peaceful existence in society and works most effectively through informal control, as we learn most effectively from people that we trust.[27] We see this in Nina Simone's song, where Wendy accepts her mother's instruction despite not understanding it. Trusted adults, such as parents and teachers, are key disseminators of the 'pre-disposition to stigmatise': in addition to direct instructions, facial expressions, behaviour and other adult responses also send cues to children which shape their cognitive development. Learnt 'responses become automatic and remain so into adulthood'.[28] Segre suggests that 'of the three sources of social control—the private morality of individuals, the customs of a circle and the compulsion of the law—the former is the most effective and convenient, although not sufficient'.[29] Stigma is unique in that it links all three sources: it is enacted by individual action, disseminated through social interaction and sometimes sanctioned by law.

Yet socialisation is not stigmatisation per se—it is not always negative. Gladwell describes socialisation as the education of the 'adaptive unconcsious', the training of the 'internal computer in the brain' that leaps to conclusions before we know why. The adaptive unconscious propels our instinctive reactions, acting as 'a kind of giant computer'[30] that quickly and quietly processes the data we need to function as human beings, and in particular, to stay safe. Gladwell argues that if, for example, a person steps out into the road and realises that she has accidentally walked into the path of a truck, it is the adaptive unconscious that

[26] BG Link and JC Phelan, 'Conceptualizing Stigma' (2001) 27 *Annual Review of Sociology* 363, 373.

[27] G Simmel, *Soziologie* (Berlin, 1968) 219.

[28] R Lenhardt, 'Understanding the Mark: Race, Stigma and Equality in Context' (2004) 79 *New York University Law Review* 803, 828.

[29] Segre, 'A Simmelian Theory of Marginality' (n 24) 144.

[30] Gladwell, *Blink* (n 16) 11.

propels her out of the way without needing to think through a series of options. The adaptive unconscious 'does an excellent job of sizing up the world, warning people of danger, setting goals and initiating action in a sophisticated and efficient manner'.[31] However, there is a 'dark side' of rapid cognition that is at the root of discrimination.[32] As shown by the numerous police shootings of unarmed black men,[33] rapid cognition utilises stigma.

II. Erwin Goffman and Stigma

Canadian sociologist Erwin Goffman was the first to examine stigma from a social psychological perspective as a 'stimulus feature' in inter-group relations.[34] Born in Winnipeg, Alberta, he studied sociology at the University of Toronto. He later worked with the National Film Board of Canada, a job that took him into many remote villages of Canada to document everyday life. During graduate work at the University of Chicago, he worked with sociologists including Dewey, Mead and Blumer to develop ideas of how the individual becomes a social creature, or socialisation. His work was based on observation, and his first book, *Asylums*,[35] explored aspects of the social life of those in a particular institution, the mental asylum. The same approach was taken in *Stigma*.[36] Goffman observed how stigma affects general social interaction. His main concern was with the issue of individual behaviour during 'mixed contacts' or 'moments when the stigmatized and normal'[37] are in each other's presence, in particular the coping strategies employed. He was primarily interested in 'impression management'.

Goffman identified different 'varieties' of stigma.[38] His first variety was framed using language acceptable at the time but out of place in the twenty-first century. Stigmas, he wrote, could, first, arise from 'abominations of the body' or limitations of physical ability; second, they could be 'blemishes of individual character' such as 'weak will, domineering or unnatural passions, treacherous and rigid beliefs, and dishonesty, these being inferred from a known record of, for example, mental disorder, imprisonment, addiction, alcoholism, homosexuality, unemployment, suicidal attempts and radical behaviour'; finally, there were 'tribal stigma'

[31] Gladwell, *Blink* (n 16) 12.
[32] Gladwell, *Blink* (n 16) 76.
[33] See http://mappingpoliceviolence.org/unarmed/; http://gawker.com/unarmed-people-of-color-killed-by-police-1999-2014-1666672349.
[34] I Katz, 'Some Thoughts About the Stigma Notion' (1979) 5 *Personality and Social Psychology Bulletin* 447, 448.
[35] E. Goffman, *Asylums: Essays on the Social Situation of Mental Patients and Other Inmates* (New York, Anchor Books, 1961).
[36] n 5 above.
[37] Goffman, *Stigma* (n 5) 23.
[38] Goffman, *Stigma* (n 5) 14.

that were 'transmitted through lineages and equally contaminate all members of a family'—these centre on race, sex, religion or nation. According to Goffman, a stigma could thus arise from a status, condition or an identity: it can be biological or biographical, psychological or physical, mutable or immutable, direct or indirect (associative). Beatrice is being subjected to a 'tribal' stigma: race.

Scholars have since added to and adapted these categories. For example, 20 years later, a schema was developed with six varieties of stigma. The descriptive schema set out by Jones[39] focuses on the nature of the 'mark': 'conceal-ability' (visibility of the mark or 'information control');[40] the 'course of the mark' (does it become progressively worse or stay the same over time?); 'disruptiveness' (to what extent does it interrupt everyday interactions?); 'aesthetics' (how unattractive is it?); 'origin' (is it congenital or immutable?); and 'peril' (to what extent does it endanger others?). Other scholars have also added temporal aspects, making stigma contingent on time and place—some stigmas emerge at specific historical moments but then disappear, or exist in certain places but not others.[41] Stigma can also be differentiated by the responses they evoke, or their 'stimulus properties': do observers feel threatened by the stigma, sympathise/pity or perhaps even blame the possessor for the stigma?[42] Punishment can be avoided if the person is blameless.[43] We may believe that the mark is the result of misfortune, or some inherent personal defect: for example, blindness is a misfortune but obesity is a defect, taking the view that people are fat because they lack the discipline to stop eating. Skin colour and nationality may fall somewhere between the two; however, white people may feel threatened when they encounter an individual with black or brown skin whereas an encounter with a white person of a different nationality may not evoke fear.

III. The Process of Stigmatisation

Even without the branding iron, stigmatisation is neither a pleasant nor benign process. It poisons cognitive interaction and pollutes social relationships. Stigmatisation can be subtle or overt. It can manifest as subtle shunning, such as avoidance or refusal to make eye contact, as well as more blatant 'social rejection, discounting, discrediting, dehumanization and personalization of others'.[44] For

[39] EE Jones et al, A Farina, AH Hastorf, H Marcus, DT Miller and RA Scott, *Social Stigma: The Psychology of Marked Relationships* (New York, Freeman and Company, 1984).

[40] Also mentioned by Goffman (*Stigma* (n 5) 64).

[41] See Heatherton et al, *Social Psychology of Stigma* (n 6). Goffman also acknowledges that attributes can lose their force as a stigma, such as divorce or Irish ethnicity, and that the history of stigma can change, by for example social action (*Stigma* (n 5) 163–64).

[42] Katz, 'Stigma Notion' (n 34) 454.

[43] Jones et al (n 39) 57.

[44] JB Pryor and AER Bos (eds), *Social Psychological Perspectives on Stigma: Advances in Theory and Research* (Abingdon, Routledge, 2014) 1. Special Edition of *Basic and Applied Social Psychology* Vol 35(1) Feb 2013.

Goffman, to be stigmatised was to be *made* 'abnormal' and as a result subjected to a power-filled public shaming. The representation of the mark in the dominant culture[45] confirms that the bearer is 'criminal, villainous or otherwise deserving of social ostracism, infamy, shame and condemnation'.[46] For the individual, to be stigmatised means to be seen as 'flawed, compromised and less than fully human'.[47] To stigmatise an individual is to 'define the individual in terms of this negative attribute'[48] and then devalue them. The public response to stigma is not only negative but often also punitive.[49]

Goffman used the term 'stigma' to refer to an 'attribute that is deeply discrediting'. He described stigma in relational terms as a 'special discrepancy' between a virtual social identity (that which is expected based on social norms) and an actual social identity (that of the individual concerned). Stigma emerges from an incongruity between these identities due to the 'information' 'conveyed' by a particular attribute or condition. Possession of the attribute or condition made a person 'different' not in a general sense but more specifically different from 'others in the category of persons available for him to be'. The person thereby became not only less desirable but also, as in ancient Greece, bad and dangerous, reduced by the attribute from a 'whole and usual person to a tainted, discounted one'.[50] By discrediting the individual, we believe that the person 'is not quite human' and

> exercise varieties of discrimination, through which we effectively, if often unthinkingly, reduce his life chances. We construct a stigma theory, an ideology to explain his inferiority and account for the danger he represents … we use specific stigma terms such as cripple, bastard, moron in our daily discourse as a source of metaphor and imagery, typically without giving thought to original meaning. We tend to impute a wide range of perfections on the basis of the original one, and at the same time to impute some desirable but undesired attributes …[51]

He described the *stigmatised* individual as a person who possesses 'an undesirable difference' and *stigmatisation* as the social response to a person who has a 'spoiled identity'. Identity is spoiled in social settings because stigma 'obtrudes' itself in the process of social interaction, overwhelming all other attributes and causing people to turn away from the holder of the stigma.

Goffman distinguished cases where individuals are 'discreditable' rather than 'discredited'; a person with an invisible 'mark' is discreditable whereas a person born with black or brown skin, whose 'mark' can be seen by all, is discredited. Stigmatisation can be avoided if the bearer alone is aware of the discrediting

[45] S Levin and C van Laar, *Stigma and Group Inequality* (London: Lawrence Erblaum Associates Publishers, 2006) 4–5.
[46] Herek, 'Thinking About AIDS and Stigma' (n 4) 595.
[47] Heatherton et al (eds), *Social Psychology of Stigma* (n 6) 3.
[48] Neuberg et al, 'Why People Stigmatise' (n 6).
[49] S Cohen (ed), *Images of Deviance* (Harmondsworth, Penguin, 1971) 11.
[50] Goffman, *Stigma* (n 5) 3.
[51] Goffman, ibid 15–16.

attribute or condition—such individuals can 'pass' as 'normal'.[52] In this case, identity remains untarnished. However, a person can be stigmatised/discredited without knowing it if, for example, the individual has not incorporated into her life standards from the wider society,[53] but adheres to different social norms—this may be the case with migrants settling in a new country. However, stigmatisation can still occur—individual ignorance of stigma does not interrupt the stigmatisation. Stigma is therefore at the same time knowledge-dependent and knowledge-independent: the stigmatiser must know of its existence[54] but an individual may be stigmatised while being oblivious to the social meaning and consequence of a status, condition or attribute.

Goffman spoke of stigmatisation in general terms as something that occurs between individuals. He described it as a 'pervasive two-role social process in which every individual participates in both roles, at least in some connections and in some phases of life. The normal and the stigmatized are not persons but perspectives.'[55] Goffman noted America's 'centralising norm':

> … in an important sense, there is only one complete unblushing male in America: a young, married, white, urban, northern, heterosexual protestant father of college education, fully employed, of good complexion, weight and height and a recent record in sports. Every American male tends to look out upon the world from this perspective, this constituting one sense in which one can speak of a common value system in America … the general identity-values of a society may be fully entrenched nowhere, and yet they can cast some kind of shadow on the encounters encountered everywhere in daily living.[56]

Also, he acknowledged that 'the lifelong attributes of a particular individual may cause him to be type-cast: he may have to play the stigmatized role in almost all of his social situations, making it natural to refer to him … as a stigmatized person whose life situation places him in opposition to normal'.[57]

Goffman was unequivocal on the origin of this. He stressed the central role of society in the stigmatisation process: he argued that the real source was social because:

> society establishes the means of categorising persons and the complement of attributes felt to be ordinary and natural for members of each of these categories. Social settings establish the categories of persons likely to be encountered there. The routines of social

[52] For example, writer Anatole Broyard passed as white in order to pursue his literary career free of racial stigma. More recently white women have 'passed' as African American (Rachel Dolezal) and Native American (Andrea Smith) in order to *promote* their careers.

[53] Goffman, *Stigma* (n 5) 18.

[54] But see JE Beatty and SL Kirby, 'Beyond the Legal Environment: How Stigma Influences Invisible Identity Groups in the Workplace' (2006) 18 *Employee Responsibilities and Rights Journal* 1, challenging the notion that attributes must be visible for stigmatisation to occur. Based on Jones (n 39), they propose four dimensions relevant to 'invisible identities': the person's responsibility for the stigma; the course of the stigma over time; its moral threat; and its effects on performance.

[55] Goffman, *Stigma* (n 5) 163–64.

[56] Goffman, *Stigma* (n 5) 153.

[57] Goffman, *Stigma* (n 5) 164.

intercourse in established settings allow us to deal with anticipated others without special attention or thought.[58]

Goffman also held that as stigma are rooted in social relations they are contextual. Although contextual, like culture, stigma travels with the individual. Where the home stigma correlates with the stigma in the host country it will be strengthened. Where the stigma in the home country is not repeated in the host country, it will likely remain at the level of prejudice—a personal dislike in the mind of an individual.

IV. Developments in the Theory of Stigma

Goffman's work attracted a broad audience. A 'PsycINFO' search of all articles published between 1963 and 2012 produced 9,939 hits, with attention to social stigma growing significantly in the last decade.[59] Since 1963—to give just a flavour of the breadth of application—stigma has been applied to studies on intergroup relations between persons with different forms of disability (for example, an amputee in a wheelchair vs somebody with a less severe disability), obesity,[60] bullying,[61] epileptics and hunchbacks, mental illness and mental health care,[62] personality disorders[63] and hearing loss.[64] Stigma has also been applied to particular illnesses such as urinary incontinence, HIV/AIDs, leprosy and cancer;[65] social statuses such as 'ex-cons',[66] debtors, the unemployed or working relationships[67]

[58] Goffman, *Stigma* (n 5) 2.

[59] Pryor and Bos (eds), *Social Psychological Perspectives* (n 44).

[60] EB King, SG Rogelberg, MR Hebl, PW Braddy, LR Shanock, SC Doerer and L McDowell, 'Waistlines and Ratings of Executives: Does Executive Status Overcome Obesity Stigma?' (2016) 55(2) *Human Resource Management* 283; DA Frederick, AC Saguy, G Sandhu and T Mann, 'Effects of Competing News Media Frames of Weight on Antifat Stigma, Beliefs About Weight and Support for Obesity-Related Public Policies' (2016) 40 *International Journal of Obesity* 543; J Whitelsel, *Fat Gay Men: Girth, Mirth, and the Politics of Stigma* (New York, New York University Press, 2014); S Mooney and AM El-Sayed 'Stigma and the Etiology of Depression Among the Obese: An Agent-Based Exploration' (2016) 148 *Social Science & Medicine* 1.

[61] R Thornberg, 'School Bullying as a Collective Action: Stigma Processes and Identity Struggling' (2015) 29 *Children and Society* 310.

[62] RP Brown, M Imura and L Mayeux, 'Honor and the Stigma of Mental Healthcare' (2014) 40(9) *Personality and Social Psychology Bulletin* 1119; G Thornicroft et al, 'Evidence for Effective Interventions to Reduce Mental-Health-Related Stigma and Discrimination' (2016) 387 *The Lancet* 1123.

[63] See Katz, 'Stigma Notion' (n 34) for research conducted in the 1960s and 1970s.

[64] M Simmons, *Hearing Loss—From Stigma to Strategy* (London and Chester Springs, Peter Owen, 2005).

[65] Link and Phelan, 'Conceptualizing Stigma' (n 26) 363–64.

[66] TA Winnick and M Bodkin, 'Anticipated Stigma and Stigma Management Among Those to Be Labeled "Ex-Con"' (2008) 29 *Deviant Behavior* 295.

[67] S Bornstein, 'The Legal and Policy Implications of the "Flexibility Stigma"' (2013) 69 *Journal of Social Issues* 389; TD Johnson and A Joshi, 'Dark Clouds or Silver Linings? A Stigma Threat Perspective on the Implications of an Autism Diagnosis for Workplace Well-Being' (2016) 101(3) *Journal of Applied Psychology* 430.

and step-parents,[68] sexuality,[69] stigmatised relationships,[70] occupations such as exotic dancing or what has been described as 'dirty work'[71] and health outcomes for sexual minorities.[72] It has even been used to explain commercial behaviour.[73]

These scholars predominantly focus on individual behaviour in interaction and varieties of stigma. As with Goffman, much of the interest has been on the reactions of the 'normal' subject when encountering difference, as well as the effect of this treatment on the stigmatised person. Development of the concept has taken two forms: first, Goffman's general theory of stigmatisation was refined with the introduction of three specific triggers; and, second, the idea of structural stigma was developed to enhance understanding of the sociological aspects of stigma, in particular the role of power. These developments have produced new understandings that take the meaning of stigma far beyond the Simmelian philosophy of the 'face to face'.

A. Three Models of Stigmatisation

Goffman's general theory of stigmatisation was refined by Katz, in an attempt to clarify the meaning of 'stigma' as a social psychological concept.[74] Katz drew upon research on inter-group relations to suggest three causal models of the stigmatisation process. First, in the '*attribute-as-sufficient-cause*' model, the possession of the attribute is enough to trigger stigmatisation. Hostility and rejection occur because the attribute *per se* has a strongly negative social meaning. Under this model, a 'mere difference' has the power to discredit—stigma inheres in the attribute itself. With such attributes, attribute and possessor are seen as one and the same; the attribute adopts a 'master status' in social intercourse and 'essentialises' the individual so that the multiplicity of biography is lost. However, as Goffman pointed out, this only holds true if the difference is visible, such as skin colour or some forms of disability.[75]

[68] Link and Phelan, 'Conceptualizing Stigma' (n 26).

[69] A Fulle, IJ Chang and D Knox, 'Female Sexual Hedonism: Navigating Stigma' (2016) *College Student Journal* 29.

[70] C Han, K Proctor and KH Choi, 'I Know a Lot of Gay Asian Men who Are Actually Tops: Managing and Negotiating Gay Racial Stigma' (2014) 18 *Sexuality & Culture* 219.

[71] JJ Vzquez, 'The Stigma of Making a Living from Garbage: Meta-Sterotypes of Trash-Pickers in Len (Nicaragua)' (2016) 57(2) *Scandinavian Journal of Psychology* 122.

[72] T Poteat, D German and D Kerrigan, 'Managing Uncertainty: A Grounded Theory of Stigma in Transgender Health Care Encounters' (2013) 84 *Social Science & Medicine* 22; A Brandes, 'The Negative Effect of Stigma, Discrimination, and the Health Care System on the Health of Gender and Sexual Minorities' (2014) 23 *Tulane Journal of Law and Sexuality* 155.

[73] O Armantier, E Ghysels, A Sarkar and J Shrader, 'Discount Window Stigma During the 2007–2008 Financial Crisis' (2015) 118 *Journal of Financial Economics* 317.

[74] Katz, 'Stigma Notion' (n 34) 447.

[75] Goffman, Stigma (n 5) 92.

In the second model, *labelling*, the attribute is a necessary but insufficient stimulus for stigmatisation. The power of the attribute is dependent upon how the majority choose to view it: this choice depends upon contextual variables such as the power and resources of the individual, the proximity between the 'normals' and 'deviants', as well as the visibility of the attribute. Under this mode of stigmatisation, context plays an important role in determining how 'normals' react to the 'marked' individual. Finally the 'scapegoat' model suggests that animosity precedes stigmatisation: it is hostility that drives a focus on 'defects' and in order to justify hostility, certain attributes are singled out. Under the scapegoat model of stigmatisation, 'disparagement is an attempt on the part of the stigmatiser to reduce moral discomfort by lowering the worth of the victim'.[76] For example, the overweight are stigmatised as personally inadequate[77] or immigrants are stigmatised as criminal in order to defend the social system as fair.

As Katz stressed, these models are not mutually exclusive and should be seen as guides to understanding the triggers of the stigmatisation process rather than strict causal categories. Most importantly, all three models acknowledge the role of society in stigmatisation. Katz did not, however, delve into this aspect—his was a categorisation of the psychological aspects of stigma. Like Goffman he did not concern himself with how society in general contributes to this. It was individuals who stigmatised. Although central to his theory, the social remained under-theorised in the process of stigmatisation.

B. Structural Stigma—Beyond the face-to-face

Although Goffman acknowledged the role of society in stigmatisation, he did not explore the contextual aspects of stigma in depth. His studies, for example on asylums, observed practices but did not consider their history or evolution,[78] and thus his 'language of relationships' referred to interpersonal interaction alone. Even though stigma is based on shared social cognition, the 'social' aspect of cognition became under-theorised. The behavioural emphasis of stigma studies pushed the social aspect of stigma into the background and reduced the potency of the concept—stigma was attached to a spectrum of social phenomena ranging from name-calling to dislike. This omission exacerbated over time as Goffman's ideas took on their own trajectory and came to be seen as a dilution because it made the stigma 'something *in the person* rather than a designation or tag that

[76] Katz, 'Stigma Notion' (n 34) 452.

[77] Recent research has found that this also applies to overweight high achievers such as CEOs. See EB King et al, 'Waistlines and Ratings of Executives: Does Executive Status Overcome Obesity Stigma?' 55(2) *Human Resource Management* Volume 283–300.

[78] I Hacking, 'Between Michel Foucault and Erwin Goffman: Between Discourse in the Abstract and Face-to-Face Interaction' (2004) 33 *Economy and Society* 277.

others affix to the person'.[79] This dilution had two consequences: first, it teetered towards presentation of an innocent view of stigma;[80] and, second, the individualistic application identified people alone as the transmitters of stigma.

Mainstream stigma studies undertaken by cognitive social psychologists thus ignored an important aspect of stigma: its roots in social power. Critics, including but not limited to critical social psychologists, took issue with and sought to address this. They argued that these 'micro approaches' ignore the structural aspects of stigma or its roots in the 'conditions that exclude people from social and economic life'.[81] They challenged the 'sanitation' of the concept by re-emphasising the ostracism of the stigmatised—a person who acquires stigma loses their 'normal' status and the social 'advantages' that accompany it, while a person who loses stigma gains a 'normal' status.[82] The former loses social power and access to a range of basic resources such as healthcare, education and employment, while the latter gains it.

In 2001, psychologist Bruce Link and sociologist Jo Phelan set out to respond to the 'vaguely defined and individually focused' stigma concept as used by social psychologists. They were especially concerned by the long-term policy consequences of this: when combined with researchers lacking personal experience of living with stigma, it resulted in research with misleading and patronising conclusions. For example in relation to disability, the study of stigma informed by behavioural theories and devised from the perspectives of persons without disabilities led to conclusions such as that disability is located solely in biology; that the problems of the disabled are due to disability-produced impairment; that the disabled person is a 'victim'; that disability is central to the disabled person's self-concept, self-definition, social comparisons and reference groups; and that having a disability is synonymous with needing help and social support.[83]

Link and Phelan identified two sources of these problems: first, the application of the stigma concept to a broad range of facts and circumstances; and, second, the inherently multidisciplinary nature of research on stigma, including, as seen above, contributions by psychologists, sociologists, anthropologists, political scientists, educationalists, doctors and social geographers. As each study and discipline had its own emphasis, 'people approach the stigma concept from different theoretical orientations that produce somewhat different visions of what should be included in the concept. Thus, different frames of reference have led to different conceptualisations.'[84] In restoring the social perspective in studies of stigma,

[79] Link and Phelan, 'Conceptualising Stigma' (n 26) 366.

[80] Crocker et al (1998) 'Social Stigma', in D Gilbert and S Fiske, *Handbook of Social Psychology*, Vol II., 504, when they suggest that it is transmitted by individuals and that what one person may view discrediting, another sees as 'charming'.

[81] Maluwa, Aggleton and Parker, 'Health HIV- and AIDS-Related Stigma' (n 20).

[82] Although this is not a straightforward process—for example, weight loss does not equate to loss of the stigma associated with weight. See BR Levy and CE Pilver, 'Residual Stigma: Psychological Distress Among the Formerly Overweight' (2012) 75 *Social Science & Medicine* 297.

[83] Link and Phelan, 'Conceptualizing Stigma' (n 26) 366.

[84] Link and Phelan, 'Conceptualizing Stigma' (n 26) 365.

they had two goals: first, to clarify the concept; and, second, to construct a revised concept to improve its application. Thus was born the idea of 'structural stigma'.

'Structural stigma' creates a frame for a broader conception of stigma based on the 'relationships between a set of interrelated concepts' that link psychological practices with social conditions. The result is a schema comprising five elements that trigger stigma when they converge. The components are summarised in the quote below:

> In the first component, people distinguish and label human differences. In the second, dominant cultural beliefs link labeled persons to undesirable characteristics—to negative stereotypes. In the third, labeled persons are placed in distinct categories so as to accomplish some degree of separation of "us" from "them." In the fourth, labeled persons experience status loss and discrimination that lead to unequal outcomes. Finally, stigmatization is entirely contingent on access to social, economic, and political power that allows the identification of differentness, the construction of stereotypes, the separation of labeled persons into distinct categories, and the full execution of disapproval, rejection, exclusion, and discrimination. Thus, we apply the term stigma when elements of labeling, stereotyping, separation, status loss, and discrimination co-occur in a power situation that allows the components of stigma to unfold.[85]

They therefore created a dynamic procedural definition of stigma that explicitly includes the idea of power. The first component of structural stigma is the everyday human practice of distinguishing between objects and assigning labels. This practice is integral to cognition. If labelling is thought of as a continuum, stigmatisation can be described as at 'one end of the continuum of the process of assigning positive or negative labels to those we come across, and then valuing or devaluing them as their labels warrant'.[86] At the stigmatising end of the continuum, there is a conscious selection of the human differences that will matter socially: skin colour has significant social meaning but eye colour does not.

This deliberate creation of a 'spoiled identity' at the beginning of stigmatisation is highlighted by health rights scholars:

> Stigma is, however, not a thing but a process. The *qualities of the individual on which stigma operates* (e.g., skin or hair color, a manner of speaking or acting) are essentially arbitrary. Particular cultures or settings fixate on certain attributes and define them as discreditable or unworthy. 'Undesirable differences' and 'spoiled identities' do not naturally exist but are created by individuals and by communities. Stigmatization is therefore a process of devaluation rather than a thing … Stigma neither occurs naturally nor does it necessarily spring from the minds of individuals. Rather, stigma is always a reaction to a social history that influences when and where it appears and the forms it takes. Understanding this history can help us combat it better.[87]

It is important that this selective creation is described as 'labelling' so as to highlight first, that the social designation of difference has no validity and second, to

[85] Link and Phelan, 'Conceptualizing Stigma' (n 26) 367.
[86] Lenhardt, 'The Mark' (n 28) 827.
[87] Maluwa, Aggleton and Parker, 'Health HIV- and AIDS-Related Stigma' (n 20) 5.

enable these categories to be questioned: we can ask 'Why is it that some human differences are singled out and deemed salient by human groups while others are ignored?' or ' What are the social, economic, and cultural forces that maintain the focus on a particular human difference?' These questions problematise not only the theme of differentiation but also endurance: Why is it that some human differences continue while others disappear?[88]

The second component highlights treatment of these labels: Why are these human differences linked to negative values? There is, after all, nothing inherently good or bad, dangerous or safe, about skin colour. This component emphasises the cognitive processes that propel categorisation and linkage between those categories and stereotypes. It raises 'critical questions of a psychological nature about the thought processes that facilitate connections between labels and stereotypes'.[89] For example how automatic is categorisation? While categorisation may be used to facilitate 'cognitive efficiency', when does this mutate into cognitive laziness?

The third key component of the stigmatisation process is the use of negative stereotyping to create crude dichotomous categories: male/female; black/white; rich/poor etc. These 'us' and 'them' binaries facilitate justification for what may otherwise be irrational and questionable treatment of groups. Categorisation suggests that the person is so different from 'us' as to be not really human—this idea is the precursor to inhuman and degrading treatment, such as under Apartheid or during the Holocaust. At its most extreme, binary thinking leads to embodiment, where the stigmatised person comes to epitomise a negative label, for example, a person with epilepsy becomes an 'epileptic'.

The fourth component is a combination of two separate but related elements. It emphasises that disadvantage is inherent in stigmatisation. It focuses on status loss and, most importantly for this book, discrimination. Discrimination is a deeper manifestation of status loss on the continuum of stigmatisation. Status loss occurs when 'the person is connected to undesirable characteristics that reduce his or her status in the eyes of the stigmatizer'. It is an inevitable consequence of negative labelling and stereotyping. Status loss as a result of stigmatisation is all encompassing: devaluation in the wider society spills over into face-to-face social interaction within smaller groups, such as in the workplace, religious organisations and even the family. Research has found that

> external statuses, like race and gender, shape status hierarchies within small groups of unacquainted persons even though the external status has no bearing on proficiency at a task the group is asked to perform. Men and whites are more likely than women and blacks to attain positions of power and prestige—they talk more frequently, have their ideas more readily accepted by others, and are more likely to be voted group leader.[90]

[88] C Tilly, *Durable Inequality* (Berkeley, University of California Press, 1998).
[89] Link and Phelan, 'Conceptualizing Stigma' (n 26) 368.
[90] Link and Phelan, 'Conceptualizing Stigma' (n 26) 371.

In addition, groups use these devalued external statuses to create 'performance expectations' which are then used to inform a complex matrix of behaviour and responses in mixed settings. In the context of public spaces such as the workplace, this includes practices such as making suggestions, taking and holding the floor, referring to the contributions of others, head nodding to show affirmation and even accepted behaviour towards interrupting.[91] The idea of status loss can thus sharpen observation and understanding of the *cumulative* disadvantage experienced by stigmatised groups.

Discrimination is discussed separately to status loss. Link and Phelan identify three forms of discrimination arising from stigmatisation: individual, structural and internalised.[92] In relation to individuals, stigmatisation can lead to the experience of direct discrimination from others: being treated with less regard because of the 'mark' resulting in the experience of social inequalities in individual life circumstances.

Structural—or institutional—discrimination can also be experienced because of a 'mark'. This does not arise from individual actions, but from accumulated practices that work to the disadvantage of minority groups. These practices can be overt or covert actions or omissions to act. An example of structural discrimination by omission can be seen in the medical field: in some regions medical practitioners are neither trained to treat nor encouraged to specialise in specific ailments, such as mental health or HIV/AIDs, because these illnesses are stigmatised. Consequently persons with stigmatised conditions suffer discrimination in relation to resource allocation and access to treatment and cure. Where treatment facilities are provided, these may be difficult to access due to cost or location, perhaps because powerful groups have lobbied to keep them out of central neighbourhoods.[93] The stigmatisation of particular illnesses can thus affect the social, political and emotional economy around the illness, and result in decisions that subject sufferers to discrimination.

A third form—internalised discrimination—is also linked to stigma: if people feel that 'a negative label has been applied to them and that other people are likely to view them as less trustworthy and intelligent, and more dangerous and incompetent'[94] they may suffer a series of negative outcomes including low self-esteem, social awkwardness, depression, stress and chronic illness, and constrained achievements including limited educational qualifications, unemployment and low career attainments. These outcomes may arise even in the absence of direct discrimination. Steele has described this phenomenon as 'stereotype threat'.[95]

[91] Link and Phelan, 'Conceptualizing Stigma' (n 26) 371.
[92] BG Link and JC Phelan, 'Stigma and Its Public Health Implications' (2006) 367 *Lancet* 528.
[93] Link and Phelan, 'Public Health Implications' (n 93) 528.
[94] Link and Phelan, 'Public Health Implications' (n 93) 528.
[95] CM Steele, *Whistling Vivaldi* (New York, WW Norton and Company, 2010).

Link and Phelan posit discrimination as a deliberate intensification of stigmatisation:

> If stigmatized persons cannot be persuaded to voluntarily accept their lower status and inferior rewards, direct discrimination can be used to accomplish the same outcome. If direct discrimination becomes ideologically difficult, sophisticated forms of structural discrimination—such as tests that induce stereotype threat—can achieve some of the same ends. The mechanisms are mutually reinforcing as well. To the extent that stigmatized groups accept the dominant view of their lower status, they are less likely to challenge structural forms of discrimination that block opportunities they desire.[96]

They did not define in detail the means used to put and keep stigmatised groups 'in their place' but this latter observation took them to their most important contribution to the study of stigma: its dependence upon 'power'.

V. Power

Link and Phelan are unequivocal on the role of power in stigma:

> Stigma is entirely dependent on social, economic, and political power—it takes power to stigmatize. In some instances the role of power is obvious. However, the role of power in stigma is frequently overlooked because in many instances power differences are so taken for granted as to seem unproblematic.[97]

Power pervades all components of stigmatisation, from attribution labelling to discrimination. None of the components are benign—they can only operate when infused with power. A stigma can only be such if social power supports it; if it only exists in the mind of an individual it is prejudice.

However, what is 'power' and how is it defined? The 'zero-sum' model of power is the most prevalent—Dahl[98] for example argued that there are only those who have it and those that do not. Bachrach and Baratz identify two 'faces' of power: it is not only seen in decision-making but also in silencing: 'to the extent that a person or group—consciously or unconsciously—creates or reinforces barriers to the public airing of policy conflicts, that person or group has power'.[99] They give the example of a person determined to raise objections to a policy at a meeting but ultimately sitting 'frozen in silence' when the time to speak arrives. In explaining such loss of courage, they argue that the 'dominant values and the political myths, rituals and institutions which tend to favor the vested interests of one or more groups, relative to others' creates what Schattschneider called a

[96] Link and Phelan, 'Conceptualizing Stigma' (n 26) 375.
[97] Link and Phelan, 'Conceptualizing Stigma' (n 26) 375.
[98] R Dahl, 'A Critique of the Ruling Elite Model' (1958) 52(2) *American Political Science Review* 463.
[99] P Bachrach and MS Baratz, 'Two Faces of Power' (1962) 56 *The American Political Science Review* 947, 949.

'mobilisation bias':[100] an environment enabling some to act and handicapping others. Thus investigation of the mobilisation bias is their starting point for the study of power: their research inquires into '... which persons or groups, if any, gain from the existing bias and which, if any, are handicapped by it'.[101]

Gaventa and Lukes identify three dimensions of power. The first dimension of explicit force can be seen by watching the winners and losers in competition or conflict. The second dimension highlights process, in particular indirect manipulation of rules to secure advantages, since architects of processes construct both the terms of entry and engagement to favour themselves. This type of power can be seen by identifying how underlying rules and structures work to favour their creators.

The third dimension mirrors the 'mobilisation bias' discussed above. It focuses on immobilisation and mobilisation, including through psychological means, of 'biases or tacit understandings that operate to exclude or to include individuals or groups in the collective decision-making or conflict'.[102] In this third dimension, power is exercised less through open conflict and more through subtle myths, symbols and stories that construct and reconstruct reality to the disadvantage of the powerless.[103] This diffuse power requires exploration of (cultural) narratives that are used to gain support for the rules operating at the second dimension of power. When successful, these third dimension narratives secure the co-operation of the powerful and the powerless, making the latter complicit in their own disempowerment.

The 'mobilisation bias' of Bachrach and Baratz and the third dimension of Gaventa and Lukes can be seen in the first component of structural stigma—why are some attributes stigmatised and others not? Or even more fundamentally, why are some attributes mobilised to become a 'semantic unit'[104]—that is, an articulated feature of the environment—yet others are not. Power determines this: even if 'relatively powerless groups create labels and stereotypes about more powerful groups and treat members of the more powerful group in accordance with those stereotypes' this will not result in stigma, because powerless groups lack the mobilisation bias to stigmatise the powerful. For example, institutionalized groups—the elderly, learning impaired, orphaned—may stereotype their carers, nurses and doctors as 'pill-pushers' and thus shun them, insult them and treat them with disrespect. Yet this negative label will only become a 'semantic unit' in the discourse of the patients; their cognitions do not carry 'sufficient clout in social, cultural, economic, and political spheres to lead to important consequences for the group that has been labelled as different'.[105] The carers would not end up

[100] EF Schattschneider, *The Semi-Sovereign People* (New York, New York University Press, 1960) 71.
[101] Bachrach and Baratz, 'Two Faces' (n 99) 952.
[102] Gaventa and Lukes in L Guinier and G Torres, *The Miners Canary* (Boston, Harvard University Press, 2002) 110.
[103] Gaventa in Guinier and Torres, *Miners Canary* (n 102) 110.
[104] Harre, *Social Being* (n 13) 200.
[105] Link and Phelan, 'Conceptualizing Stigma' (n 26) 378.

being a stigmatised group because the groups labelling them are unable to imbue their cognitions with social power.[106] Without the authority to prevail upon the social imaginary, their cognitive biases are incapable of producing any status loss or discriminatory consequences.

Power is therefore the ultimate and overarching component of stigmatisation: stigma does not 'spring from the minds of "bad" people but is inextricably linked to power, domination and subordination in the society as a whole'.[107] In the absence of power, even if some components of stigma might appear, 'what we generally mean by stigma would not exist'.[108] Adding to this, I would argue that in the absence of arbitrariness, stigma does not exist. Thus, for example, people who smoke are not stigmatised: smoking may be negatively evaluated but persons who smoke are not as a group powerless and do not suffer discrimination that affects their life opportunities and well-being. Indeed, many prime ministers and presidents—such as Nick Clegg or Barack Obama—are smokers. By contrast, corpulence is an example of an arbitrary attribute that has been given a host of negative labels such that those who do not conform to 'normal' body size may suffer status loss, discrimination and limited life opportunities.[109] Yet very few countries offer protection against weight discrimination. The same arguably applies to body tattoos, which continue to be subject to negative stereotypes—employers discriminate against those with tattoos with impunity. In the UK, individuals may damage their job prospects if they get 'inked'.[110]

VI. Conclusion

The study of stigma spans at least five decades and twice as many disciplines, including criminology, sociology, social psychology, psychology, psychiatry, medicine and public health.[111] Research in these disciplines has shown that it is a complex idea that has a variety of manifestations, mechanisms and outcomes. Whereas Goffman started from the face-to-face and neglected the social, the last 50 years of interdisciplinary research on stigma has both broadened and reversed the perspective on stigmatisation. Stigma now refers not only to the 'mark' but also to the potentially persistent social approbation which it triggers—its key elements are 'difference and devaluation'.[112] It is now widely accepted that stigma resides not in

[106] Link and Phelan, 'Conceptualizing Stigma' (n 26) 376.
[107] Maluwa, Aggleton and Parker, 'Health HIV- and AIDS-Related Stigma' (n 20).
[108] Link and Phelan, 'Conceptualizing Stigma' (n 26) 376.
[109] King et al, 'Waistlines and Ratings of Executives' (n 60).
[110] 'No tattoo if you want the job!', available at http://rt.com/uk/190572-tattoo-convention-jobs-fired/ [03/10/2014]. Discussed in Ch 8.
[111] J Stuber, I Meyer and B Link, 'Stigma, Prejudice, Discrimination and Health' (2008) 67 *Social Science & Medicine* 351.
[112] Pryor and Reeder, *Social Psychological Perspectives* (n 44) 1.

the person but is hosted by the social environment. As social environments differ, what is stigmatising in one context may not be so in another.

Put together, this interdisciplinary research allows creation of an understanding of stigma that starts with public power and moves to the face-to-face, recognising both as equally important. Stigma begins with the deliberate social creation of a 'mark' and results in individual discrimination. Five key aspects can be identified: first, the attribute or condition upon which stigma operates is *arbitrary*. 'Marks' are neither self-creating nor per se discrediting, and have no inherent meaning. Second, 'marks' are *given* a negative meaning by a larger group or society. As Fassin points out, 'the object of phobia is not to be mistaken for its source'.[113] Third, this meaning is *supported* by a diffuse yet oppressive and thus difficult to challenge social power. Fourth, the larger group or society *shares knowledge* of the negative evaluation associated with the mark—everybody knows how society views those in possession of this mark (even if nobody knows how the mark came to be evaluated in this way).[114] Fifth, because stigma resides in 'common sense' and is surrounded by ambivalence,[115] it is *inescapable*—unlike other social norms, the stigmatised cannot control or 'wish away'[116] the societal definition, although they may use different methods to manage it. Such methods can include concealment ('passing') or 'over-embracement' (the 'gift' of HIV-positive status). Although stigma cannot be escaped, the mark may lose its power over time as social habits change.

The role of power is important. A stigmatised person experiences status loss and discrimination. As ever, social power hierarchies inform and are played out in interpersonal power relations:

> By virtue of their position in a social hierarchy, members of marginalized groups such as the uneducated, poor, or overweight have lower status than their more educated, wealthy, thin, or otherwise better socially situated counterparts. Status dynamics also play out in the interpersonal relations among people. The belief that others hold about whether someone possesses resources and/or personal characteristics that are important for the achievement of collective goals also influences perceptions of status. Members of stigmatized groups are unlikely to be viewed as contributors to these goals. Structural and interpersonal stigma, combining experiences of both a diminished control over resources and a devalued social identity, are defined by both low power and low status.[117]

Stigma plays a key role 'in producing and reinforcing relationships of power and control. It causes some groups to be devalued and others to be considered superior.'[118] Stigmatisation is not the work of any single individual but is

[113] E Fassin, 'Why the Roma' (2010) *Theory, Culture and Society*, available at http://www.theoryculturesociety.org/eric-fassin-why-the-roma/.

[114] C Stangor and CS Crandall, 'Threat and the Social Construction of Stigma' in Heatherton et al (eds) (n 6), 62.

[115] Katz, 'Stigma Notion' (n 34).

[116] K Plummer, *Sexual Stigma* (London, Routledge and Kegan Paul, 1975) 26.

[117] Richman and Lattamer. See also Kurzban & Leary, 2001; Phelan, Lucas, Ridgeway & Taylor, 2014; Leary, Jongman-Sereno & Diebels, 2014.

[118] Maluwa, Aggleton and Parker, 'Health HIV and AIDS-Related Stigma' (n 20).

perpetuated by the 'collective attitude which society as whole adopts'.[119] Likewise stigma does not change due to efforts of stigmatised individuals: the Irish did not become 'white'[120] because they wanted to do so, but because general social attitudes changed. Suicide and divorce are also examples of a statuses that has become de-stigmatised as social attitudes have changed. However, some stigma have not changed: in 1963, when Goffman wrote, the 'urban unrepentant poor' were 'second class citizens', and they remain so today, as do their offspring.[121]

Yet, despite its clear link to discrimination, stigma has rarely been studied by lawyers even though the idea arises regularly in case-law. It is worth considering if, just as stigma is integral to discrimination, stigma can also be integrated into anti-discrimination law? If social psychological, sociological and criminological approaches to stigma can assist our understanding of discrimination, can they also assist in the development of anti-discrimination law? If stigma lies at the heart of every discrimination case, can it be used in the design of anti-discrimination law? Before addressing this question, it would be useful to think about the current design of anti-discrimination law.

[119] Sandro Segre 'A Simmelian Theory of Marginality, Deviance and Social Control', in F Doerr-Backes and L Nieder (eds) *Georg Simmel: Between Modernity and Post Modernity* (Wuerzburg: Koenigshausen & Neumann, 1995) 149.

[120] N Ignatieff, *How the Irish Became White* (New York, Routledge, 1995).

[121] M Fitzpatrick, 'Stigma' (2008) 58(549) *British Journal of General Practice* 294.

2

Legal Protection from Discrimination

I. Introduction

When is discrimination so wrong that it must be prevented by law? One answer to this normative question invokes ideas of dignity[1] and 'immutability'—the latter, drawing upon attribution theory,[2] emphasises the absence of blame and the former the deprivation of humanity. International human rights law and domestic anti-discrimination law have traditionally relied upon both, although human rights law[3] seems to emphasise dignity rather than immutability.

Both of these ideas can to some extent explain the varieties of anti-discrimination law that exist in civil law and common law legal systems. Limitations and concerns have been expressed in relation to both concepts. It is questionable whether they have the requisite combination of rigour and versatility to guide the creation of laws to prevent and protect from discrimination in the twenty-first century. Are they robust enough to explain to a teenager why the overweight and persons with tattoos are not protected from discrimination at work or in relation to enjoyment of goods and services? Arguably, dignity is too broad while immutability is too narrow. There seems, therefore, to be scope for another concept—such as stigma—to make a significant theoretical and practical contribution to anti-discrimination law. Stigma offers an alternative that incorporates both dignity and immutability. It adds a social backdrop to clarify the difference between discrimination that is lawful under anti-discrimination law and that which is not.

The main purpose of this chapter is to provide a historical review of the development of the anti-discrimination principle in international law. The creation of law in this area was a key part of the renewal of political morality in the post-war period and creation of an international society based upon democracy. The discussion begins below with an examination of Aristotelian notions of equality and traces its evolution to expression and entrenchment in international and national law. This is followed by a review of the uses and limitations of the concepts of

[1] According to 'attribution theory', the more a person is seen as responsible for their condition, the more others will blame and react negatively, and the less social sympathy will be expressed—and the less likely it is to be protected under anti-discrimination law.

[2] C Dupre, *The Age of Dignity: Human Rights and Constitutionalism in Europe* (Oxford, Hart Publishing/Bloomsbury, 2015).

[3] B Turner, *Vulnerability and Human Rights* (Pennsylvania, Penn State University Press, 2006).

dignity and immutability as a prelude to closer consideration of the idea of stigma in Chapter 3.

II. Equality and Inequality in Political Philosophy

Aristotle promoted equality in Ancient Greece as a conditional value, necessary for political stability. His vision of equality was by no means universal: equality was only for those otherwise equal; inequality was appropriate and just for the unequal. Likewise, equality in one respect did not mean equality in all respects: he described it as an error when men equal in one regard imagine themselves equal in every aspect or when men unequal in one respect, such as financial security, consider themselves unequal in all aspects. With these caveats, he promoted the pursuit of equality as essential for the stability of the political system and maintenance of the status quo.

By the time of the Enlightenment, equality had become an ethical dilemma. Philosophers such as Montesquieu, Rousseau and Paine all promoted the idea of natural equality, according to which all men were born equal. Montesquieu blamed society for the gradual loss of equality and saw it as the role of the state to restore equality through use of the law. Rousseau augmented natural equality with the idea of political equality. His first form of inequality, natural, was linked to the species of *Homo sapiens.* These inequalities arose from biological or psychological qualities such as age, health and strength. They were unavoidable—'when a giant and a dwarf walk the same road, every step each takes gives an extra advantage to the giant'. However, his second form—political or moral inequality—was avoidable: it arose due to human habits of bestowing power and privileges to some persons but not others. These forms of inequality interacted with and entrenched each other: natural inequality increased in humanity due to the effects of 'instituted inequality', the embedding of natural differences such as age or physique in social conventions and norms. Rousseau offered no remedy for this unjust outcome. By contrast Tom Paine, who fervently opposed inequality as the source of poverty, offered revolution as the only way to overcome the most invidious inequality of all: the difference between 'Kings' and 'Subjects'.

Romantics such as Hegel and Herder also started from the idea of natural equality, but this was not seen as unjust per se. Natural inequality was seen as fate: the inevitable consequence of the natural distribution of talents and traits. That the distribution may have been unequal was not of itself a problem. Romantics thus held that inequality was the unavoidable outcome of natural equality and, furthermore, that to deny this or attempt to change this would be folly. The uniqueness of people meant that difference was to be tolerated. At its most extreme this appreciation of particularism supported the establishment of systems and rules that treated people according to their specific 'natures' and abilities, such as slavery, apartheid, colonialism and national socialism. It was to revise this particularist notion of equality and restore the humanity of those demeaned under these systems that the universalist anti-discrimination principle was developed in international law. The long term goal was to use law to establish a new baseline for international morality.

III. The Anti-discrimination Principle in International Law

An important articulation of the anti-discrimination principle in the post war period was set out in the United Nations Declaration of Human Rights (UNHDR).[4] The Declaration was steered through the Commission of Human Rights (CHR) by John Humphries, a professor of law at McGill University in Canada. Humphries was appointed Director of the Human Rights Division by Henri Laugier[5] who became the UN Assistant Secretary General in 1946, responsible for Social Affairs. The chief task given to Humphries was preparation of the CHR to start work on an International Bill of Rights. Humphries regularly kept a diary of his work at the UN. He had a unique perspective on the proceedings and the diaries record his insights as well as his frustrations. It relates how over two years, he negotiated every provision of the Declaration with diplomats from countries holding diverse and often conflicting social visions and religious convictions.

For example, he noted that the 'two special interests that have tried hardest to influence the Declaration are the Catholic Church and the Communist Party—the former with considerably more success than the latter!'[6] His diary also noted the importance of 'creative emotion' to the enterprise: influenced by the philosopher Bergson,[7] he wrote that moral rules could not emerge from society:

> The reason, of course, why moral rules englobing the whole of humanity cannot emanate from the first source is that the instrument of society when it forges moral rules is habit. Even if it is admitted, therefore, that a new universal society is emerging or has emerged that society has not yet had the time by the instrumentality of habit to forge the moral rules necessary for its maintenance. It follows therefore that we must have recourse to creative emotion.[8]

According to Bergson, the first source of public morality is the collection of prevailing norms, rules and practices dictated by society; the second source goes beyond this—it is something higher than society described as 'creative emotion.' A new morality could not emerge from the first source because society could not see beyond itself. Creative emotion was therefore necessary for genuine social regeneration.

[4] Adopted 7 December 1948, Paris.
[5] Henri Laugier was Professor of Physiology at the Sorbonne before World War II.
[6] Humphries Diary Entry, 22 November 1948.
[7] CT Curle, *Humanite: John Humphrey's Alternative Account of Human Rights* (Toronto, University of Toronto Press, 2007).
[8] Humphries Diary Entry, Tuesday 21 December 1948.

However, creative emotion could not override political reality. Some articles were less controversial than others. Article 2 ('everyone is entitled to all the rights and freedoms set forth in the Declaration, without distinction of any kind, such as race, colour, sex, language, religion, political or other opinion, property or other status, birth or national or social origin') was adopted with 37 votes in favour, none against and one abstention (Panama) on 14 October 1948 in Paris,[9] whereas Article 3 (Everyone has the right to life, liberty and security of the person') was almost defeated by an amendment from the Lebanon proposing inclusion of the concepts of honour and physical integrity. It was eventually adopted by 36 votes in favour, none against and 12 abstentions.[10]

Despite reservations about the impact of the political manoeuvring on the quality of the Declaration, Humpries was 'firmly convinced' that the Declaration would 'prove to be a tremendously important document'.[11] A year after its adoption, he wrote:

> My own belief is that, while the declaration is not now legally binding on States, it could become binding; and our job is to encourage that development. It is a political document of the very highest importance and represents a preliminary or perhaps even first stage in the law making process. If it is not yet legislative it at least manifests a legal conviction[12] [...] the Declaration provides a standard by which the conduct of governments can be measured; and this even although the declaration may not be legally binding on governments. Indeed, this political or moral function of the Declaration would probably be its most important function even though it were also possible to invoke it before an international tribunal.[13]

He may have seemed idealistic at the time, but history has proved him correct. The Declaration has acquired a moral and political authority perhaps stronger than any legal value it may have held.

Yet for all his work on the Declaration, it was only when dealing with an allegation of anti-Semitism in the UN that Humphries linked discrimination to prejudice. He wrote in his diary that the case had 'forced me to think through the whole problem of discrimination based on prejudice'.[14] This omission may explain his lack of understanding of the work of the Sub-Commission on Discrimination, which prepared the groundwork for the International Convention on the Elimination of All Forms of Racial Discrimination (ICERD). Diary entries show he was impatient with it and dismissive of its work:

> The time and effort devoted to the Sub-Commission is largely a waste ... Individually some of the members are outstanding—Masani, Spanien, Miss Monroe etc.—but insofar

[9] John Humphries records in his diary that this provision was adopted with 37 votes in favour, none against and one abstention (Panama). Humphries Diary Entry, 14 October 1948.

[10] Humphries Diary Entry, 19 October 1948.

[11] Humphries Diary Entry, 19 October 1948.

[12] Humphries Diary Entry, 18 September 1949.

[13] Humphries Diary Entry, 27 September 1949.

[14] Humphries Diary Entry, 10 November 1949.

> as this work is concerned they can be classified into defeatists (of the type of Nisot) and naïve 'do-gooders'. It would be better for the UN if the Sub-Commission were abolished and specific question referred to the Ad Hoc committees of responsible experts.[15]

Time has proved Humphries wrong in his estimation of the work of the Sub-Commission—as discussed below, the ICERD has exerted significant moral and political authority, influencing many countries in their legal entrenchment of the anti-discrimination principle. Some, for example Britain, the USA and Australia carefully iterate every group to which it applies (closed or exhaustive lists), while others (including Canada and South Africa) provide examples and leave scope for other grounds to be included under its scope (open lists).

IV. Closed Lists

The law of England and Wales incorporated the anti-discrimination principle in 1965, when an anti-racial discrimination law—the Race Relations Act (RRA)[16]—was adopted. In 1970, an Equal Pay Act was created, followed by a Sex Discrimination Act (SDA) in 1975. No further anti-discrimination statute was introduced until the Disability Discrimination Act in 1995, and Regulations prohibiting discrimination on grounds of age, religion and sexual orientation in employment and vocational training were promulgated in 2006. A Gender Recognition Act was adopted in 2004. These diverse statutes were brought together under a single Equality Act in 2006, revised in 2010. Chapter 1 of the Equality Act 2010 now lists all of the 'protected characteristics' to which the anti-discrimination principle applies: age; disability; gender reassignment; marriage and civil partnership; race, religion or belief; and sex and sexual orientation.[17]

Legal protection from discrimination began in the USA a year earlier, in 1964, with the Civil Rights Act (CRA). In the USA, racial discrimination was entrenched in law—cases such as *Plessey v Ferguson*[18] gave legal status to the idea of 'separate but equal' public facilities for black and white Americans. The CRA ended this sanctioned segregation in public places and also banned employment discrimination on the basis of race, colour, religion, sex or national origin. Over time, state law and city codes have extended the anti-discrimination principle to other attributes such as height and weight, for example the Elliot Larsen Civil Rights Act[19] in Michigan or the municipal codes in Santa Cruz, California and San Francisco.[20] The Human Rights Law of the District of Columbia[21] also bans

[15] Humphries Diary Entry, 27 January 1950.
[16] Repealed by the Race Relations Act 1968, which was amended in 1976, 2000 and 2003.
[17] Equality Act 2010, Chapter 1.
[18] *Plessy v Ferguson*, 163 US 537 (1896).
[19] Act 453 of 1976, Sec 209.
[20] San Francisco Administrative Code Chapters 12a, 12b and 12c.
[21] DC Code Ann 1-2501 (1987 and Supp 1993).

employment discrimination based upon family responsibilities, matriculation or political affiliation. Many states have also included protection from employment discrimination on the basis of sexual orientation and gender identity.[22] The proposed Equality Act[23] is designed to amend the federal Civil Rights Act of 1964 to explicitly include sex, sexual orientation[24] and gender identity[25] among the prohibited categories of discrimination or segregation in public places.

In 2008 a new federal statute focusing on health insurance and employment was created to prohibit 'genetic' discrimination. Genetic discrimination is defined as differential treatment of any person because of a predisposition to a genetic disease. The USA has a history of such discrimination: sterilisation laws adopted between 1907 and 1981 perpetuated genetic discrimination, allowing persons presumed to have genetic 'defects' (such as mental illness, epilepsy or blindness) to be prevented from having children. In the 1970s, some states also enacted discriminatory laws for obligatory screening for sickle cell anemia, leading to stigmatisation and discrimination against African Americans.[26] While many of these laws have been repealed, the Genetic Information Nondiscrimination Act (GINA) remains necessary, especially in the workplace—individuals with a genetic mutation can experience genetic discrimination if considered less employable[27] because of this. Employees can be demoted or excluded from promotion because employers do not want to invest in training individuals who may be unable to perform certain roles due to illness caused by their genes. Different groups of people regularly associated with genetic diseases in the media suffer genetic discrimination if they are considered unemployable without tests to confirm their genetic status.[28] The GINA is the only statute of its kind in the world to address this problem.

Australia also follows the pattern of closed and exhaustive lists. As in the USA, the Australian Constitution entrenched discrimination. Section 127 of the Australian Constitution originally stated: 'In reckoning the numbers of the people of the Commonwealth, or of a State or other part of the Commonwealth, aboriginal natives shall not be counted.'[29] Section 127 was repealed by Referendum

[22] See map and table at https://www.aclu.org/map/non-discrimination-laws-state-state-information-map.

[23] H.R.3185—114th Congress (2015–2016), available at https://www.congress.gov/bill/114th-congress/house-bill/3185.

[24] Homosexuality, heterosexuality or bisexuality.

[25] Gender-related identity, appearance, mannerisms, or characteristics, regardless of the individual's designated sex at birth.

[26] To alleviate some of this stigma, Congress in 1972 passed the National Sickle Cell Anemia Control Act, which withholds Federal funding from States unless sickle cell testing is voluntary.

[27] Pre-employment genetic screening was conducted at Lawrence Berkeley Laboratory: see *Norman-Bloodsaw v Lawrence Berkeley Laboratory* (135 F.3d 1260, 1269 (9th Cir. 1998).

[28] W Zukerman, 'Genetic Discrimination in the Workplace: Towards Legal Certainty in Uncertain Times' (2009) 16 *Journal of Law and Medicine* 770, 773 (see also http://geneticliteracyproject.org/2014/11/canada-gearing-up-to-pass-law-against-genetic-discrimination/ and http://ukhumanrightsblog.com/2012/05/09/should-we-outlaw-genetic-discrimination/).

[29] 1901 Australian Constitution, Section 25, 'Provisions as to races disqualified from voting: For the purposes of the last section, if by the law of any State all persons of any race are disqualified from

in 1967, and in 1975 the anti-discrimination principle was entrenched in the first federal race equality law. The Racial Discrimination Act 1975[30] was followed by the Sex Discrimination Act 1984[31] and the Disability Discrimination Act 1992.[32] Both the federal Racial Discrimination Act 1975 and the Sex Discrimination Act 1984 are explicitly based on international Conventions—the ICERD and the Convention on the Elimination of all Forms of Discrimination Against Women (CEDAW)—which are attached as schedules to the respective Acts.[33]

In addition, each State and Territory in Australia has its own anti-discrimination laws, with a unique range of protection. A review of these illustrates how context-driven protection from discrimination can be, even within the same country. The Anti-Discrimination Act 1977 of New South Wales (NSW)[34] is perhaps the most limited in scope. It covers race; sex transgender; marital/domestic status; disability; responsibility as a carer; homosexuality; age; and HIV/Aids. The Anti-Discrimination Act 1992 of the Northern Territory (NT) adds more categories, covering race; sex; sexuality; age; marital status; pregnancy; parenthood, breastfeeding; impairment; trade union or employer association activity; religious belief or activity; political opinion; affiliation or activity; irrelevant medical record; irrelevant criminal record; and association with a person who has, or is believed to have, one of these attributes. The Anti-Discrimination Act 1991 of Queensland (Qld) is also broad. It includes sex; relationship status; pregnancy; parental status; breastfeeding; age; race; impairment; religious belief or religious activity; political belief or activity; trade union activity; lawful sexual activity; gender identity; sexuality; family responsibilities; association with, or relation to, a person identified on the basis of any of the above attributes.

The Equal Opportunity Act 1984 of South Australia (SA) covers sex; chosen gender; sexuality; race; disability; age; marital or domestic partnership status; identity of a spouse or domestic partner; pregnancy; the ground of association

voting at elections for the more numerous House of the Parliament of the State, then, in reckoning the number of the people of the State or of the Commonwealth, persons of the race resident in that State shall not be counted'. See A Twomey, 'An Obituary for s 25 of the Constitution' (2012) 23 *Public Law Review* 125.

[30] Rogers reminds that, as elsewhere, 'Despite these genuine measures, Indigenous Australians are still suffering various, less explicit forms of racial discrimination. Legislative discrimination in public space law is one such example. This article will examine how Queensland's police "move on" powers discriminate against Indigenous Australians.' D Rogers, 'Crime and Misconduct Commission: Review of Police Move-on Powers' (2011) *Queensland Lawyer* 31.

[31] J Seeman '*Discrimination*' (2010) 1 Weekly Report 115.

[32] N Rees, S Rice and D Allen, *Australian Anti-Discrimination Law*, 2nd edn (The Federation Press, 2014).

[33] G McCarry 'Landmines Among the Landmarks: Constitutional Aspects of Anti-Discrimination Laws' (1989) 63 *The Australian Law Journal* 327, 328. McCarry discusses the case of *Viskauskas v Niland*, where the question of consistency between the Racial Discrimination Act 1975 and the sections of the Anti-Discrimination Act 1977 (NSW) dealing with discrimination on the ground of race was considered.

[34] I Moss and M Newton, 'The Anti-Discrimination Board of New South Wales: Eight Years of Achievement in a New Area of Law' (1986) 60 *The Australian Law Journal* 162.

with a child; the ground of caring responsibilities; and the ground of religious appearance or dress. The Anti-Discrimination Act 1988 in Tasmania (Tas) uses groups and sub-groups to prohibit discrimination on the grounds of the following attributes: race; age; sexual orientation; lawful sexual activity; gender; gender identity; intersex;[35] marital status; relationship status; pregnancy; breastfeeding; parental status; family responsibilities; disability; industrial activity; political belief or affiliation; political activity; religious belief or affiliation; religious activity; irrelevant criminal record; irrelevant medical record; association with a person who has, or is believed to have, any of these attributes.[36] Tasmania is one of the few places in the world to recognise intersex discrimination.

Meanwhile, the Equal Opportunity Act 1995/ 2010 of Victoria (Vic)[37] iterates age; carer and parental status; disability (including physical, sensory and intellectual disability; work related injury; medical conditions; and mental, psychological and learning disabilities); employment activity; gender identity, lawful sexual activity and sexual orientation; industrial activity; marital status; physical features; political belief or activity; pregnancy and breastfeeding; race (including colour, nationality, ethnicity and ethnic origin); religious belief or activity; sex; and personal association with someone who has, or is assumed to have, one of these personal characteristics.

The Equal Opportunity Act 1984 of Western Australia (WA) provides protection on grounds of sex, marital status, pregnancy or breast feeding; gender history grounds in certain cases; family responsibility or family status; sexual orientation;[38] race;[39] religious or political conviction;[40] impairment;[41] age;[42] and finally publication of relevant details of persons on the Fines Enforcement Registrar's website.[43] Finally, the Discrimination Act 1991/2013 in the Australian Capital Territory (ACT) states in Section 7(1) that the Act applies to discrimination on the ground of sex; sexuality; gender identity; relationship status; status as a parent or carer; pregnancy; breastfeeding; race; religious or political conviction; disability; industrial activity; age; profession, trade, occupation or calling; association (whether as a relative or otherwise) with a person identified by reference to one of these attributes; and a spent conviction within the meaning of the Spent Convictions Act 2000.

[35] Re intersex in the EU, see M Travis, 'Accommodating Intersexuality in EU Anti-Discrimination Law' (2015) 21(2) *European Law Journal* 180.

[36] Section 16.

[37] G Orr and JC Tham, 'Work and Employment' (2012) 19 *Australian Journal of Administrative Law* 180.

[38] Part II.

[39] Part III.

[40] Part IV.

[41] Part IV A.

[42] Part IV B.

[43] Part IV C.

V. Open Lists

Open lists adopt a flexible approach to the anti-discrimination principle. This open approach applies to the prohibition of discrimination as set out in Article 15(1) of the Canadian Charter of Rights and Freedoms:[44]

> Every individual is equal before and under the law and has the right to the equal protection and equal benefit of the law without discrimination and, in particular, without discrimination based on race, national or ethnic origin, colour, religion, sex, age or mental or physical disability.

This is an inclusive equality[45] guarantee because in addition to the enumerated grounds, Article 15 (1) accomodates unspecified 'analogous grounds', thereby enabling other groups to enjoy legal protection from discrimination. The meaning of 'analogous grounds' was discussed by the Canadian Supreme Court in *Miron v Trudel*,[46] where the Justices stated that factors to consider include whether the group sharing the characteristic has been the object of historical stereotyping, prejudice or disadvantage; whether the group constitutes a 'discrete and insular minority' which is lacking in political power or influence; whether the characteristic is beyond an individual's control or 'changeable only at unacceptable personal cost'; and whether the characteristic is 'recognized as a prohibited ground of discrimination under other human rights laws, or is similar in any other way to the grounds explicitly included under section 15'.[47]

The different decisions concerning whether 'homelessness' constitutes an analogous ground illustrates that despite the guidance there is divergence. In *Tanudja*,[48] Lederer J held for the Supreme Court of Ontario that there is no such group:

> [129] … it is not possible to identify who is 'homeless' […] homelessness is not, for the purposes of this Application, restricted to those without homes. […] It may be that what is being referred to as 'the homeless' includes those without 'affordable, adequate and accessible' housing. What is adequate housing? Presumably, this depends on the circumstances of the individuals involved … [131] [T]here is no means to understand the parameters that would define those who make up the analogous group. Who would be the members? On what basis is the group said to be analogous? In these circumstances, it is impossible to come to a substantive understanding of what the analogous ground is.

Thus 'homelessness' was held to represent an indefinable ground because it did not outline an objectively ascertainable and stable group of people.

[44] Constitution Act 1982, Part I.

[45] C Sheppard, *Inclusive Equality: The Relational Dimensions of Systemic Discrimination in Canada* (Montreal, McGill-Queens University Press, 2010).

[46] *Miron v Trudel* [1995] 2 SCR 418.

[47] See RJ Sharpe and KE Swinton, 'Equality' in RJ Sharpe and KE Swinton, *The Charter of Rights and Freedoms* (Toronto, Irwin Law, 1998) 184.

[48] *Tanudjaja v Canada (Attorney General)*, 2013 ONSC 5410.

However, *Tanudja* was criticised[49] as out of line with previous judgments in other state courts. For example, in *Sparks*,[50] the Nova Scotia Court of Appeal held that poverty and reliance on public housing did constitute analogous grounds under Section 15. In this case, public housing tenants challenged local housing law that excluded them from 'security of tenure' protections enjoyed by private sector tenants. Writing for the Court, Hallett J focused less on the transitory nature of the groups (people may move in and out of public housing) and more on the social attitudes towards residency in public housing. He recognised the stigma and discriminatory treatment directed at those living in public housing and noted that attitudes toward public housing tenants were linked to the over-representation of racialised households and single mothers among those living in poverty and relying on public housing. Thus he concluded that 'the impugned provisions amount to discrimination on the basis of race, sex and income'. His reasoning was subsequently adopted by the Nova Scotia Supreme Court in *R v Rehberg*,[51] where Section 15 was used to challenge a 'spouse in the house' rule that disentitled sole support parents, mainly women, from receiving social assistance benefits if they were co-habiting with a man. The Justices in Nova Scotia found that the differential treatment of co-habitants when they relied on social assistance constituted discrimination on the ground of poverty.[52]

The *Sparks* and *Rehberg* decisions were cited by the Ontario Court of Appeal in *Falkiner v Ontario (Ministry of Community and Social Services)*, which involved a similar challenge to 'spouse in the house' rules. Harrington is, therefore, highly critical of the rejection by the Ontario Supreme Court:

> The denial of analogous grounds claims on the basis that people may move in and out of poverty or homelessness represents a misapplication of the concept of immutability as set out in *Corbiere* … Judicial decisions predating *Corbiere*, which recognize poverty as an analogous ground, are not inconsistent with the focus on socially constructed identity which the majority in *Corbiere* relied on in developing the concept of 'constructive immutability.

As in the USA and Australia, the anti-discrimination principle is also expressed in state law. For example, Article 10 of Quebec's Charter of Human Rights grants 'full and equal recognition and exercise of his human rights and freedoms, without distinction, exclusion or preference' regardless of 'race, colour, sex, sexual orientation, civil status, religion, political convictions, language, ethnic or national origin, social condition or the fact that he is a handicapped person or that he uses

[49] J Sealy-Harrington, 'Should Homelessness be an Analogous Ground? Clarifying the Multi-Variable Approach to Section 15 of the Charter' available at http://ablawg.ca/wp-content/uploads/2015/04/Blog_JSH_Tanudjaja_ONCA_April20152.pdf; JR Belcher and BR De Forge, 'Social Stigma and Homelessness: The Limits of Social Change' (2012) 22(8) *Journal of Human Behaviour in the Social Environment* 929.

[50] *Dartmouth/Halifax County Regional Housing Authority v Sparks* (1993), 119 NSR (2d) 91, 101 DLR (4th) 224 (NSCA) [*Sparks*].

[51] *R v Rehberg* (1993), 127 NSR (2d) 331, 111 DLR (4th) 336 (NSSC) [*Rehberg*].

[52] Sealy-Harrington, 'Should Homelessness be an Analogous Ground?' (n 49).

any means to palliate his handicap'. Likewise the Ontario Human Rights Charter states in Part I that 'every person has a right to equal treatment ..., without discrimination because of race, ancestry, place of origin, colour, ethnic origin, citizenship, creed, sex, sexual orientation, gender identity, gender expression, age, marital status, family status or disability'.[53] In addition, Canada's Human Rights Act of 1985 prohibits discrimination on grounds of race, national or ethnic origin, colour, religion, sex, age or mental or physical disability, sexual orientation, marital status, family status, disability and spent or suspended conviction.

Like Canada, South Africa also uses an open list. The 'Promotion of Equality and Prevention of Unfair Discrimination Act 2000' implements Section 9 of the Constitution. It aims to prevent and prohibit unfair discrimination and harassment, to promote equality and eliminate unfair discrimination, to prevent and prohibit hate speech. The prohibited grounds set out in Chapter 1 are:

> (a) race, gender, sex, pregnancy, marital status, ethnic or social origin, colour, sexual orientation, age, disability, religion, conscience, belief, culture, language and birth; or
> (b) any other ground where discrimination based on that other ground ...

The enumerated grounds therefore act as specific examples rather than the totality of the application of the principle.

This brief perusal illustrates that the anti-discrimination principle can and has been applied to a range of attributes, statuses and conditions. Whether open or closed, there are clearly no inherent limits to the range of prohibitions that can be set out in anti-discrimination law. The range is contextual—there are specific reasons why the ACT includes protection for spent convictions but NSW does not, or why WA is the only place to include publication of relevant details of persons on the Fines Enforcement Registrar's website. The Canadian law may come the closest to universal application of the anti-discrimination principle, yet the additional concept of 'analogous grounds' is used to limit it. Can dignity or immutability explain this variety in anti-discrimination law?

VI. Dignity, Immutability and the Anti-discrimination Principle

The idea of dignity is central to the United Nations (UN). The UN Charter is based on the principles of the dignity and equality inherent in all human beings, and this is also reflected in the Declaration on Human Rights. The first article of the Declaration adopted by the UN Commission of Human Rights (CHR) declares: 'All human beings are born free and equal in dignity and rights. They are endowed with reason and conscience and should act towards one another in

[53] R.s.o. 1990, c H.19, s 1; 1999, c 6, s 28 (1); 2001, c 32, s 27 (1); 2005, c 5, s 32 (1); 2012, c 7, s 1.

a spirit of brotherhood.'[54] During debate, South Africa had proposed an amendment to replace 'dignity and rights' in Article 1 with the more limited 'fundamental rights and freedoms'. In his diaries, Humphries describes this suggestion as 'shocking'.[55] His response indicates the high value placed upon this idea. In 2008, on the anniversary of the UN Declaration, Pope Benedict XVI stated that the 'universality, indivisibility and interdependence of human rights all serve as guarantees safeguarding human dignity'.[56]

The idea of dignity was also central to the development of the anti-discrimination principle in the UN. The CHR created a Sub-commission on prevention of discrimination and protection of minorities (SPDPM) in 1946 which was tasked with drafting the ICERD to institutionalise anti-discrimination. This work began in 1949 with a systematic study into the 'main types of discrimination which impede the equal enjoyment by all of human rights and fundamental freedoms and the causes of such discrimination'.[57] The direct concern was prevention of the discriminatory enjoyment of the rights listed in the Declaration of Human Rights and identification of possible remedies—legal, administrative and educational—for racial discrimination. The first step however was to articulate the problem of racial discrimination. This was defined as 'any act or conduct which denies to certain individuals equality of treatment with other individuals because they belong to particular groups in society'.

Three elements had to be satisfied in order for an act to be discriminatory. First, there had to be negative or pejorative act (thus a failure to act could not be discriminatory). Second, the perjorative act had to be motivated by a *social* rather than individual identity—the focus was conduct 'based on a distinction made on grounds of natural or social categories, which have no relation either to individual capacities or merits, or to the concrete behaviour of the individual person'.[58] The act therefore had to be an affront to a person's individuality. Finally, the affront had to have harmful results—acts that affronted human dignity by negating individual freedom and equality were always harmful. 'Prevention of discrimination', as per the UN, was therefore 'the prevention of any action which denies to individuals or groups of people equality of treatment which they may wish' and required measures to 'suppress or eliminate inequality of treatment … on grounds of race, colour, sex, language, religion, political or other opinion, national or social origin, property, birth or status' which may have 'harmful results'. The SPDPM did not offer a comparative approach: the treatment did not have to be 'like' or 'less

[54] Humphries Diary Entry, 12 October 1948.

[55] Humphries Diary Entry, 6 October 1948.

[56] F Brennan, 'Religion, Multiculturalism and Legal Pluralism' in N Hosen and R Mohr (eds), *Law and Religion in Public Life: The Contemporary Debate* (London, Routledge, 2011) 73.

[57] UN E/EN.4/Sub.2/40/Rev.1 7 June 1949 ('United Nations—Commission on Human Rights (Sub-commission on preventing discrimination and the protection of minorities), 'The Main Types and Causes of Discrimination' (Memorandum submitted by the Secretary General, New York, 1949, p 1).

[58] UN, 'Main Types and Causes of Discrimination' (n 57) 9.

favourable'. The problem of discrimination was not to be guided by comparison but by the concept of dignity:

> Since human beings are both alike and different, the principle of equality must be based upon some criterion. That criterion is to be found in an ethical concept, namely, the idea of the dignity of the human person. Human dignity implies that human beings are to be treated as ends in themselves and not as mere means to an end.[59]

The SPDPM thus anchored the anti-discrimination principle in dignity, establishing it as the ethical impulse in action to prevent discrimination.[60]

VII. The Limits of Dignity

It is hard to reconcile barbaric systems such as (but not limited to) slavery, apartheid, colonialism and the Holocaust with the long and cherished history of the idea of dignity in Western theology and philosophy. Dignity is a complex idea, incorporating notions of social status, autonomy and personal honour. Kant described dignity as autonomy—autonomy was 'the ground of the dignity of human nature'. Rawls refers to dignity as the basis of self-respect such that a life without dignity lacks value or meaning—arguments for assisted suicide often draw upon notions of dignity. The dignity of humanity is presented as a non-negotiable fact—it is seen as an 'unassailable value, and, as such, it may serve as an irrefutable argument'.[61]

This may explain why post-war human rights texts use dignity as the common characteristic of all humanity[62] and why many constitutions drafted in the twentieth century—such as those of Germany, Hungary, Israel and South Africa—entrench it. The South African constitution links a finding of discrimination to systemic disadvantage and the undermining of dignity. The Treaty on European Union of 1992 also sets out respect for human dignity as the fundamental value in the EU.[63] It is a powerful idea in law. In the equality context, Fredman argues that 'the central aim of equality should be to facilitate equal participation of all in society, based on equal concern and respect for the dignity of each individual'.[64]

[59] UN, 'Main Types and Causes of Discrimination' (n 57) 4.

[60] A further study on the legislative and judicial practices of various countries with regard to measures of the cessation of any advocacy of national, racial or religious hostility (UN E/CN.4/Sub.2/172 9 November 1955) was completed in 1955. Reports were prepared for 67 countries using texts of constitutions, statutes and administrative instruments, preliminary studies on legislative and judicial practice concerning incitement. The information indicated that legal systems differed in the extent to which freedom of expression could be restricted in order to stop incitement to racial, religious or national hostility. This was followed in 1956 by a study of discrimination in the field of employment and occupation (E/CN.4/Sub.2/176/Rev.1 4 January 1956).

[61] R O'Connell, 'The Role of Dignity in Equality Law: Lessons from Canada and South Africa' (2008) 6(2) *International Journal of Constitutional Law* 267.

[62] O'Connell, 'The Role of Dignity in Equality Law' (n 61).

[63] Article 2 of the Treaty on European Union (TEU).

[64] S Fredman, 'What Do We Mean by Age Equality?' (London, IPPR, 2001) 2.

The idea is used to prevent leveling down: 'Dignity requires that people be treated well, and in an equality context equally well: it is not satisfied if people are treated equally badly!'[65]

Nussbaum identifies dignity as central to the capabilities approach:

> Human dignity is an idea of central importance today. It plays a key role in the international human rights movement, and it figures prominently in many documents that ground political principles for individual nations. It also plays a role in abstract theories of justice and human entitlement. I myself have given the idea a key role in my own political conception of justice, holding that a hallmark of minimum social justice is the availability, to all citizens, of ten core 'capabilities,' or opportunities to function. All citizens are entitled to a threshold level of these ten capabilities because, I argue, all ten are necessary conditions of a life worthy of human dignity.

It is also invoked in case-law—for example, in *Nachova and Others*[66] the European Court of Human Rights (ECtHR) stated that 'racial violence is a particular affront to human dignity ...' [145]; in *Hoffmann*,[67] the South African Supreme Court stated that

> [27]: At the heart of the prohibition of unfair discrimination is the recognition that under our Constitution all human beings, regardless of their position in society, must be accorded equal dignity. That dignity is impaired when a person is unfairly discriminated against ...

Yet those who recognise the longevity and centrality of this idea also acknowledge its limitations. Fredman describes its 'ambiguous almost subjective nature'[68] with the example of 'dwarf-throwing': does the prevention of this 'sport' protect dignity or undermine autonomy? She argues that dignity should be an aspect of equality: 'the aims of equality should be seen as the facilitation of choice or autonomy, the protection of dignity and the enhancement of participative democracy or social inclusion. A legislative model should be shaped to achieve these objectives.'[69] Nussbaum likewise sees the problems inherent in the influential Stoic account of human dignity, yet argues these are surmountable if substituted by the Aristotelian/Marxian account of dignity, which sees the dignity of the human being as squarely a part of the world of nature and does not posit a sharp split between rationality and other human capacities:

> Indeed, one good general way of thinking about the intuitive idea of dignity is that it is the idea of being an end rather than merely a means. If something has dignity, as Kant put it well, it does not merely have a price: it is not merely something to be used for the

[65] Sachs J in *Lesbian and Gay Equality Project v Minister of Home Affairs* (CCT10/04) [2005] (2005/12/01) at [150].

[66] *Nachova and Others v Bulgaria* (Application nos 43/577/98 and 43/579/98) 2005 ECtHR. *Nachova* was the first case where the ECtHR distinguished between a procedural and substantive violation of Art 14 (non-discrimination).

[67] *Hoffmann v South African Airways* 20 ILLR 67.

[68] S Fredman, *Introduction to Discrimination Law* (Oxford, Oxford University Press, 2002) 19.

[69] Fredman, *Discrimination Law* (n 68) 15.

> ends of others, or traded on the market. This idea is closely linked to the idea of *respect* as the proper attitude toward dignity; indeed, rather than thinking of the two concepts as totally independent, so that we would first offer an independent account of dignity and then argue that dignity deserves respect (as independently defined), I believe that we should think of the two notions as closely related, forming a concept-family to be jointly elucidated. Central to both concepts is the idea of being an end and not merely a means.[70]

By contrast, Hepple promotes a 'stewardship' notion of dignity.

However these suggestions would not address all concerns with the concept. McCrudden argues, dignity would remain open to judicial manipulation.[71] As O'Connell[72] writes:

> If the idea of dignity is sometimes used in order to expand the scope of equality law's reach, arguably its main use is to restrict it. One of the main purposes of dignity in comparative constitutional equality jurisprudence is *as a threshold requirement*, to separate those distinctions which are constitutionally improper from ones not so improper.

He draws upon examples from Canada and South Africa to illustrate how dignity can be used to restrict the reach of equality law. In the South African Constitution, dignity is 'an underlying consideration'[73] used to determine what constitutes *unfair* discrimination. Discrimination is unfair if it:

> i. causes or perpetuates systemic disadvantage; ii. undermines human dignity; or iii. adversely affects the equal enjoyment of a person's rights and freedoms in a serious manner that is comparable to discrimination on a ground in paragraph *(a)*.

Case law from Canada provides a second example of the limiting effect of dignity. In *Law*[74] the Canadian Supreme Court rejected the claim that a lower age restriction on survivor's benefits for women was discriminatory because the restriction did not undermine the claimant's dignity. Iacobucci J, speaking for the Court, established guidelines incorporating three key equality principles: Did the case involve a formal distinction or a differential impact? Was this based on one of the grounds mentioned in Section 15 of the Charter or an analogous ground? If so, does it violate the purpose of the Charter?[75] This final question imported the idea of dignity[76] in particular whether the dignity of the claimant was demeaned.[77]

[70] M Nussbaum, 'Human Dignity and Bioethics: Essays Commissioned by the President's Council on Bioethics', Washington, DC, March 2008. Part 4: The Source and Meaning of Dignity—Chapter 14: Human Dignity and Political Entitlements Martha Nussbaum, available at https://bioethicsarchive.georgetown.edu/pcbe/reports/human_dignity/chapter14.html#endnote1.

[71] C McCrudden, 'Human Dignity and Judicial Interpretation of Human Rights' (2008) 19(4) *European Journal of International Law* 655.

[72] O'Connell, 'The Role of Dignity in Equality Law' (n 61).

[73] *Robins v Volks* [79] (Ngcoco J, concurring).

[74] *Law v Canada (Minister of Employment and Immigration)* [1999] 170 Dominion Law Reports 4th 1 [1999] 1 SCR 497 (1999/3/25).

[75] ibid [39], [88].

[76] ibid [51].

[77] ibid [59]–[75].

Applying this test, Iacobucci J found that there was a distinction and that it was based on the enumerated ground of age *but* that there was no violation of human dignity. He reasoned that young people (without disability or dependent children) had a better chance to find employment. There was therefore no stereotyping of people under the age of 35 implied in the restriction. Rather, the distinction was related to the economic reality that a young person has a greater opportunity to replace the lost income.[78]

Even where dignity is just one of a range of considerations, it can upset equality aims. In *Ayinde and Thinjom*,[79] consideration of dignity did not convince a British court to respect the preferences of an elderly citizen to be cared for by his wife, who as a non-national was subject to a deportation order:

> 41. Reliance on broad principles of human dignity as contained within the Charter of the Fundamental Rights of the European Union does not assist the appellants. Whilst the principle is inviolable and must be respected and protected, it does not lead to the conclusion that, in order for there to be compliance, it is necessary to secure the presence of a relative as a carer.[80]

While in theory dignity should always promote equal treatment, in practice it can too often tolerate discrimination. Consequently, there is reason to approach with caution the 'shadowy figure of dignity.'[81] For many scholars it is an ambiguous concept which conceals very different ideas of what constitutes a dignified life: 'What one person regards as an intolerable assault on human dignity, another may see as incidental, part of the common everyday life. Or what one person may see as an assault on dignity, another may see as necessary positive action.'[82]

VIII. The Idea of Immutability

An alternative or complement to dignity is immutability. Immutability describes something that is not chosen and cannot be changed. Like dignity, it has an air of irrefutability but in addition hints at perpetuity and irreversibility. This may be because it is closely linked to biology as well as morality. Immutability refers to an 'eternal truth',[83] thus to be immutable is not merely to be unchanging, but also to be *unable* to change. As put by Marcossen, 'few arguments offered on behalf of ending discrimination or inequality resonate more powerfully than immutability.

[78] ibid [101]–[103].
[79] *Ayinde and Thinjom* (Carers—Reg.15A—*Zambrano*) [2015] UKUT 560 (IAC) 21 May 2015.
[80] ibid [41].
[81] O'Connell, 'The Role of Dignity in Equality Law' (n 61).
[82] O'Connell, 'The Role of Dignity in Equality Law' (n 61).
[83] D Kaufman, 'God's Immutability and the Necessity of Descartes's Eternal Truths' (2005) 43(1) *Journal of the History of Philosophy* 1.

It reflects the universal appeal of the concept that it is unfair to disadvantage people based on a characteristic over which they exercise no control.'[84]

Immutability has played a central role in determining where the anti-discrimination principle should be active. Application of the anti-discrimination principle is only politically legitimate if it serves to protect people from mistreatment for reasons over which they have little or no control, and are impossible or very difficult to change—in other words, are immutable. Immutability was the reason why protection from discrimination on the grounds of religion was removed from drafts of the Race Relations Act 1965: the Society for Labour Lawyers stressed that the law should 'protect those attacked for what they are, not for what they may believe or do'.[85] Therefore religious groups were not included among those who it proposed should be protected, unless religion was proxy for ethnicity. This distinction between immutable and mutable characteristics was less relevant for other groups, such as the Campaign Against Racial Discrimination (CARD), that proposed a prohibition which included religion.[86] The Labour government settled the content of the legislation based upon two considerations: first, what would be practical to apply and thus effective and, second, what would be compatible with the emerging international instrument, the International Convention on the Elimination of All Forms of Racial Discrimination (ICERD). The ICERD focused on race and consciously excluded religion because it was seen as a chosen rather than inherent attribute. This pattern was followed by the British government and remains potent in cases of discrimination: protection focuses on characteristics similar to sex that are 'innate and largely immutable [characteristics] closely connected with an individual's personality and life chances'.[87]

Regional frameworks adopt the same logic: in the case of *TEST-Achat*[88] before the CJEU Advocate General Kokott described race, ethnic origin and gender as characteristics which are 'inseparably linked' to an individual, 'over which he has no influence' and which are 'not subject to any natural changes'. Immutability is also central in the protection from discrimination in the USA. It has long served as a limiting principle[89] to determine when legal protection from discrimination should be provided, and has an especially strong imprint on American constitutional law. The United States Supreme Court has made it clear that immutability determines when a classification is 'suspect' and therefore subject to a strict rather than standard level of scrutiny.[90] This test applies only to scrutiny under the

[84] SA Marcosson, 'Constructive Immutability' (2001) 3(2) *University of Pennsylvania Journal of Constitutional Law* 673.

[85] Public Records Office, London: 'LAB 8/3070, Memorandum on Draft Bill'.

[86] Public Records Office, London: 'LAB 8/3070, CARD Proposals for Legislation'.

[87] *Reg (RJM) v Work & Pensions Secretary* [2008] UKHL 63, [2009] 1 AC 311 [5].

[88] Case C-236/09 *Association belge des Consommateurs Test-Achats ASBL and Others v Conseil des Ministres.* [50] AG Opinion. See also paras 62–63, where the AG seems to challenge the modern utility of categories per se.

[89] *McClesky v Kemp* 481 US 279, 283 (1987).

[90] A classification subject to 'strict scrutiny' must demonstrate that it 'serves a compelling state interest' and is 'necessary … to the accomplishment' of its objective.

Equal Protection Clause of the 14th Amendment—under Title VII,[91] which covers employment discrimination, there is just one level of protection. The determination of whether a classification is 'suspect' depends upon a number of factors. The Court asks: whether the group so defined has suffered a history of purposeful discrimination; whether it lacks political power to obtain redress; and whether the discrimination constitutes a level of unfairness invidious to the ideal of equal protection. When seeking to answer this final question, the Court considers, amongst other aspects, whether the trait defining the group is immutable.[92] Immutability is therefore integral to the question of fairness—it is unfair to be burdened by a classification which has not been chosen. Immutability in the USA therefore performs the role given to 'dignity' in South Africa.

The US Supreme Court's use of immutability in the context of equal treatment has been traced to *Weber*, a case concerning discrimination against children born outside of marriage, at that time described as 'illegitimate'.[93] The Court noted that 'imposing disabilities on the illegitimate child is contrary to the basic concept of our system that legal burdens should bear some relationship to individual responsibility or wrongdoing'. It reasoned that if the state wanted to discourage adults from engaging in particular behaviours, it was unfair to burden the 'disincentives on their unwitting children'. Justice Brennan adopted this language from *Weber* in *Frontiero* where he emphasised the unfairness of gender discrimination. Writing for the majority, he presented the 'immutability' of sex as one reason why such discrimination was wrong. Specifically, quoting *Weber*, he wrote that:

> Moreover, since sex, like race and national origin, is an immutable character determined solely by the accident of birth, the imposition of special disabilities upon the members of a particular sex because of their sex would seem to violate the basic concept of our system that legal burdens should bear some relationship to individual responsibility.

The Supreme Court clarified that immutability meant that the group had to be defined by a permanent and unchanging feature 'determined solely by accident of birth'.[94] Accordingly, race, gender and national origin are treated as immutable characteristics.[95]

The Supreme Court has been criticised for not providing a clearer rationale to explain its approach to immutability.[96] For example, in *Rogers v American Airlines*

[91] Title VII 42 U.S.C 2000e-2(a) (2004).

[92] MR Shapiro, 'Treading the Supreme Court's Murky Immutability Waters' (2002) 38 *Gonzaga Law Review* 409.

[93] *Weber v Aetna Casualty & Surety Co*, 406 US 164, 168 (1972).

[94] *Frontiero v Richardson* 411 US 677 (1973). See also *Garcia v Gloor* 618 F.2d 264 (5 Cir. 1980), cert denied, 499 US 1113 (1981); *Caban v Mohammad*, 441 US 380 (1979); *Holland v Illinois* 493 US 474 (1990). Balog asks whether the trait has to be visible. See K Balog, 'Equal Protection for Homosexuals: Why the Immutability Argument is Necessary and How it is Met' (2005) 53 *Cleveland State Law Review* 545.

[95] MKB Darmer, 'Immutability and Stigma: Towards A More Progressive Equal Protection Rights Discourse' (2010) *The American University Journal of Gender, Social Policy & the Law* 5.

[96] Shapiro, 'Treading the Supreme Court's Murky Immutability Waters' (n 92).

the Supreme Court argued that a braided hairstyle could easily be changed and was therefore mutable, while an afro was natural and thus immutable.[97] Ms Rogers argued that the policy of American Airlines prohibiting braided hairstyles discriminated specifically against her as a black woman. She had worked for American Airlines for 11 years before a new dress policy was instituted that prohibited the wearing of braids. She argued that the policy discriminated indirectly against black women because braids have been 'historically, a fashion and style adopted by Black American women, reflective of cultural, historical essences of the Black women in American society'. However as braids can be undone, the Court saw them as mutable and therefore the policy as non-discriminatory. This perhaps illustrates the problem with immutability: how do we decide what can and what can't be changed? That gender can in fact now be changed does not make it less immutable. Being in a caring relationship has little to do with immutability[98] yet carers in Australia are protected from discrimination.[99]

Like dignity, immutability works both ways—it has blocked some claims for protection but enabled others. Sexual orientation discrimination was prohibited in law in the USA when it was recognised as immutable.[100] As documented by Clarke, state courts in Wisconsin,[101] Texas,[102] Michigan[103] and California[104] and supreme courts in New Mexico,[105] Iowa,[106] California[107] and Connecticut[108]

[97] ML Turner, 'The Braided Uproar: A Defense of My Sisters Hair and an Indictment of *Rogers v American Airlines*' (2001) 7 *Cardozo Women's Law Journal* 115.

[98] J Herring, *Caring and the Law* (Oxford, Oxford University Press, 2014).

[99] B Smith, 'Its About Time—For a New Regulatory Approach to Equality' (2008) 36(2) *Federal Law Review* 1.

[100] JA Clarke, 'Against Immutability' (2015) 125 *Yale Law Journal* 1.

[101] *Wolf v Walker*, 986 F. Supp. 2d 982, 1013 (W.D. Wis. 2014) the state court held that as it is 'fundamental to a person's identity', sexual orientation satisfied the test of immutability.

[102] *De Leon v Perry*, 975 F. Supp. 2d 632, 651 (W.D. Tex. 2014) ('[S]exual orientation is so fundamental to a person's identity that one ought not be forced to choose between one's sexual orientation and one's rights as an individual—even if one could make a choice').

[103] *Bassett v Snyder*, 951 F. Supp. 2d 939, 960 (E.D. Mich. 2013) ('Even if sexual orientation were not immutable, sexual orientation is an integral part of personal identity').

[104] *Golinski v US Office of Pers Mgmt*, 824 F. Supp. 2d 968, 986 (N.D. Cal. 2012), hearing en banc denied, 680 F.3d 1104 (9th Cir. 2012), appeal dismissed, 724 F.3d 1048 (9th Cir. 2013) ('[A] person's sexual orientation is so fundamental to one's identity that a person should not be required to abandon it').

[105] *Griego v Oliver*, 316 P.3d 865, 884 (N.M. 2013) ('This [immutability] requirement cannot mean that the individual must be completely unable to change the characteristic. … Instead, the question is whether the characteristic is so integral to the individual's identity that, even if he or she could change it, would it be inappropriate to require him or her to do so in order to avoid discrimination?').

[106] *Varnum v Brien*, 763 N.W.2d 862, 886–89 (Iowa 2009) ('[W]e agree with those courts that have held the immutability "prong of the suspectness inquiry surely is satisfied when … the identifying trait is 'so central to a person's identity that it would be abhorrent for government to penalize a person for refusing to change [it].'"' (quoting *Watkins v US Army*, 875 F.2d 699, 703 (9th Cir. 1989)).

[107] *Re Marriage Cases*, 183 P.3d 384, 442 (Cal. 2008) ('Because a person's sexual orientation is so integral an aspect of one's identity, it is not appropriate to require a person to repudiate or change his or her sexual orientation in order to avoid discriminatory treatment').

[108] *Kerrigan v Comm'r of Pub Health*, 957 A.2d 407, 426 (Conn. 2008) ('gay persons, because they are characterized by a "central, defining [trait] of personhood, which may be altered [if at all] only at the expense of significant damage to the individual's sense of self" are no less entitled to consideration

have accepted a new approach to immutability linked not to permanent and unchanging but *fundamental* characteristics. For example, in *Latta*[109] a District Court stated: 'We have recognized that sexual orientation and sexual identity are immutable; they are so fundamental to one's identity that a person should not be required to abandon them.' In *Obergefell I*[110] the United States Supreme Court confirmed this approach, declaring that immutability arises not only where a characteristic is 'strictly unchangeable' but also where 'the characteristic is a core trait or condition that one cannot or should not be required to abandon'. In *Obergefell II*,[111] the Supreme Court accepted the submission from the American Psychological Association, which argued that sexual orientation should be seen as a core trait or condition that one 'cannot or should not be required to abandon' and that 'Most gay men and lesbians do not experience their sexual orientation as a voluntary choice'.

Obergefell appears to incorporate something similar to the Canadian idea of 'constructive immutability', introduced in *Corbiere*,[112] to limit the meaning of 'analogous grounds' in the Charter. While reiterating that the analogous ground inquiry must consider the general purpose of Section 15, the majority of the Court went on to suggest that analogous grounds must either be 'actually immutable, like race, or constructively immutable, like religion' and that other factors to be considered in the analogous grounds analysis 'may be seen to flow from the central concept of immutable or constructively immutable personal characteristics'. If a characteristic is immutable, it qualifies as analogous. The Court explained that the basis for recognising constructively immutable characteristics as analogous grounds is that these characteristics either cannot be changed or 'the government has no legitimate interest in expecting us to change to receive equal treatment under the law'. The Court concluded that the distinction at issue in *Corbiere* (on-reserve versus off-reserve residential status) 'goes to a personal characteristic essential to a band member's personal identity, which is no less constructively immutable than religion or citizenship'.

However the move to 'constructive immutability' has not been welcomed by all in the USA. The acknowledgement of a link between immutability and sexual orientation has been seen as a mixed blessing. While some support the adoption of a 'soft'[113] or 'new'[114] immutability others are strongly against this and argue

as a suspect or quasi-suspect class than any other group that has been deemed to exhibit an immutable characteristic' (quoting *Jantz v Muci*, 759 F. Supp. 1543, 1548 (D. Kan. 1991) rev'd, 976 F.2d 623 (10th Cir. 1992).

[109] *Latta v Otter*, 771 F.3d 456, 464 n.4 (9th Cir. 2014). See also *Hernandez–Montiel v INS*, 225 F.3d 1084, 1093 (9th Cir 2000).

[110] *Obergefell v Wymyslo*, 962 F. Supp. 2d 968, 990 (S.D. Ohio 2013).

[111] *Obergefell v Hodges*, 135 S. Ct. 2584, 2596 (2015).

[112] *Corbiere v Canada (Minister of Indian and Northern Affairs)* [1999] 2 SCR 203. See http://www.socialrightsontario.ca/jurisprudence/domestic-jurisprudence-2/section-15-of-the-charter-equality-rights/.

[113] J Landau, '"Soft Immutabilty" and "Imputed Gay Identity": Recent Developments in Transgender and Sexual Orientation Based Asylum Law' (2005) 32 *Fordham Urban Law Review* 237–64.

[114] Clarke, 'Against Immutability' (n 100).

it should be discarded completely.[115] According to Darmer, 'arguments regarding immutability have hampered the attainment of true equality for LGBTs'.[116] The problem is that immutability suggests a norm: the subtext is that this norm is preferred but those who cannot satisfy the norm will be 'tolerated' and even 'forgiven' as the deviation from the norm (skin colour, sex, sexual orientation or impairment) is not their 'fault' – they did not choose it and can do nothing to change it. Immutability suggests a kind of paternalistic social forgiveness for the biological 'misfortune' of being black, female, disabled or gay, rather than an acceptance of the legitimacy of these attributes. Thus,

> it is not only inherently stigmatizing to ask whether a person's sexual orientation can be 'changed' but this approach to sexual orientation also suggests a heterosexual norm: heterosexuality is the 'preferred' sexual orientation and that it would be better if folks could change their sexual orientation if it deviates from that norm. The attitude that an unchosen sexual orientation should not be criminalized or penalized, while perhaps preferable to a society that terrorizes members of the LGBT community, is still not an embracing theory that is truly accepting of the legitimacy of being LGBT.[117]

The further problem is that immutability enables society to continue to 'punish' those who may choose not to subscribe to its norms, such as those who are considered to be overweight. Weight discrimination is acceptable largely due to the widespread belief that avoirdupois is a behavioural or voluntary condition. As a result, there is a low level of public sympathy for discrimination against those who are overweight or obese, and 'anti-fat' attitudes are entrenched in society. Immutability therefore does nothing to tackle the stigma attached to various attributes, but, in fact, supports that stigma. It makes the characteristic the problem, rather than the social meaning given to it. As Clarke notes, reliance on immutability promotes 'luck egalitarianism'[118] and harbours fundamental moral and economic judgments lurking 'below the surface of policy and legal doctrine that are not interrogated or theorized. Is obesity more morally blameworthy than heart disease, which is protected from discrimination despite having behavioral components?'[119]

There is still no clear definition of immutability. In *Obergefell II* the Court neither defined 'immutable', nor explained its role in the ground-breaking decision that the Constitution requires states to license and recognize same-sex marriages.[120] Nonetheless, the prohibition of sexual orientation discrimination

[115] DL Hutchinson, '"Unexplainable on Grounds Other Than Race": The Inversion of Privilege and Subordination In Equal Protection Jurisprudence' (2003) *University of Illinois Law Review*, 615–700.

[116] SB Goldberg, 'Equality Without Tiers' (2004) 77 *Southern California Law Review* 481, 582; Darmer, 'Immutability and Stigma' (n 95); ER Gill, 'Beyond Immutability: Sexuality and Constitutive Choice' (2014) 76 *The Review of Politics* 93; G Mucciaroni and ML Killian, 'Immutability, Science and Legislative Debate over Gay, Lesbian and Bisexual Rights' (2004) 47 *Journal of Homosexuality* 1; E Stein 'Sexual Orientations, Rights, and the Body: Immutability, Essentialism, and Nativism' (2011) 78(2) *Social Research* 633.

[117] Darmer, 'Immutability and Stigma' (n 95).

[118] E Anderson, 'What is the Point of Equality?' (1999) 109 *Ethics* 287, 289.

[119] Clarke, 'Against Immutability' (n 100) 8.

[120] Clarke, 'Against Immutability' (n 100).

has changed the nature of the immutability enquiry. Contrary to *Rogers*, it is no longer just a question of changeability. The requirements seem now to be tenacity, and how integral or constitutive, the characteristic is to identity. In *Baskin*[121] Posner, J described the immutability enquiry as looking for 'some immutable or at least tenacious characteristic … biological, such as skin color, or a deep psychological commitment, as religious belief often is'. Courts now consider not just whether a characteristic can change but 'whether the characteristic is so integral to a person's identity that it would be inappropriate to require her to change it to avoid discrimination'.[122] Choice is therefore also a part of the immutability test. Yet this new approach is just a small step away from the previous biological essentialism: immutability now refers to a choice that an individual should not be forced to change as well as something that has not been chosen, and cannot be changed.[123] Clarke suggests that '[r]ather than replacing the old theory of immutability, which entails problematic moral judgments about individual responsibility, the new version reinvigorates the ideology behind the old'.[124]

IX. Conclusion

This chapter has shown that there is at present a wide divergence in the range of statuses, conditions and attributes that are protected under anti-discrimination law, both across countries and even within them. For example, although federal anti-discrimination law in Australia prohibits only race,[125] sex,[126] age[127] and disability,[128] state anti-discrimination codes are far more extensive, including specifics such as pregnancy, parenthood and breastfeeding as well as irrelevant medical and criminal record.[129] Only one state—Western Australia—prohibits discrimination related to publication of fine enforcement details. The variety of prohibited grounds illustrates how much more sensitive both society and legislators are to inequality. It also demonstrates the importance of context—it can only be assumed that fines enforcement is a problem peculiar to Western Australia.

While the increased social recognition of discrimination can only be positive, an unintended consequence of this may be a diminution of the notion of

[121] *Baskin v Bogan*, 766 F. 3d 648, 655 (7th Cir. 2014).

[122] *Love v Beshear*, 989 F. Supp. 2d 536, 546 (W.D. Ky. 2014) in Clarke, 'Against Immutability' (n 100).

[123] Helfand in McColgan 2014: 49. M. Helfand 'The Usual Suspect Classifications: Criminals, Aliens and the Future of Same-Sex Marriage' (2009) 12 *University of Pennsylvania Journal of Constitutional Law* 1, 1.

[124] Clarke, 'Against Immutability' (n 100).

[125] 1975.

[126] 1984.

[127] 2004.

[128] 1992.

[129] Northern Territory and Tasmania.

discrimination. In the absence of a clear logic, any differential treatment becomes discrimination, and discrimination in turn becomes weaker, and less able to afford protection to those who really need it. Perhaps now more than ever, anti-discrimination law needs a rationale: increasing breadth of protection should not undermine the depth of protection.

Both dignity and immutability continue to be valuable principles. However, they may no longer be enough to guide democratic action to promote equality. Immutability may provide a principle to ensure that a remedy exists for the most invidious forms of discrimination, suffered as a result of characteristics—such as skin colour, gender, or national origin—over which an individual has no, or little, control. However, if the test of immutability excludes other vulnerable groups from access to legal protection against discrimination, how helpful is it in the goal of ameliorating discrimination?

Clarke's critique of immutability also applies to dignity: it fails to provide 'a theoretically satisfying basis for understanding which characteristics deserve protection, and invites normatively problematic judgments that are at odds with the purposes of antidiscrimination law'. In addition, 'the new immutability's focus on valued traits leaves out many stigmatised identities—identities that might have the strongest claims to protection precisely because judgments based on them are superficial and perpetuate systemic subordination'.[130]

How can dynamism be retained in anti-discrimination law while retaining the boundaries? 'Softening the edges' of immutability may make it more appealing but does not provide a clear rationale for anti-discrimination law. Is it useful to search for such a rationale? Is it possible to have a unifying principle to guide the application of the anti-discrimination principle? Some have abandoned this idea. Fredman, for example, suggests four rationales: immutability; discrete and insular minorities; dignity; and a history of disadvantage.[131] This would create a multi-dimensional equality law that is redistributive (breaks the cycle of disadvantage); promotes respect for dignity and worth; addresses stigma; and is pluralistic, transformative and participative (promotes inclusion). The targets of intervention would be those 'suffering disadvantage, stigma and exclusion'.[132] Shin also suggests that the best moral explanation for the legal concept of discrimination is that it 'embodies a collection of approaches that together express our society's commitment to identify, disavow, and disallow in our institutional practices the categories of actions that tend to reinforce or resonate with historic and persistent patterns of unjust inequalities'.[133]

[130] Clarke, 'Against Immutability' (n 99).
[131] Fredman, *Discrimination Law* (n 68) 130–39.
[132] Fredman, *Discrimination Law* (n 68) 26.
[133] P Shin, 'Is There a Unitary Concept of Discrimination?' in D Hellman and S Moreau (eds) *Philosophical Foundations of Discrimination Law* (Oxford, Oxford University Press, 2013).

Perhaps rather than abandon the search for a unifying principle, the search area could be broadened, for example relocated from dignity and immutabilty in philosophy to stigma in social psychology. This will be the aim of Chapter 3. Stigma may provide the theoretically satisfying basis for understanding which characteristics deserve protection, in line with the purposes of anti-discrimination law, that Clarke seeks.

3

Stigma and Litigation

As seen in Chapter 1, the concept of stigma has travelled far beyond Goffman's face-to-face interaction. It is increasingly acknowledged that stigma has negative consequences for individual well-being, although positive uses of stigma have also been identified.[1] Stigma affects public perceptions and so can influence the distribution of public resources, both those that are tangible, such as funding, as well as those that are intangible, such as well-being. For example, medical research, especially that concerned with public health issues such as HIV/AIDs, mental illness or obesity, is particularly concerned with the effects of stigma on management, recovery and avoidance of ill health.[2]

Increasingly, discriminatory behaviour is seen as the end result of stigma. If stigma is the source of discriminatory behaviour, can it also be used as a starting point for anti-discrimination law? Could it perhaps address the current challenges facing this field of law? Lawyers, including discrimination lawyers, rarely speak of stigma and the concept hardly appears in legislative discussion or judicial decision-making. However, I am not the first to draw upon the work of Goffman to address shortcomings in anti-discrimination law—as will be seen below, both Robin Lenhardt and Glenn Loury use Goffman's idea of stigma in this way. My proposal goes further than previous suggestions as I incorporate the considerable developments that have strengthened the idea of stigma. Lenhardt and Loury also focus only on racial discrimination, whereas I would apply the anti-stigma principle to all forms of discrimination. My argument is that a guiding logic is necessary to ensure that this law retains the capacity to help those suffering from discrimination and remains focused on remedying discrimination. It is possible that the theoretical developments in understanding stigma can help anti-discrimination law in general to focus and yet retain its potency to address socially damaging and dangerous discrimination.

This chapter begins with a discussion of how Goffman's study on stigma was used in legal scholarship. It then continues with a review of the use of stigma in judicial decisions in both common law and civil law jurisdictions including Australia, England and Wales, Canada, South Africa and in the European Courts.

[1] For a rare positive application of stigma see WS Helms, KD Patterson and W Helms, 'Eliciting Acceptance for "Illicit" Organizations: The Positive Implications of Stigma for MMA Organizations' (2014) 57(5) *Academy of Management Journal* 1453.

[2] K Roche and C Keith, 'How Stigma Affects Healthcare Access for Transgender Sex Workers' (2014) 23(21) *British Journal of Nursing* 1147.

I. Goffman in Legal Scholarship

Legal scholar Robin Lenhardt argues in her article on 'the mark'[3] that racial stigma is the main source of racial harm in the USA. Drawing upon the seminal work of Charles Lawrence on unconscious bias,[4] she suggests that the US Supreme Court needs to concern itself with the *meanings* associated with race—her argument is that 'racial stigma, not intentional discrimination or unconscious racism, is the true source of racial injury in the United States'[5] and racial stigma should thus be the focus of equality jurisprudence. She defends the need to incorporate analysis of unconscious racial bias into jurisprudence on the Fourteenth Amendment.[6] This focus on racial stigma rather than direct or indirect discrimination will lead judges to the core of racial harm: by reframing its enquiry to focus on stigma, the Supreme Court will not only ameliorate discrimination in particular cases but also strengthen democracy in society by removing the 'citizenship harms' that prevent full participation of racial minorities.

Lenhardt brings Goffman together with the work of economist Glenn Loury. Recalling Loury, she defines racial stigma as:

> a problem of negative social meaning, of 'dishonorable meanings socially inscribed on arbitrary bodily marks [such as skin color], of "spoiled collective identities."' To be racially stigmatized, ... implies more than merely being referred to by a racial epithet or even the denial of a particular opportunity on the basis of one's race. It involves becoming a disfavored or dishonored individual in the eyes of society, a kind of social outcast whose stigmatized attribute stands as a barrier to full acceptance into the wider community. As Loury recently explained, racial stigmatization 'entails doubting the person's worthiness and consigning him or her to a social netherworld. Indeed, although the language is somewhat hyperbolic, it means being skeptical about whether the person can be assumed to share a common humanity with the observer.[7]

Although not focusing on the Supreme Court and law, Loury like Lenhardt suggests that 'a proper study of contemporary racial inequality requires that we understand the extent to which an inherited "racial stigma"' undermines the efforts of African Americans to 'realize their full human potential'. He uses stigma rather than discrimination, to 'probe beneath the cognitive acts of individuals and investigate the structure of social relations within which those individuals operate'.[8]

Lenhardt and Loury present good arguments but stigma remains in the shadow of the law. It appears most frequently in legal scholarship concerned with HIV/

[3] Lenhardt, 'Understanding the Mark: Race, Stigma, and Equality in Context' (2004) 79 NYUL Rev 803.

[4] Lawrence suggests that the unconscious is the primary source of racism.

[5] Lenhardt, 'The Mark' (n 3) 809.

[6] Lenhardt, 'The Mark' (n 3).

[7] Lenhardt, 'The Mark' (n 3) 809.

[8] G Loury, *The Anatomy of Racial Inequality* (Harvard University Press, 2003).

Aids or mental health law. Judges rarely speak of stigma and the concept is largely absent from legislation. Nonetheless, a review of cases shows that the idea of stigma does appear in law. It has been used by common law courts in England, Canada and Australia across a wide field of case-law. For the most part, the use is not well defined and mention is often fleeting. However, there are cases where the idea of stigma is central to tackling the issues before the court. There is little indication of the theoretical developments in understanding stigma. The common approach appears to be that promoted by Goffman—in all cases stigma is referred to as a negative, and as something that tarnishes the individual. Only in relation to criminal law is stigma recognised as a positive tool, which is used for social control.

As a precursor to the proposal that stigma can be used in legislation, this chapter reviews the use of the concept in case-law from England and Wales, Australia and Canada. The review shows that judges do invoke the idea of stigma, although rarely in a deep and meaningful way. It is worth noting that the idea of stigma is not foreign to the common law, even if it is not yet used in legislation.

A. Australia

A search of all Australian High Court cases in AustLii returned just 26 cases where stigma was mentioned. The use was always negative and very brief: in 21 of these cases, stigma was mentioned just once and only in passing without any definition or detail. For example in *Amalgamated Society of Engineers*, the court mentioned the 'stigma of illegality'[9] or in *Perre*, the 'stigma of unacceptable business practice'.[10] The High Court has spoken of the stigma of bankruptcy,[11] the social stigma of illegitimacy[12] as well as the 'stigma of dishonor'.[13] In *A v New South Wales*, the court referred to a charge of child abuse as being 'likely to leave a stigma upon the parent even if the charge fails'.[14] In *MacFarlane*, the court also noted the 'stigma which will attach in the event of an adverse finding' of a criminal charge.[15] A tax case mentioned the absence of holiday pay as placing a 'grave stigma on the

[9] *Amalgamated Society of Engineers v Smith* [1913] HCA 44; (1913) 16 CLR 537 (5 September 1913).

[10] *Perre v Apand Pty Ltd* [1999] HCA 36; 198 CLR 180; 64 ALR 606; 73 ALJR 1190 (12 August 1999) [160].

[11] *Marek v Tregenza* [1963] HCA 40; (1963) 109 CLR 1 (15 October 1963) [12].

[12] *Attorney-General (Vic) v Commonwealth* ('Marriage Act case') [1962] HCA 37; (1962) 107 CLR 529 (1 August 1962) [19].

[13] *Commonwealth Life Assurance Society Ltd v Smith* [1938] HCA 2; (1938) 59 CLR 527 (14 February 1938).

[14] *A v New South Wales* [2007] HCA 10; (2007) 233 ALR 584; 81 ALJR 763 (21 March 2007) [185].

[15] *R v MacFarlane* [1923] HCA 39; (1923) 32 CLR 518 (23 August 1923). See also *Ziems v Prothonotary of the Supreme Court of NSW* [1957] HCA 46; (1957) 97 CLR 279 (2 July 1957) [4] and *KBT v R* [1997] HCA 54; (1997) 191 CLR 417; (1997) 149 ALR 693; (1997) 72 ALJR 116 (9 December 1997) [5] where the court spoke of the stigma of a conviction, and *Charlie v R* [1999] HCA 23; 199 CLR 387; 162 ALR 463; 73 ALJR 809 (13 May 1999) [27] where it spoke of the stigma of a murder conviction.

patriotism of war workers'.[16] In *HG v R*, the court referred to the Parliamentary papers explaining legislation as being designed to ameliorate and 'remove the stigma attached to the rape victim'.[17]

Social stigma was specifically mentioned in *Dinsdale v R*,[18] as a form of mitigation as the court considered the appropriate sentencing for a criminal offence: the court wondered whether the 'social stigma that would follow the conviction' should have the effect of suspending the prison term. Likewise, in *Ryan v Ross*[19] the court considered whether 'factors such as public opprobrium and a permanent and public stigma entitle a convicted person to a lesser sentence than otherwise would be the case'. The case concerned the re-sentencing of a paedophile, whose identity had become public due to the criminal proceedings. On the one hand, it was argued that 'the stigma will commonly add a significant element of shame and isolation to the prisoner and the prisoner's family' which may comprise a special burden that is 'just' to take into account. However, on the other it was argued that this idea should be rejected as, first, it suggested that a 'well known individual should get a lesser sentence than the person who is hardly known in his or her community' and, second, it would mean that the greater the public outrage, the lesser the sentence imposed.[20] Stigma was also mentioned in one employment case,[21] where the court considered the implied terms of employment contract and referred specifically to the idea of stigma damages developed in the British case of *Malik*, discussed below.[22]

B. England and Wales

'Stigma' has appeared in around 200 cases dealt with in the courts of England and Wales between 1948 and 2014. These cases address a wide variety of issues: property; banking; employment; family law; criminal law and human rights. Only one case has linked stigma and discrimination.

Judges refer regularly to the stigma of bankruptcy, divorce, 'illegitimacy' or a criminal conviction. Immigration law cases mention the 'stigma of deportation'.[23] The word has never been clearly defined but the use in adjudication is always negative, indicating a 'taint',[24] a 'social sanction'[25] or a 'stain'.[26] Stigma has

[16] *R v Commonwealth Court of Conciliation & Arbitration* [1942] HCA 39; (1942) 66 CLR 488 (26 November 1942).

[17] *HG v R* [1999] HCA 2; 197 CLR 414; 160 ALR 554; 73 ALJR 281 (9 February 1999).

[18] *Dinsdale v R* [2000] HCA 54; 202 CLR 321; 175 ALR 315; 74 ALJR 1538 (12 October 2000) [88].

[19] *Ryan v Ross* [1916] HCA 43; (1916) 22 CLR 1 (1 August 1916) [52].

[20] ibid [53]–[55].

[21] *Commonwealth Bank of Australia v Barker* [2014] HCA 32 (10 September 2014) [34] and [70].

[22] See note and text at n 49 below.

[23] *R v Secretary of State for the Home Department, ex parte Oladehinde; R v Secretary of State for the Home Department, ex parte Alexander* [1990] 2 All ER 367.

[24] *Egerton and Others v Esplanade Hotels London Ltd and Another* [1947] 2 All ER 88.

[25] *Hill v William Hill (Park Lane) Ltd* [1949] 2 All ER 452.

[26] *P v T Ltd* [1997] 4 All ER 200.

been used to describe a temporary blemish arising from social status (divorcee, 'illegitimacy'), unethical behaviour ('moral stigma'[27] or dishonesty)[28] as well as a more permanent taint associated with a form of activity, as in criminal law where 'stigma' is used functionally.

Stigmatisation is deliberate and inherent in criminalisation—serious crime, convictions and imprisonment arising therefrom are intentionally stigmatised.[29] The 'deep stigma' associated with, for example, murder is intended to act as a deterrent from the commission of this act. Although there are exceptions, for example in one case in 1964 where a wife killed her terminally ill husband, the judge stated:

> I, therefore, wish to make it perfectly plain that, though the wife must be held by me to have feloniously killed the husband, nevertheless it is not, in my judgment, a crime which should attract the deep stigma which still, rightly and fortunately for good order in our country, attaches to the commission of crime. This is clearly a case for compassion rather than for condemnation. Deciding the question as I have decided it, nevertheless I am concerned that the family should not feel that this is a matter which ranks for the high degree of condemnation which is rightly associated with serious criminal offences[30]

De-criminalisation of an act is also a de-stigmatisation; suicide was decriminalised because the common law offence not only stigmatised the members of the suicide's family but also left those who failed in their suicide attempt open to subsequent prosecution.[31]

Courts have applied stigma to property as well as to acts. For example, in 1948, the use of premises as a brothel was found to cast a 'stigma … and impose a taint'. However, this was seen to be temporary—the judge went on to say that the taint could 'be removed if those who have brought it about are no longer associated

[27] *R v Bates and Another* [1952] 2 All ER 842; *Sayce v Coupe* [1952] 2 All ER 715; *S v E* [1967] 1 All ER 593—sex outside of marriage.

[28] *Akerhielm and Another v De Mare and Others* [1959] 3 All ER 485; *Dingle v Associated Newspapers Ltd and Others* [1961] 1 All ER 897; *Shelley v Paddock and Another* [1978] 3 All ER 129.

[29] *Warner v Metropolitan Police Commissioner* [1968] 2 All ER 356—serious crime; *Sweet v Parsley* [1969] 1 All ER 347; *R (on the application of North Yorkshire Police Authority) v Independent Police Complaints Commission (Chief Constable of North Yorkshire Police and Another, interested parties)* [2011] 3 All ER 106—criminal conviction; *Nishina Trading Co Ltd v Chiyoda Fire & Marine Insurance Co Ltd* [1969] 2 All ER 776; *Kennedy v Spratt* [1971] 1 All ER 805—convictions; *Spill v Spill* [1972] 3 All ER 9—stigma of a charge of 'cruelty'; *R v Phekoo* [1981] 3 All ER 84; *R v Lambert* [2001] 3 All ER 577; *R v K* [2009] 1 All ER 510—criminal conviction; *R v Inland Revenue Commissioners, ex parte Mead and Another* [1993] 1 All ER 772; *B (a minor) v Director of Public Prosecutions* [2000] 1 All ER 833—conviction; *S-T (formerly J) v J* [1998] 1 All ER 431—stigma of criminality; *R v Cooney; R v Allam; R v Wood* [1999] 3 All ER 173—imprisonment; *R v H* [2003] 1 All ER 497—stigma of indecent assault; *R v Drew* [2003] 4 All ER 557—stigma of life imprisonment.

[30] *Re Dellow's Will Trusts Lloyds Bank Ltd v Institute of Cancer Research and Others* [1964] 1 All ER 771.

[31] As explained by Lord Bingham *R (on the application of Pretty) v DPP* [2002] 1 All ER 1 at [35], [2002] 1 AC 800 at [35]. The stigma of suicide has been discussed in cases concerning assisted dying: *R v Inner West London Coroner, ex parte De Luca* [1988] 3 All ER 414; *Reeves v Commissioner of Police of the Metropolis* [1998] 2 All ER 381; *R (on the application of Pretty) v Director of Public Prosecutions* [2002] 1 All ER 1; *R (on the application of Nicklinson and another) v Ministry of Justice; R (on the application of AM) v Director of Public Prosecutions* [2014] 2 All ER 32.

with the premises'.[32] Yet in more recent cases concerning breach of covenant, illegal or immoral use which fixes 'the premises with some sort of irremovable stigma' has been deemed incapable of remedy.[33] Legal persons can also be stigmatised—company law cases talk of the stigma on a company's commercial reputation.[34] The courts have also referred to the 'stigma of being a bad employer'.[35]

Stigma attached to natural persons can be temporary because social norms change: cases in family courts note the demise of stigma attached to birth and marital status. A case in 1949 noted the 'stigmas of birth',[36] while another in 1955 acknowledged the natural desire of a young mother to start a new life without the 'stigma of having borne such a child', that is, out of wedlock.[37] In *Re O*[38] the court referred to legislative attempts to remove the stigma of 'bastardy' and in *Re L*, illegitimacy was described as a 'grave stigma with serious consequences for the child.[39] By 1970 a more positive note was sounded in *W*:

> An illegitimate child was not only deprived of the financial advantage of legitimacy but in most circles of society, other than those considered disreputable, it carried throughout its life a stigma which made it a second class citizen. But now modern legislation has removed almost all the financial disadvantages of illegitimacy and it has become difficult to foretell how grave a handicap the stigma of illegitimacy will prove to be in later life.[40]

In 2002, the court confidently stated that 'illegitimacy with its stigma has been legislated away'.[41]

The stigma associated with divorce[42] also diminished due to parliamentary intervention: in *Wachtel v Wachtel*,[43] the court stated:

> When Parliament in 1857 introduced divorce by the courts of law, it based it on the doctrine of the matrimonial offence. This affected all that followed. If a person was the guilty party in a divorce suit, it went hard with him or her. It affected so many

[32] See *Egerton and Others v Esplanade Hotels London Ltd and Another* [1947] 2 All ER 88; *Hoffman v Fineberg and Others* [1948] 1 All ER 592; *Borthwick-Norton and Others v Romney Warwick Estates Ltd* [1950] 1 All ER 362—'stigma of having been known as a house of illfame …'; *Central Estates (Belgravia) Ltd v Woolgar* [1971] 3 All ER 647 (I & II) and *Scala House and District Property Co Ltd v Forbes and Others* [1973] 3 All ER 308.

[33] In *Akici* the court seemed concerned to prevent a lessee avoiding the risk of forfeiture simply by ceasing an illegal use on being given notice of it. *Akici v LR Butlin Ltd* [2006] 2 All ER 872 drawing upon *Rugby School (Governors) v Tannahill* [1935] 1 KB 87; [1934] All ER Rep 187 and *British Petroleum Pension Trust Ltd v Behrendt* [1985] 2 EGLR 97.

[34] *Columbia Picture Industries Inc and Others v Robinson and Others* [1986] 3 All ER 338; *Al-Rawas v Pegasus Energy Ltd and Others* [2009] 1 All ER 346.

[35] *Furnell v Whangarei High Schools Board* [1973] 1 All ER 400.

[36] *L v L* [1949] 1 All ER 141.

[37] *Re A (an infant)* [1955] 2 All ER 202. See also *Re D (an infant)* [1958] 3 All ER 716.

[38] *Re O (an infant)* [1964] 1 All ER 786. See also *Re Adoption Application No 41/61 (No 2)* [1963] 2 All ER 1082 and *Re E (P) (an infant)* [1969] 1 All ER 323.

[39] *Re L* [1968] 1 All ER 20.

[40] *S v S; W v Official Solicitor* [1970] 3 All ER 107.

[41] *Bellinger v Bellinger* [2002] 1 All ER 311. See also *Re B (a child) (adoption by one natural parent)* [2002] 1 All ER 641.

[42] *Bater v Bater* [1950] 2 All ER 458; *Williams v Williams* [1963] 2 All ER 994; *Collins v Collins* [1972] 2 All ER 658.

[43] *Wachtel v Wachtel* [1973] 1 All ER 829. See also *Rogers v Rogers* [1974] 2 All ER 361.

> things. The custody of the children depended on it. So did the award of maintenance. To say nothing of the standing in society. So serious were the consequences that divorce suits were contested at great length and at much cost. All that is altered. Parliament has decreed: 'If the marriage has broken down irretrievably, let there be a divorce'. It carries no stigma, but only sympathy. It is a misfortune which befalls both. No longer is one guilty and the other innocent. No longer are there long contested divorce suits.

However this varies across cultures: in some communities and countries there is still a strong stigma attached to divorce.[44]

The same also applies to stigma of co-habitation; although this is still a precarious status for women, it is no longer seen as 'living in sin':

> It is, I think, not putting it too high to say that between 1950 and 1975 there has been a complete revolution in society's attitude to unmarried partnerships of the kind under consideration. Such unions are far commoner than they used to be. The social stigma that once attached to them has almost, if not entirely, disappeared. The inaccurate but expressive phrases 'common law wife' and 'common law husband' have come into general use to describe them. The ordinary man in 1975 would, in my opinion, certainly say that the parties to such a union, provided it had the appropriate degree of apparent permanence and stability, were members of a single family whether they had children or not.[45]

In *Fitzpatrick*,[46] the idea of the common law family was fully accepted.

By contrast, behavioural stigma has been seen as more permanent. Bankruptcy,[47] fraud[48] and employment cases often mention stigma, especially in relation to dismissal or allegations of misconduct. The idea of 'stigma damages' first arose in cases related to the liquidation of the Bank of Credit and Commerce International SA (BCCI). Following the huge number of redundancies and difficulties in finding new employment, over 100 former employees sought compensation for stigma arising due to their former association with the bank. In *Malik*, it was argued that the employers had carried on a dishonest business which adversely affected the standing of the employees in the banking industry.[49] In *P v T*,[50] the

[44] *Re Kumar (a bankrupt), ex parte Lewis v Kumar and Another* [1993] 2 All ER 700; *Re SK (An Adult) (Forced Marriage: Appropriate Relief)* [2005] 3 All ER 421 (Bangladesh); *XCC v AA and Others* [2013] 2 All ER 988.

[45] *Dyson Holdings Ltd v Fox* [1975] 3 All ER 1030; repeated in *Helby v Rafferty* [1978] 3 All ER 1016. See also *Mitchell v Mitchell* [1983] 3 All ER 621.

[46] *Fitzpatrick v Sterling Housing Association Ltd* [1999] 4 All ER 705.

[47] *Re Liabilities (War-time adjustment) Act 1941; Re Affairs of Kirby* [1944] 1 All ER 166; *Re Royal Albion Hotel Ltd* [1943] 2 All ER 192; *Bailey v Purser* [1967] 1 All ER 188; *Re a Debtor (No 13 of 1964), Ex Parte Official Receiver v The Debtor* [1979] 3 All ER 15; *Re Stern (a bankrupt), ex parte Keyser Ullmann Ltd and Others v The Bankrupt and Others* [1982] 2 All ER 600; *K and Another v P and Others (J, Third Party)* [1993] 1 All ER 521; *Randhawa v Official Receiver* [2007] 1 All ER 755; *Smeaton v Equifax plc* [2012] 4 All ER 460.

[48] *R v Berry; R v Stewart* [1969] 1 All ER 689.

[49] *Malik v Bank of England (Bank of Credit & Commerce International SA* [1997] ICR 606. See also *Malik and Another v Bank of Credit and Commerce International SA (In Liq)* [1995] 3 All ER 545; *Bank of Credit and Commerce International SA (In Liq) v Ali and Others* [1999] 2 All ER 1005; *Capital Trust Investments Ltd v Radio Design TJ AB and Others* [2002] 2 All ER 159. Also *Johnson v Unisys Ltd* [1999] 1 All ER 854.

[50] *P v T* (n26).

defendant contended that he had been wrongfully accused and dismissed for gross misconduct. He also sought 'stigma damages' from the employer. While doubting the success of his claim, the court suggested that even the award of stigma damages may not, 'succeed in curing the blight on his employment prospects or fully compensate him for the damage caused to him by that blight'. More recently, stigma damages were sought against the National Crime Agency.[51]

The field of employment law has given rise to the idea of 'stigma loss'. In *Chaggar*,[52] stigma loss was described as arising 'because of the act of the employee in bringing proceedings against the employer, albeit that that was a response to the employer's unlawful act'. *Chaggar* has probably seen the most substantial discussion of stigma since *Malik*. It is a unique case in that it links stigma and discrimination. After five years' service at Abbey National, Mr Chagger was selected for redundancy out of a pool of two people, following a flawed redundancy procedure. An employment tribunal determined that this had been racially discriminatory and awarded him £2.7 million compensation. The award was so high due to the conclusion that Chaggar could never again find suitable employment—he had unsucessfully applied for over 300 posts. He argued that his lack of success was partly due to the stigma associated with bringing a successful discrimination claim against his former employer. The award was appealed and eventually came before the Court of Appeal. A key question was whether, if Mr Chaggar had been unlawfully stigmatised, his former employer, Abbey National, could be held liable for this.

In determining the calculation of compensation to Mr Chaggar, the Court of Appeal therefore considered whether Abbey should 'be liable for the so called "stigma" consequences of the dismissal, i.e. the decision by third parties not to employ Mr Chagger because he had brought discrimination proceedings against his employer'.[53] The response was sympathetic:

> [89] We see considerable force in Mr Jeans' argument, but ultimately we reject it. We consider that the original employer must remain liable for so-called stigma loss. First, we do not accept Abbey's broad submission that the mere fact that third party employers contribute to, or are the immediate cause of, the loss resulting from their refusal to employ of itself breaks the chain of causation. If those employers could lawfully refuse to employ on the grounds that they did not want to risk recruiting someone who had sued his employer and whom they perceived to be a potential trouble maker, we see no reason why that would not be a loss flowing directly from the original unlawful act. Indeed, it is now firmly established that if a stigma attaches to employees from the unlawful way in which their employer runs his business, then the employer will be liable for losses which may result from the fact that other employers will not want to recruit employees because of their link with the business: see *Malik v BCCI*.

[51] *Szepietowski v National Crime Agency* [2014] 1 All ER 225. See also *Triggs v GAB Robins (UK) Ltd* [2007] 3 All ER 590.

[52] *Chaggar v Abbey National plc* [2009] EWCA Civ 1202.

[53] ibid [54].

> [90] … the mere fact that third party employers are the immediate cause of the loss does not free the original wrongdoer from liability. The fact that the direct cause is their decision not to recruit does not of itself break the chain of causation …
>
> [93] It is also material to note that it is only in the context of discrimination laws that the concept of victimisation discrimination has been developed. Each of the discrimination statutes provides for a free standing wrong of victimisation, but it is not always unlawful for third party employers to refuse to recruit someone who has sued his own employer. For example, an employee who has taken proceedings for unfair dismissal could be stigmatised in that way quite lawfully. It would be unsatisfactory and somewhat artificial if tribunals were obliged to discount stigma loss in the context of discrimination law but not in other contexts.
>
> [94] In our judgment the stigma loss is in principle recoverable. It is one of the difficulties facing an employee on the labour market.

The case was remitted to the original tribunal for calculation of compensation. Subsequent cases have built upon *Chaggar:* in *Mattu*[54] the court accepted that 'the stigma of dismissal will in some cases render an employee effectively unemployable'.

More recently, stigmatisation has been linked to respect for human rights. A 2013 case held that 'the stigma of removal from a post for allegedly immoral or criminal conduct might engage Article 8 ECHR'[55] unless the employees could be held responsible for their own wrong. Likewise, courts have highlighted that the stigma associated with being declared unfit to work with vulnerable adults or children can interfere with human rights,[56] as can unnecessary retention of data. When the Metropolitan Police refused to destroy the data collected after dropping all charges against a suspect, the Supreme Court stated that this could constitute discrimination because certain sections of the population,

> [62] … in particular men and people from the black and minority ethnic communities, run a disproportionate risk of arrest and therefore of having their data taken and kept. This is a detriment with a discriminatory impact. (e) The detriment is the stigma, certainly felt and possibly perceived by others, involved in having one's data on the database. This stigma, together with wider concerns about potential misuse, is sufficient to outweigh the benefits in the detection and prosecution of crime.[57]

[54] *Mattu v University Hospitals of Coventry and Warwickshire NHS Trust* [2012] 4 All ER 359. See also *Norton Tool Co Ltd v Tewson* [1973] 1 All ER 183; *Heath and Another v J F Longman (Meat Salesmen) Ltd* [1973] 2 All ER 1228; *Stock v Frank Jones (Tipton) Ltd* [1976] 3 All ER 218; *Thompson v Eaton Ltd* [1976] 3 All ER 384.

[55] *Turner v East Midlands Trains Ltd* [2013] 3 All ER 375.

[56] *R (on the application of L) v Metropolitan Police Commissioner* [2010] 1 All ER 113; *R (on the application of Gallastegui) v Westminster City Council* [2012] 4 All ER 401; *R (on the application of T) v Chief Constable of Greater Manchester and Others; R (on the application of JB) v Secretary of State for the Home Department* [2014] 4 All ER 159.

[57] *R (on the application of GC) v Metropolitan Police Commissioner; R (on the application of C) v Metropolitan Police Commissioner* [2011] UKSC 21; *R (on the application of GC) v Metropolitan Police Commissioner; R (on the application of C) v Metropolitan Police Commissioner* [2011] 3 All ER 859.

C. Canada

Stigma is used in various legal contexts in Canada. The Canadian Supreme Court has spoken of 'the social stigma attached to sexual offenders',[58] the stigma attached to removal of a child from the parental home,[59] or the lack of stigma in being checked at border crossings.[60] Stigma is also regularly mentioned in relation to criminal proceedings and convictions—as in British law, these are seen to stigmatise the accused.[61] In *Mabior*, the Supreme Court confirmed: 'A criminal conviction and imprisonment, with the attendant stigma that attaches, is the most serious sanction the law can impose on a person, and is generally reserved for conduct that is highly culpable—conduct that is viewed as harmful to society, reprehensible and unacceptable.'[62] In the landmark freedom of expression case *Keegstra*, the Court stated: 'Given the stigma that attaches and the freedom which is at stake, the contest between the individual and the state imposed by a criminal trial must be regarded as difficult and harrowing in the extreme.'[63] A plea of insanity to avoid criminal liability is regarded as a dual stigma: 'the stigma of being held to be both a criminal and insane'.[64] Thus in *Dermers*, the Court promoted use of mental health legislation instead of the criminal law to deal with a person permanently unfit to stand trial (the defendant in this case suffered from Down Syndrome and had been accused of sexual assault) in order to avoid those with a mental disorder 'being stigmatized by criminal proceedings'.[65]

However, convicted persons are protected from indefinite stigmatisation by s 18(2) of the Charter—as explained in *Maksteel*, the purpose of this section is 'to protect individuals from *unjustified* social stigma that operates to exclude a person with a criminal conviction from the labour market'. Thus two types of stigma are recognised—while stigma arising from conviction is legitimate, 'unjustified stigma is the product of prejudice or stereotyping'.[66]

In *Finta*,[67] the Supreme Court mentioned the 'special stigma' that attaches to war crimes. In contrast to the discussion in Australia, the Canadian Supreme Court held that a higher level of public opprobrium is indeed warranted for such crimes. They stated that

> there are certain crimes where, because of the special nature of the available penalties or of the stigma attached to a conviction, the principles of fundamental justice require

[58] *R v Ewanchuk* [1999] 1 SCR 330 [66].

[59] *New Brunswick (Minister of Health and Community Services) v G (J)* [1999] 3 SCR 46.

[60] *R v Kang-Brown* [2008] 1 SCR 456, 2008 SCC 18.

[61] *Canadian Foundation for Children, Youth and the Law v Canada (Attorney General)* [2004] 1 SCR 76, 2004 SCC 4 [204].

[62] *R v Mabior* 2012 SCC 47, [2012] 2 SCR 584 [19].

[63] *R v Keegstra* [1990] 3 SCR 697.

[64] *R v Swain* [1991] 1 SCR 933.

[65] *R v Demers* [2004] 2 SCR 489, 2004 SCC 46 [92].

[66] *Quebec (Commission des droits de la personne et des droits de la jeunesse) v Maksteel Québec Inc* [2003] 3 SCR 228, 2003 SCC 68.

[67] *R v Finta* [1994] 1 SCR 701.

> a mental blameworthiness or a *mens rea* reflecting the particular nature of that crime. It follows that the question which must be answered is not simply whether the accused is morally innocent, but rather, whether the conduct is sufficiently blameworthy to merit the punishment and stigma that will ensue upon conviction for that particular offence. In the present case there must be taken into account not only the stigma and punishment that will result upon a conviction for the domestic offence, but also the additional stigma and opprobrium that will be suffered by an individual whose conduct has been held to constitute crimes against humanity or war crimes. In reality, upon conviction, the accused will be labelled a war criminal and will suffer the particularly heavy public opprobrium that is reserved for these offences. Further the sentence which will follow upon conviction will reflect the high degree of moral outrage that society very properly feels toward those convicted of these crimes.[68]

Stigma also appeared in a case where a local newspaper argued that a prohibition on reporting certain aspects of matrimonial proceedings breached the Charter. In responding to the assertion that persons might refrain from seeking divorce if they thought their private family matter would appear in the press, the Canadian Supreme Court noted: 'Many allegations that might once have been acutely embarrassing and painful are today a routine feature of matrimonial causes to which little, if any, public stigma attaches.'[69]

In *Blencoe*,[70] it was argued that protection from stigma is itself a human right. In March 1995, while serving as a Government Minister in the province of British Columbia, Blencoe was accused by one of his assistants of sexual harassment. A month later, he was fired. In July and September 1995 complaints against him of sexual harassment were filed with the British Columbia Human Rights Commission. Hearings before the British Columbia Human Rights Tribunal were, however, scheduled for March 1998, over two years after the initial complaints had been filed. Blencoe argued that the delay prolonged his public humiliation and degradation contrary to Section 7 of the Charter, which he asserted provided a right to be free from the stigma associated with a human rights complaint.

This was rejected: stigma was recognised as a form of suffering but seen as 'extrinsic' to the human rights process. Prior to 1995, Blencoe had already suffered stigmatisation: he and his family were hounded by the media; he and his wife isolated themselves; his children were subjected to insults and name-calling at school; and he was put on antidepressants and took medical leave from work.[71] Thus the stigma was neither caused by the process nor likely to end with it. In addition, the Charter did not include a general right to be free from stigma:

> First, the Section 7 rights of 'liberty and security of the person' do not include a generalized right to dignity, or more specifically a right to be free from the stigma associated with

[68] *R. v. Finta*, [1994] 1 S.C.R. 701.

[69] *Edmonton Journal v Alberta (Attorney General)* [1989] 2 SCR 1326 [5]. See also *Nova Scotia (Attorney General) v. Walsh* [2002] 4 SCR 325, 2002 SCC 83.

[70] *Blencoe v. British Columbia (Human Rights Commission*, [2000] 2 S.C.R. 307.

[71] ibid [63].

> a human rights complaint. While respect for the inherent dignity of persons is clearly an essential value in our free and democratic society which must guide the courts in interpreting the Charter, this does not mean that dignity is elevated to a free-standing constitutional right protected by Section 7. The notion of 'dignity' is better understood as an underlying value. Like dignity, reputation is not a free-standing right. Neither is freedom from stigma.[72]

The Court also noted that 'stress, anxiety and stigma may arise from any criminal trial, human rights allegation, or even a civil action, regardless of whether the trial or process occurs within a reasonable time'.[73]

In *Taylor*, stigma was described as dividing criminal from civil law: 'attached to a criminal conviction is a significant degree of stigma and punishment, whereas the extent of opprobrium connected with the finding of discrimination is much diminished and the aim of remedial measures is more upon compensation and protection of the victim'.[74] Nonetheless, the idea of stigma has been used in civil law, such as discrimination law cases. In *Law*,[75] Section 15 of the Canadian Charter of Rights and Freedoms was affirmed as a 'means of protecting discrete and insular minorities and of shielding vulnerable groups against stigmatization, stereotyping, and prejudice'.[76] The Supreme Court stated that stigmatisation is integral to a finding of discrimination—if the court decides that a policy does not stigmatise, it also finds that there has been no discrimination. In *Tétreault-Gadoury*, La Forest J noted 'the stigmatising effect of discriminatory treatment' and 'the role of Section 15(1) in preventing the imposition of such stigma and the perpetuation of negative stereotypes and vulnerability.'[77] In *McKinney* the appellant lost because it was held she was not a member of a 'traditionally disadvantaged group, an insular minority or a segment of society that is or may be stigmatized, stereotyped or subjected to prejudice'.[78] The Court decided no stigma was 'attached to being retired at 65. It conforms as well to what most people would do voluntarily.' Likewise, Gosselin lost her case because she could not show membership of a group that 'suffered from pre-existing disadvantage and stigmatisation on the basis of their age'.[79] Gosselin had challenged the use of age to determine welfare payments: persons under 30 years of age received less financial assistance than those over 30. She argued that this regime (which was ultimately abolished) violated both the Charter (Sections 7 and 15(1) as well as Section 45 of the Quebec Charter of Human Rights and Freedoms.

[72] See ibid [80].

[73] ibid [59].

[74] *Canada (Human Rights Commission) v Taylor* [1990] 3 SCR 892.

[75] *Law v Canada (Minister of Employment and Immigration)* [1999] 1 SCR 497. See CD Bavis, '*Vriend v Alberta, Law v Canada, Ontario v M. and H.*: The Latest Steps on the Winding Path to Substantive Equality' (1999) 37 *Alberta L Rev* 683.

[76] *Law v Canada* (n 76) [16].

[77] *Tetreault-Gadoury v Canada (Employment and Immigration Commission)* [1991] 2 SCR 22 cited in *Lawv Canada* [47].

[78] *McKinney v University of Guelph* [1990] 3 SCR 229.

[79] *Gosselin v Quebec (Attorney General)* [2002] 4 SCR 429, 2002 SCC 84.

However, this position may have changed. Family law has used the idea of stigma in a less restrictive way. In *A*,[80] the Supreme Court was asked to consider whether certain provisions of the Quebec Civil Code infringed Article 15(1) of the Charter. The Civil Code contained provisions that excluded cohabiting—or *de facto* spouses—from enjoyment of the rules on family patrimony, the family residence, compensatory allowance, the partnership of acquests[81] and the obligation of support to persons who are married or in a civil union. Consequently *de facto* dependent spouses in Quebec had no right to claim support, no right to divide the family patrimony, and were not governed by any matrimonial regime. A, who had three children with her wealthy partner, argued that these provisions had the effect of creating a disadvantageous distinction based on the ground of marital status.[82]

A 5:4 court answered in the affirmative—the absence of stigmatisation did not change this finding of disadvantage. Writing for the majority, Abella J noted that

> Historically, unmarried spouses in Canada were stigmatized; but as social attitudes changed, so did the approaches of legislatures and courts, which came to accept conjugal relationships outside a formal marital framework ... The exclusion of *de facto* spouses from the economic protections available to formal spousal relationships is a distinction based on marital status, an analogous ground. That it imposes a disadvantage is clear [...] The disadvantage this exclusion perpetuates is an historic one: it continues to deny *de facto* spouses access to economic remedies of which they have always been deprived, remedies Quebec considered indispensable for the protection of married and civil union spouses.

Even in the absence of an intention to stigmatise de facto spouses, the denial of the benefits was discriminatory and perpetuated historical disadvantages.

II. Litigation in Europe

Stigma has also made an appearance before each of the European Courts—the European Court of Human Rights (ECtHR) in Strasbourg and the Court of Justice of the European Union (CJEU) in Luxembourg. Recent discrimination cases before these two Courts have used the concept: in *Alajos Kiss*,[83] and *BS*[84] the

[80] *Quebec (Attorney General) v A* [2013] 1 SCR 61, 2013 SCC 5.

[81] Under Canadian law, marriage creates a matrimonial regime. Couples can choose their matrimonial regime, such as a partnership of acquests. 'Acquests' is the term for property acquired by the spouses during the marriage—salaries, property, investment income etc. Private property is that acquired before marriage or received via gift or inheritance. Under this matrimonial regime, all property not considered private by law is treated as an 'acquest'. If the marriage ends, the value of the property accumulated during the marriage, ie the acquests, is divided between the spouses.

[82] Although marital status is not explicitly mentioned in Art 15(1), it has been recognised as an 'analogous ground' in *Withler v Canada (Attorney General)* [2011] SCC 12, [2011] 1 SCR 396.

[83] *Alajos Kiss v Hungary* (Application no 38832/06) 20 May 2010.

[84] *BS v Spain* (Application no 47159/08) (ECtHR, 24 July 2012). See K Yoshida, 'Towards Intersectionality in the European Court of Human Rights: the case of B.S. v Spain' (2013) 21 *Feminist Legal Studies* 195.

ECtHR in Strasbourg implicitly adopts a stigma-led approach by referring to the social status of the complainant. However the ECtHR went further in *Kiyutin*[85] and in *CHEZ*[86] the CJEU in Luxembourg also explicitly refers to stigma.

A. The European Court of Human Rights in Strasbourg

Kiss[87] was the first case where the highest human rights court in Europe spoke at length on stigma and gave it a central place in its reasoning. Alajos Kiss, a Hungarian, was diagnosed with manic depression in 1991 at the age of 37. In 2005 he was placed under partial guardianship using powers contained in the Hungarian civil code, which also triggered the activation of Article 70(5) of the Constitution stating that those under total or partial guardianship—for whatever reason—automatically lose the right to vote. He thenceforth could not participate in any elections. He only realised this in 2006 when he noted he was omitted from the electoral register. His complaints to the national authorities were rejected, and he brought an application under Article 3 of Protocol No 1, read alone or in conjunction with Articles 13 and 14 of the European Convention, complaining that the disenfranchisement, imposed on him because he was under partial guardianship for manic depression, constituted an unjustified and discriminatory deprivation of his right to vote. His challenge was to the loss of the right to vote as an automatic consequence of the guardianship, rather than the guardianship per se.

The Strasbourg judges refused to accept the blanket ban, especially on this group of vulnerable persons. The judgment did not mention stigma directly but spoke of enduring historical prejudice and legislative stereotyping. It held:

> 42. … if a restriction on fundamental rights applies to a particularly vulnerable group in society, who have suffered considerable discrimination in the past, such as the mentally disabled, then the State's margin of appreciation is substantially narrower and it must have very weighty reasons for the restrictions in question […] The reason for this approach, which questions certain classifications per se, is that such groups were historically subject to prejudice with lasting consequences, resulting in their social exclusion. Such prejudice may entail legislative stereotyping which prohibits the individualised evaluation of their capacities and needs.

In *BS*[88] the ECtHR also alluded to stigma. This case concerned a 26-year old Nigerian woman who had resided in Spain since 2003. She worked as a prostitute in Palma de Mallorca. On three separate occasions, she was stopped by local police and physically assaulted—medical reports presented to the Court documented a number of bruises and inflammation of the hands and knee. She was also subjected to racist remarks and degrading treatment: the police had apparently

[85] *Kiyutin v Russia* (Application no 2700/10) 10 March 2011.
[86] Case C-83/14 *CHEZ Razpredelenie Bulgaria AD*.
[87] *Alajos Kiss v Hungary* (Application no 38832/06) 20 May 2010.
[88] *BS v Spain* (Application no 47159/08) (ECtHR, 24 July 2012).

said, 'get out of here you black whore' and while subjecting her to controls had not questioned the other women with a 'European phenotype' carrying on the same activity nearby.

Her complaint to the local judge was discontinued due to lack of evidence and her appeal challenging this decision was dismissed. She then lodged an appeal to the Constitutional Court, relying upon Articles 10 (right to dignity), 14 (prohibition of discrimination), 15 (right to physical and mental integrity) and 24 (right to a fair trial) of the Constitution. Citing a lack of constitutional basis for the complaints, the Constitutional Court dismissed the appeal. She then brought a complaint under Articles 3 (torture or to inhuman or degrading treatment or punishment) and 14 (non-discrimination) of the ECHR.

Her case focused on the attitude towards investigation of her complaints, which she argued breached the State's procedural obligations under Article 3. For example, the court had been ineffective: it had disregarded her medical reports and had not responded to her request for an identity parade of the police officers behind a two-way mirror so that she could identify the officers involved. In addition, the State had shifted the obligation to investigate on to her and imposed the burden of proving the alleged offence on her, in contravention of Strasbourg case-law holding it incumbent upon the State to prove that its behaviour was not discriminatory. She also alleged that the attitude and conduct of the police and the courts was tainted by prejudice. In perhaps the first intersectional case before the ECtHR, she explicitly argued that her position as a black woman working as a prostitute made her particularly vulnerable to discriminatory attacks.[89]

In coming to its decision, the Court considered evidence submitted in reports on structural discrimination presented by third party intervenors including the AIRE Centre and researchers at the University of Barcelona.[90] *BS* also highlighted a report by the United Nations Human Rights Committee which had already found a violation by Spain on grounds of discrimination.[91] Taking these into consideration, it held that the Spanish courts had 'failed to take account of the applicant's particular vulnerability inherent in her position as an African woman working as a prostitute'.[92] In light of the failure of the State to take all possible steps to ascertain whether or not a discriminatory attitude might have played a role in the events, the Court therefore found a violation of Article 14 ECHR taken in conjunction with the lack of an effective investigation under Article 3 ECHR.

Stigma was, however, directly mentioned in *Kiyutin*.[93] In 2003, Kiyutin, an Uzbek national, applied for a residence permit to settle in Russia. During the mandatory medical examination as part of this application, he tested positive for HIV. As a consequence, his application for a residence permit was refused. An appeal failed in 2004. He filed a second unsuccessful application for a temporary

[89] ibid [52].
[90] ibid [56] and [57].
[91] ibid [36]–[38].
[92] ibid [62].
[93] *Kiyutin v Russia* (Application no 2700/10) 10 March 2011.

residence permit in 2009, upon which he was informed that he was considered an unlawful resident and fined 2,500 Russian roubles. That year he also received a definitive rejection of his application for a residence permit on the basis of Section 7(1)(13) of the Foreign Nationals Act, which restricted the issue of residence permits to foreign nationals who could not show their HIV-negative status. The decision gave him three days to leave Russia.

He challenged this decision in court. However, given the existing law barring residence permits to aliens who are unable to show their HIV-negative status, his HIV-positive status made it conclusively impossible for him to gain lawful residence in Russia. Following successive rejection of his appeals at the national level, he brought a complaint in Strasbourg under Articles 8, 13, 14 and 15 of the ECHR that the decision to refuse him authorisation to reside in Russia was a breach of his right to family life and disproportionate to the legitimate aim of the protection of public health.

The Court decided to examine the issues under Articles 8 and 14 ECHR. In its reasoning, it repeated the section in paragraph 42 in *Alajos Kiss v Hungary*, before directly applying the idea of stigma to justify the identification of people living with HIV/Aids as a vulnerable group:

> 64. Since the onset of the epidemic in the 1980s, people living with HIV/Aids have suffered from widespread stigma and exclusion, including within the Council of Europe region [...] Ignorance about how the disease spreads has bred prejudice which, in turn, has stigmatised or marginalised those who carry the virus. As the routes of transmission of HIV/Aids became better understood, it was recognised that HIV infection could be traced to specific behaviours—such as same-sex sexual relations, drug injection, prostitution or promiscuity—that were already stigmatised in many societies, thereby creating a false nexus between the infection and personal irresponsibility and reinforcing other forms of stigma and discrimination, such as racism, homophobia or misogyny. [...] The Court therefore considers that people living with HIV are a vulnerable group with a history of prejudice and stigmatisation and that the State should be afforded only a narrow margin of appreciation in choosing measures that single out this group for differential treatment on the basis of their HIV status.

Thus, as the case concerned a vulnerable group, Russia enjoyed a narrower margin of appreciation than usual and the Court found that this had been over-stepped: Kiyutin was held to have been a victim of discrimination due to his health status, in violation of Article 14 ECHR taken in conjunction with Article 8 on respect for family life.

B. The European Court of Justice in Luxembourg

CHEZ[94] directly raised the question of whether stigma constitutes discrimination under EU law. The case concerned the practices of a utility company specifically

[94] Case C-83/14 *CHEZ Razpredelenie Bulgaria AD.*

adopted in a region populated predominantly by Bulgarian Roma. In areas with a large population of Roma in the Bulgarian town of Dupnitsa, electricity meters for domestic consumers are fixed about 6m from the ground, making normal visual checks by consumers impossible. In areas with no or a low number of Roma residents, the same electricity meters are installed at a height of approximately 1.70m, making them visible to consumers. CHEZ placed its electricity meters in 'Roma districts' at a height of 6metres to avoid alleged tampering and unlawful usage.

AG Kokott highlighted the relevance of stigma in her opening remarks on the case:

> 1. Discussion of discrimination problems sometimes focuses on the specific fate of one individual. That is not the situation in this case, which concerns the prohibition of discrimination based on ethnic origin under EU law. The case does ultimately stem from a complaint lodged by one individual; however, the centre of interest is the wholesale and collective character of measures which affect an entire community and are liable to stigmatise all the members of that community and their social environment.

AG Kokott had previously referred in *Belov*[95] to 'the context of the social exclusion of Roma and the very poor socio-economic conditions in which that community lives in many places in Europe'. *CHEZ* provided an opportunity to revisit this idea and also to consider 'the possible justifications for collective measures with stigmatising character'. She concluded that justification is only possible if the measures actually prevented fraud and abuse, and contributed to securing a stable electricity supply to all consumers. In addition, the measure had to be proportionate and avoid 'undue adverse effects' on the residents of the district concerned,

> due account being taken of:
>
> — the fact that the threat of stigmatisation of an ethnic group appreciably outweighs purely economic considerations and
> — the interest of final customers supplied with electricity in monitoring their individual energy consumption by means of a regular visual check of their electricity meters.

The CJEU agreed with her: it held that the measure constituted direct discrimination[96] as well as unjustifiable indirect discrimination. Two distinct types of detriment were suffered by the Roma: first, a moral disadvantage, due to the 'offensive and stigmatizing nature of the practice' and, second, a practical disadvantage that made it almost impossible for final consumers to read their meters in order to ascertain their level of electricity consumption.[97]

[95] Case C394/11 *Valeri Hariev Belov v CHEZ Elektro Balgaria AD and Others.*
[96] Case C-83/14 *CHEZ Razpredelenie Bulgaria AD* [91].
[97] ibid [105]–[108].

C. South Africa

A South African court has also explicitly referred to stigma and HIV positive status in a case of employment discrimination. In *Hoffmann*,[98] the South African Constitutional Court used stigma to address the refusal of South African Airlines (SAA) to employ a man with HIV positive status. Mr Hoffmann passed all the employment tests, but a health check revealed that he carried the HIV virus. He was then refused a job with SAA: SAA policy was to refuse employment as cabin crew to people living with HIV. SAA defended its policy as first, promoting the safety and health of its passengers and, second, its own competitive position. Hoffmann challenged the constitutionality of this. The policy was upheld by the High Court but upon appeal the Constitutional Court found that SAA had infringed Mr Hoffmann's constitutional right under Section 9 of the Constitution not to be unfairly discriminated against.[99] The decision revolved around the stigmatisation of people living with HIV.

The Constitutional Court recognised being HIV positive as a stigmatised status, resulting in a marginalisation that condemned sufferers to 'intense prejudice', 'systematic disadvantage and discrimination', denial of employment and yet, paradoxically, invisibility as fear of exclusion forces many not to reveal their status. Invisibility in its turn leads to isolation and deprivation of the help and support they need and could receive. The Court described HIV positive people as 'one of the most vulnerable groups in our society' and in view of the prejudice against them, the Court found that 'any discrimination against them can ... be interpreted as a fresh instance of stigmatization and [...] an assault on their dignity'.

Constitutional Court had no doubt that SAA discriminated against Hoffmann because of his HIV status. It took an equivocal stance to protect him from this and promoted instead 'ubuntu', compassion and understanding towards people living with HIV. Refusing to condemn HIV sufferers to 'economic death' by the denial of equal opportunity in employment, it stated:

> Prejudice can never justify unfair discrimination. This country has recently emerged from institutionalised prejudice. Our law reports are replete with cases in which prejudice was taken into consideration in denying the rights that we now take for granted ... Our constitutional democracy has ushered in a new era—it is an era characterised by respect for human dignity for all human beings. In this era, prejudice and stereotyping have no place. Indeed, if as a nation we are to achieve the goal of equality that we

[98] *Hoffmann v South African Airways* (CCT17/00) [2000] ZACC 17; 2001 (1) SA 1; 2000 (11) BCLR 1235; [2000] 12 BLLR 1365 (CC) (28 September 2000).

[99] '(1) Everyone is equal before the law and has the right to equal protection and benefit of the law ... (3) The state may not unfairly discriminate directly or indirectly against anyone on one or more grounds, including race, gender, sex, pregnancy, marital status, ethnic or social origin, colour, sexual orientation, age, disability, religion, conscience, belief, culture, language and birth ... (5) Discrimination on one or more of the grounds listed in subsection (3) is unfair unless it is established that the discrimination is fair.'

> have fashioned in our Constitution we must never tolerate prejudice, either directly or indirectly. SAA, as a state organ that has a constitutional duty to uphold the Constitution, may not avoid its constitutional duty by bowing to prejudice and stereotyping.[100]

III. Conclusion

This brief review illustrates that the idea of stigma is not alien to law. Judges in national (Australia, England and Wales, Canada and South Africa), as well as European (the European Union and the Council of Europe) courts recognise stigma and use it across various fields of law. The Greek meaning dominates: a stigma is something that is always negative and leads to a punitive response. Interestingly, Canadian law recognises different categories of stigma: legitimate stigma (that is associated with conviction), unjustified stigma (arising from prejudice and stereotype) and a heightened stigma associated with crimes against humanity in general rather than specific individuals. Although in Canada stigma was in the past used to limit access to a remedy under discrimination law, this seems to have been reversed in the more recent case of *A*.

The distinction used by the Canadian Supreme Court highlights that not all stigma need be protected by anti-discrimination law. The legislative antennae should be attuned to unjustifiable stigma, that is, those arising from the arbitrary ascription of a negative value and resulting in a punitive social response that leads to persistent and historical disadvantage. 'Overweight' persons would fall into this category—weight is no indicator of ability, yet larger persons, especially women, are routinely punished (by the withholding of jobs and promotions) for their size. As explored in Chapter 7, weight is an example of the type of unjustifiable stigma that should be the focus of anti-discrimination law. It is an arbitrary ascription to which the public response is always punitive.

Stigma would remain legitimate where associated with, for example, actions of a criminal nature. Persons stigmatised for harming others, such as war criminals or paedophiles, would not become a group protected by anti-discrimination law. Likewise persons with substance dependency issues—including smokers and alcoholics—would not be protected since as a group, they are not *per se* reviled by society for their habits (many smokers for example, such as Barack Obama, occupy leadership positions). These persons would not be recognised and protected as groups under anti-discrimination law, but other laws might be designed for this purpose.

Not withstanding *Law*, stigma may be useful to anti-discrimination law in three ways. First, it reverses the traditional approach to discrimination. Whereas immutability resulted in a pre-occupation with the individual, stigma by definition

[100] *Hoffmann* (n 91) [37].

throws a spotlight on society. It therefore roots discrimination in society rather than in individual behaviour. A focus on stigma restores the connection between discrimination law and society. Anti-discrimination law rooted in society deals with fairness: the demand for non-discrimination is not fuelled by interest group resentment but by a broader belief in social equality. It is a tool for social renewal and cohesion rather than a facilitator of individual or group progress.

This connection is crucial because in the absence of this link, positive and affirmative measures to tackle discrimination are vulnerable to criticism as 'reverse discrimination'. By starting with social attitudes rather than the individual attribute, stigma raises what has heretofore been on the margins in anti-discrimination law—the social level—to the same status as the individual level. As the recent successful attacks on affirmative action in the USA show,[101] measures to ameliorate the effects of discrimination that are separated from social reality can easily be reduced to a battle between economic or political 'interests'. As a consequence, stigma can alter the focus of protection offered by anti-discrimination law—for example, positive action measures would no longer be the exception but the starting point for anti-discrimination law. Positive action and similar 'fifth generation' measures become the norm.

Second, stigma can help anti-discrimination law in general to both see existing problems differently as well as to see different problems. Stigma provides a common divisor over which different forms of discrimination can be set: just as the numbers 2 and 3 have a common divisor of 6, so the current grounds of discrimination have a common divisor in stigma. Although the following quote mentions mental health, it could apply to many of the current protected characteristics:

> [a]t the heart of the issue is the overwhelming stigma attached to mental illness. It means that many people living with these disabilities are effectively rendered invisible and unheard. It is not that they do not have the ability to advocate for themselves, it is that they are not allowed to: after all, they are 'crazy.' Because of this, the enormity of the problem is hidden [...] stigma results in an entire section of communities being, at best, overlooked by their own society and, at worst, being severely maltreated.[102]

The persistence of unequal pay between women and men or disability harassment—all become subject to a broader question focusing on the social norms that support this disadvantageous treatment by employers, colleagues and service providers. The emphasis is not on individual motivation: the individual remains responsible but society is held complicit. Individual freedom to act is linked with the social context and structure within which that individual acts.[103] The restoration of this link locates some moral responsibility for discrimination

[101] For example, Proposal 209 in California, or more recently, Proposal 2 in Michigan, where voters decided in 2006 to amend the state constitution to prohibit the use of criteria such as race or gender in admissions decisions to public institutions.

[102] R Hammond, 'Breaking the Chains' (2014) 115 *Transition* 34.

[103] J Turner, 'American Individualism and Structural Injustice: Tocqueville, Gender and Race' (2008) 40 *Polity* 2.

in society. If society supports the perpetuation of discrimination, then society also bears the responsibility to address this.

Finally, stigma would enable anti-discrimination law to address complex complaints of discrimination such as intersectionality. The idea of stigma provides the synergy[104] that is a prerequisite of intersectionality—it differentiates intersectional discrimination from additive or compound multiple discrimination. These ideas will be developed in Chapter 4.

[104] I Solanke, 'Infusing the Silos in the Equality Act 2010 with Synergy' (2011) 40 *Industrial Law Journal* 336.

4

The Anti-stigma Principle

The previous chapter illustrated that the concept of stigma has a footprint in common law jurisprudence. Even if undefined, it is used in litigation before national and international courts in various ways. Seeing stigma used in case-law makes it more tenable to suggest that it be used in a systematic way in legislation to strengthen anti-discrimination law. My specific proposal is that stigma be used to inform the protected characteristics set out in anti-discrimination law rather than influence the determination of a finding of discrimination. This would provide a clear logic to guide identification of the grounds upon which discrimination is prohibited. This differs to the use of stigma in *Law*,[1] as I argue that stigma can determine whether marital status should be protected by anti-discrimination law per se.

This chapter develops my proposal to give stigma a fundamental place in the design of anti-discrimination law. It suggests that the idea of stigma, as developed by the critical scholars of stigma discussed in Chapter 1, should be fashioned into an 'anti-stigma principle' that can act as a guide to inform the boundaries of anti-discrimination law as well as set new priorities for this field of law. It proposes that the anti-stigma principle should be informed not only by structures of power, but also by patterns of consequences, so as to accommodate the difference between those stigma that will be protected by anti-discrimination law and those that will not.

In order to think about how this can be done, is helpful to look at the models developed by scholars of stigma to depict the spheres in which stigma is active, from the inter-personal level to macro structures of power, and the links between them. It becomes clear from these models that stigma is closely connected to an area that is far away from discrimination law—public health. A question that therefore arises from centralising stigma in anti-discrimination law is whether in so doing discrimination can be framed as a public health issue as well as an equality matter.

Section I discusses the critical approaches to stigma that emerged following the work of Link and Phelan. Thereafter, I present three models of stigma, comparing and contrasting their aims and elements before bringing them together into a heliocentric model of stigma. Once explained, this model will be applied in subsequent chapters.

[1] *Law v Canada (Minister of Employment and Immigration)* [1999] 1 SCR 497.

I. Linking Interpersonal and Structural Stigma

It is clear that the understanding of stigma has been considerably refined since Goffman published his seminal text in 1963. Critical studies of stigma identify it as a complex concept with multiple components[2] that is structurally embedded[3] and multi-level.[4] It is a far more intricate concept than the 'face to face'. This section will discuss these developments and the new models of stigma that have emerged linking the face to face with structural stigma. Recognition of social power is inherent in all of them.

A. Critical Approaches to Stigma

Link and Phelan re-conceptualised the sociology of stigmatisation: in contrast to the simple face-to-face, they defined it as 'a convergence of interrelated components … stigma exists when elements of labeling, stereotyping, separation, status loss, and discrimination occur together in a power situation that allows them'.[5] Their conceptualisation recognises three key elements of stigma: its *arbitrary* nature, its *dynamic* nature and its *embeddedness* in a society that has specific relationships of power. They retain aspects found in the traditional usage of ancient Greece and add others, most significantly the concept of power. By centralising power in the definition of stigma, Link and Phelan reduce attention upon the individual person and attributes—understanding of power imbalances in status thus become as important as individual attributes.

The work of Link and Phelan was as influential as Goffman's. Their re-conceptualisation inspired a new generation of stigma scholars. The idea of structural stigma provided new objects of study and levels of analysis. In psychology, Herek defined stigma as 'an enduring condition, status or attribute that is negatively valued by society' and that is 'rooted in social history, produced and maintained by relationships of power and control'.[6] Researchers in psychiatry linked law to stigma and discrimination, arguing that '[s]tructural discrimination is formed by sociopolitical forces and represents the policies of private and

[2] B. Link and J. Phelan, 'Conceptualising Stigma' (2001) 27 *Annual Review of Sociology* 363–385.

[3] S Hannem and C Bruckert (eds), *Stigma Re-visited: Re-examining the Mark* (University of Ottowa Press, 2012).

[4] BA Pescosolido, JK Martin, A Lang and S Olafsdottir, 'Rethinking Theoretical Approaches to Stigma: A Framework Integrating Normative Influences on Stigma (FINIS)' (2008) 67 *Social Science & Medicine* 431.

[5] Link and Phelan, 'Reconceptualising Stigma' (n 2) 377.

[6] GM Herek—Thinking About AIDS and Stigma: A Psychologist's Perspective' (2002) 30 *Journal of Law, Medicine and Ethics* 595.

governmental institutions that restrict the opportunities of stigmatized groups'.[7] Structural stigma was also found in policies of private companies, such as those refusing to employ people living with HIV.[8] In public health, researchers concluded that '[s]tructural stigma creates environments that have increased threat, punishment, lack of resources, and other social constraints'.[9]

However, the structural seemed to replace rather than complement the face-to-face—as more attention was paid to structural manifestations of stigma, researchers in sociology and criminology noticed a neglect of the interpersonal and inter-face experiences. This gap was addressed by two Canadian scholars working with the idea of structural stigma: Hannem (a sociologist) and Bruckert (a criminologist). Their emphasis that stigma is not only 'interpersonally realised but structurally embedded' linked classical and critical study of stigma to stress that stigma is not just about low social power, but also low interpersonal status.

Using Foucault to address the power vacuum in Goffman's work, they develop a multi-level theory of stigma as 'symbolically realised in individual interactions and structurally embedded in the cultural values, practices and institutions of a society'.[10] In their integrated approach, stigma is not just a process of what people do to each other (interpersonal power) but also what society entertains and allows people to do (institutional power). The essays in their collection use Foucault's work on the production of truth, knowledge and power to show the dual (vertical and horizontal) construction of stigma and its impact on individuals and groups. They define structural stigma as a process that occurs 'when stigmatic assumptions become embedded in social policies and practices'. The process results in a contamination of certain attributes. This definition recognises the insidiousness and pervasiveness of stigma—it is a co-creative and mutually reinforcing social practice engaged in by individuals and institutions.

The integration of individual and structural levels of stigma can be seen in research concerned with health disparities,[11] such as a study on the health outcomes of young gay men.[12] The study linked the individual experience of this cohort into the larger macro-structures of power, suggesting that the behaviour of these young men towards their own health can be linked to the synergy

[7] PW Corrigan, AC Watson, ML Heyrman, A Warpinski, G Gracia, N Slopen and LL Hall, 'Structural Stigma in State Legislation' (2005) 56(5) *Psychiatric Services* 557.

[8] As for example in *Hoffmann v South African Airways* (CCT17/00) [2000] ZACC 17; 2001 (1) SA 1; 2000 (11) BCLR 1235; [2000] 12 BLLR 1365 (CC) (28 September 2000) (discussed in ch 3, section II.C.).

[9] LS Richman and MR Lattanner, 'Self-Regulatory Processes Underlying Structural Stigma and Health' (2014) 103 *Social Science & Medicine* 94, 95.

[10] Hannem and Bruckert, *Stigma Re-visited* (n 3) 10.

[11] Richman and Lattanner, 'Self-regulatory Processes' (n 9).

[12] JE Pachankis, ML Hatzenbuehler and TJ Starks, 'The Influence of Structural Stigma and Rejection Sensitivity on Young Sexual Minority Men's Daily Tobacco and Alcohol Use' (2014) 103 *Social Science & Medicine* 67.

between individual stigma (rejection sensitivity) and the social environment. The researchers concluded that stigma occurs at different levels and also that there is a synergy between these levels: the more sensitive a black or minority ethnic male is to rejection, the worse his health or behaviour are:

> psychological predispositions, such as rejection sensitivity, interact with features of the social environment, such as structural stigma, to predict important health behaviors among young sexual minority men. These results add to a growing body of research documenting the multiple levels through which stigma interacts to produce negative health outcomes among sexual minority individuals.

Thus structural stigma can perpetuate self-stigmatisation, and accentuate an already existing imbalance in power relations. Research into transgender interaction with medical providers also illustrates this: studies suggest that the social and institutional stigma against transgender people allow issues specific to their care to be excluded from the curriculum in medical training. This creates an ambivalence in medical professionals and wariness in transgender patients when they encounter each other: 'transgender people anticipate that providers will not know how to meet their needs'. Nervousness about the level of care interferes with the appropriate balance of power in provider/patient relationships by reinforcing the authority of the medical provider during such interactions. Studies in the health context furthermore suggest that interpersonal stigma serves a specific sociological function: to reinforce medical power and authority in the face of provider uncertainty. Multi-level theories of stigma thus agree with Link and Phelan: functional theories of stigma need to 'acknowledge the role of power and to understand how stigmatising attitudes function to maintain systems of inequality that contribute to health disparities'.[13]

B. Models of Stigma

These insights into social power have informed multi-factoral and multi-level models of stigma. One model, produced by social psychologists, starts from the premise that 'stigmatisation occurs on societal, interpersonal and individual levels'.[14] They group the manifestations of stigma into four inter-related categories: public stigma; self-stigma; stigma by association; and structural stigma.[15] All four types involve 'cognitive, affective and behavioural aspects'. The novelty of this model lies in its positioning of the role of society—public stigma sits at the centre

[13] T Poteat, D German and D Kerrigan, 'Managing Uncertainty: A Grounded Theory of Stigma in Transgender Health Care Encounters' (2013) 84 *Social Science & Medicine* 22.

[14] AER Bos, JB Pryor, GD Reeder and S Stutterheim, 'Stigma Advances in Theory and Research' (2013) 35 *Basic and Applied Social Psychology* 1.

[15] JB Pryor and GD Reeder, 'HIV Related Stigma' in JC Hall, BJ Hall and CJ Cockerell (eds), *HIV/AIDS in the Post-HAART Era: Manifestations, Treatment and Epidemiology* (Shelton, CT: PMPH-USA, 2011) 790.

of their model: 'public stigma is at the root of self-stigma, stigma by association and structural stigma'.[16]

Public stigma can be understood as a collective negative reaction to a stigma that confers lower social status and power to those who possess the stigmatised attribute.[17] Self-stigma results from an awareness of public stigma and has three forms: 'enacted' where the individual is actually subjected to negative treatment; 'felt' where the individual anticipates stigmatisation due to a 'mark' or condition; and 'internalised' where the individuals sense of self-worth is reduced due to a stigmatised condition. 'Passing'—pretending to not have the stigmatised attribute—may help a person to avoid enacted stigma but not felt or internalised self-stigma. Stigma by association occurs when persons are devalued due to their relationship with someone bearing a 'mark'[18] where, for example, a stigmatised family member results in an individual having reduced self-esteem and psychological distress. Volunteers can also be devalued by association. Structural stigma emerges from societal ideologies and institutions and 'is perpetuated by hegemony and the exercise of social, economic and political power'.[19] It is an acknowledgment that 'power differences are essential for the production of stigma'.[20] As structures promoting stigmatisation vary across time and place, contextual studies are required—structural stigma requires 'examination of the social context in which that stigma occurs and the local knowledge systems that contribute to structural stigma'.[21]

One concern with this categorisation is that it seems to suggest the existence of stigma without power—in this model only structural stigma explicitly incorporates power. Link and Phelan and Hannem and Bruckert would arguably suggest that power is inherent in stigma *per se*: it is impossible to have any type of stigma without power. The social psychological model does, however, introduce a useful way to think about the parties involved in stigmatisation. In this model, 'target' and 'perceiver' replaces the language traditionally used in anti-discrimination law of 'victim' and 'perpetrator'. A 'target' is a person who possesses stigmatised attributes while a 'perceiver' is a person who stigmatises. This language will be useful for the anti-stigma principle as it highlights that fact that an attribute is actively magnified to justify demeaning treatment.

[16] Bos et al, 'Stigma Advances' (n 14) 6.

[17] SR Chaudoir, VA Earnshaw and S Andel, 'Discredited v Discreditable' in Bos et al, 'Stigma Advances' (n 14) 75.

[18] The *Coleman* case is an example of stigma by association—in this case Mrs Coleman claimed to have been discriminated against by her employer because she had a son who was disabled. C 303/06 S. *Coleman v Attridge Law and Steve Law.*

[19] G Scambler and F Paoli, 'Health Work, Female Sex Workers and HIV/AIDS: Global and Local Dimensions of Stigma and Deviance as Barriers to Effective Interventions' (2008) 66(8) *Social Science and Medicine* 1848.

[20] Bos et al, 'Stigma Advances' (n 14) 5.

[21] Bos et al, 'Stigma Advances' (n 14) 4.

Some of the types of self-stigma mentioned by Bos et al map onto current forms of anti-discrimination law. Enacted stigma would be direct discrimination; stigma by association would be discrimination by association; and structural stigma would be indirect or institutional discrimination. The type of stigma that has no direct correlate in anti-discrimination law is 'felt' and 'internalised' stigma—there is no legal remedy for 'passing', a phenomenon that may happen more frequently than imagined. Recent revelations demonstrate that on rare occasions people will also claim to possess a stigmatised attribute: in 2015 it emerged that two white women—Rachel Dolezal and Andrea Smith—had adopted the identity of an African American (Dolezal) and a Native Indian (Smith) respectively.[22] Dolezal led a local branch of the National Association for the Advanvement of Coloured People (NAACP) and Smith's membership of the Cherokee nation supported her successful career as law professor.

Self-stigma is the focus of another categorisation[23] specifically designed to explain how stigma 'gets under the skin' to affect individual mental and physical health. As put by Link and Phelan, 'when powerful groups forcefully label and extensively stereotype a less powerful group, the range of mechanisms for achieving discriminatory outcomes is both flexible and extensive'.[24] The 'Stigma Mechanisms in Health Disparities' model maps these mechanisms used by perceivers. Public stigma, also at the centre of this model, 'initiates a cascade of processes that ultimately lead to disparate outcomes among stigmatized and non-stigmatized individuals'. This model is also multi-level and inter-connected: the processes can occur at the sociocultural, the interpersonal and the individual level whereby 'individual beliefs and interpersonal processes are both nested within broader sociocultural phenomena'.[25] For example, at the individual level stress can lead to stigma getting 'under the skin' while at the sociocultural level lack of access to healthcare can trigger this.

The categories encompass the many mechanisms that perceivers can use to stigmatise and achieve discriminatory outcomes. These mechanisms can be overt or covert. They encourage targets of stigma 'to believe that they should not enjoy full and equal participation in social and economic life'.[26] Stigma mechanisms are also temporary—they can change and be reinvented as quickly as they are blocked or avoided. Targets of stigma may take action to avoid a negative consequence by

[22] See EV Lee, 'No, Andrea Smith is not the "Native American Rachel Dolezal"' (1 July 2015), available at https://moontimewarrior.com/2015/07/01/no-andrea-smith-is-not-the-native-american-rachel-dolezal/.

[23] SR Chaudoir, VA Earnshaw and S Andel, 'Discredited v Discreditable' in Bos et al, 'Stigma Advances' (n 14) 75.

[24] Link and Phelan, 'Re-conceptualising Stigma' (n 2) 378.

[25] Chaudoir, Earnshaw and Andel, 'Discredited v Discreditable' (n 23).

[26] Link and Phelan, 'Re-conceptualising Stigma' (n 2) 378.

challenging or evading the specific mechanism that leads to the discrimination that they seek to escape only to find that the neutralised mechanism has been easily replaced by another. When the range of possible mechanisms is broad, the benefit is only temporary.

The diversity of stigma mechanisms is one reason why stigma is so often inescapable. Link and Phelan describe this as a 'persistent predicament',[27] that is, a general pattern of disadvantage that is connected to stigma processes of labeling, stereotyping, status loss and discrimination. Stigma can also be inescapable because it can be all encompassing, and outcomes can be experienced by the individual on multiple levels:

> One can exert great effort to avoid one stigma-related outcome, like discrimination in medical insurance or injury to self esteem, but doing so can carry costs. For instance, the coping effort can be stressful, as in the case of John Henryism and hypertension levels among African Americans. In that example, the effort to eliminate one bad outcome ironically produces strain that leads to another. Also, focusing particular attention on one outcome means that less attention is available to deal with other aspects of life. As a result, while benefits may accrue in one domain, concomitant harms may result in others. It is the existence of multiple stigma mechanisms and multiple stigma outcomes that helps explain why stigma is a persistent predicament—why, on average, members of stigmatized groups are disadvantaged in a broad range of life domains (e.g. employment, social relationships, housing, and psychological well-being).

Like Goffman, they recognise that some stigmas stick for life, even if variation in personality, resources and life circumstances prevents all individuals in a group sharing the same exposure to stigma mechanisms and the same pattern of stigma outcomes. As Goffman says, some groups are permanently stigmatised. These insights are also useful for the anti-stigma principle, which does not recognise all stigmas as valid for protection under anti-discrimination law. The anti-stigma principle respects the specific goal of anti-discrimination law and its use is intended to retain the focus on arbitrary attributes that result in persistent and permanent stigmatisation.

A further and more sophisticated model of stigma has been developed by researchers of mental illness. In order to explain both the mechanisms and outcomes of this stigma, they use a multi-level interactive model: the 'Framework Integrating Normative Influences on Stigma (FINIS)'. This model illustrates the possibilities of a cross-disciplinary approach to provide a 'textured' understanding of stigma. It

> starts with Goffman's notion that understanding stigma requires a language of social relationships, but acknowledges that individuals do not come to social interaction devoid of *affect and motivation*. Further, all social interactions take place in a context in which

[27] Link and Phelan, 'Re-conceptualising Stigma' (n 2) 378.

> organizations, media and larger cultures structure normative expectations which create the possibility of marking 'difference'. Labelling theory, social network theory, the limited capacity model of media influence, the social psychology of prejudice and discrimination, and theories of the welfare state all contribute to an understanding of the complex web of expectations shaping stigma.[28]

According to the FINIS model, the process of stigmatisation of mental illness rests upon norm expectations in social life. There are three different levels of social life: the 'micro or psychological and socio-cultural level or individual factors; meso or social network or organizational level factors; and macro or societal-wide factors'.[29] The macro level includes the national context, with its economic structures, social organisations and cultural systems that set normative expectations, reflect access to social power, and establish 'the acceptability of acting on cultural biases'.[30] Action can be taken at each of these levels to ameliorate, for example, mental illness stigma.

The FINIS model is innovative due to the attention paid to the role of the mass media as a stigma mechanism. The model incorporates findings from research suggesting that the media plays a powerful role in shaping the public image of mental illness. One study that examined newspapers, movies and television found that mental illness was consistently portrayed as dangerous, unpredictable and incompetent. Even if individuals are not passive recipients of information disseminated in the mass media, the media play a central role in establishing norms. Information on traditional and social media accompanies individuals as they construct their world and community views of places and people. In addition, film and art may be mechanisms by which individuals create their world view.

The models discussed above contribute to the creation of the 'anti-stigma principle' (ASP). They share an understanding that stigma is played out between individuals but originates in and is perpetuated by broader social forces, such as the media, organisational culture or public policies. Each also makes a more specific contribution. Bos et al contribute the new designators of 'target' and 'perceiver'—these may be more useful for the anti-stigma principle than the language of 'victim' and 'perpetrator'. Chaudoir et al contribute the idea of chameleonic multi-level, interactive and malleable mechanisms that lead to discriminatory outcomes—this idea allows the anti-stigma principle to be proactive and flexible. Finally, the FINIS model highlights the need to take action—different types of action—at each level of social life: micro, meso and macro, allowing the anti-stigma principle to incorporate levels previously ignored by anti-discrimination law. In particular, an anti-discrimination law informed by the anti-stigma principle could

[28] Pescolido et al, 'Rethinking Theoretical Approaches to Stigma' (n 4) 433.
[29] ibid.
[30] Pescolido et al, 'Rethinking Theoretical Approaches to Stigma' (n 4) 435.

recognise the psychological harm endured by targets and therefore provide remedies for discrimination arising at this level of stigmatisation. The priority of anti-discrimination law moves from individual attributes and behavioural deficits to social meanings and narratives, such as the stigma of obesity and the representation of 'fat' in the media.[31] The anti-stigma principle is therefore inherently broad in its scope of action, more responsive and potentially more pro-active than the anti-discrimination principle.

The anti-stigma principle can improve the vision of anti-discrimination law in three ways. First, in relation to clarity on the scope of anti-discrimination law, it can provide a useful lens through which to ascertain which attributes, conditions and statuses should be protected by anti-discrimination law. Even if equality must be inclusive, anti-discrimination law must be limited in scope. In order to limit anti-discrimination law while remaining committed to equality, the anti-stigma principle can guide the vision of ADL, or *what* it sees, so that the prevention of discrimination remains central to the promotion of equality.

Second, the anti-stigma principle can inform *how* anti-discrimination law sees or in other words help it to remedy discrimination based upon one protected characteristic as well as multiple characteristics. Stigmas can travel alone or in groups—for example, medical research argues that stigmas can intersect:

> Inner city women with severe mental illness may carry multiple stigmatized statuses. In some contexts these include having a mental illness, being a member of an ethnic minority group, being an immigrant, being poor, and being a woman who does not live up to gendered expectations. These potentially stigmatizing identities influence both the way women's sexuality is viewed and their risk for HIV infection. This qualitative study applies the concept of intersectionality to facilitate understanding of how these multiple identities intersect to influence women's sexuality and HIV risk.[32]

Third, by foregrounding social power (macro structures), the anti-stigma principle highlights where discrimination originates: it is not only manifested in individual behaviour but also social norms. Drawing out *social responsibility* can provide a stronger rationale for collective remedies for discrimination such as positive action, especially in areas where discrimination is persistent. Under the anti-stigma principle, such measures undertaken to challenge prevailing common sense may be better described as 'public action' rather than positive action. Thus the anti-stigma principle may produce an anti-discrimination law more capable of addressing durable inequality.

[31] K Holland, RW Blood, SL Thomas and S Lewis, 'Challenging Stereotypes and Legitimating Fat: An Analysis of Obese People's Views on News Media Reporting Guidelines and Promoting Body Diversity', 51 *Journal of Sociology* 431–445.

[32] PY Collins, H von Unger and A Armbrister, 'Church Ladies, Good Girls, and Locas: Stigma and the Intersection of Gender, Ethnicity, Mental Illness, and Sexuality in Relation to HIV Risk' (2008) 67 *Social Science & Medicine* 389.

II. Models of Stigma and Public Health

Empirical medical research has contributed much to the development of the models of stigma discussed above. In particular, research on issues such as HIV/AIDs, mental health and other ailments of general public concern have played a key role. It is therefore not surprising that the models display characteristics found in approaches to public health. For example, both have a particular priority: to link the individual to external surrounding forces and identify social determinants of individual health.[33] The anti-stigma principle is therefore also linked to the field of public health, as this perspective informs the models of stigma upon which it is built.

There are many images of the field called 'public health' leading to the conclusion that a single definition is impossible. Public health is most often associated with the medical profession—the phrase conjures images of kindly medical researchers (such as Marie Curie) or investigators (such as the fictional Dr Gregory House). However, public health research is by no means always benign, as illustrated by the Tuskegee syphilis experiment.[34] It is also often linked to pandemic disease, such as avian bird flu, HIV/Aids or Ebola. When such epidemics rage through the population, the expectation is that public health experts, mainly from the medical profession, will work to address it. Indeed, medical social movements, such as *medecin sans frontiers*, have an increasingly strong profile in matters of public health, especially in the Global South. In the Global North, however, public health has two contrasting faces: in the UK it is, on the one hand, portrayed as the interfering 'Nanny State' but, on the other, as the socially concerned National Health Service, working to manage the health and wellbeing challenges of everyday life.[35]

It is the predominant image of public health in the Global South that is of relevance here: like models of structural stigma, it focuses upon an individual linked to external surrounding forces. In both, individuals are placed within a context and examined in light of their connections with their fellow beings, structures and institutions as well as the broader environment. However, alongside this fundamental similarity, there are key differences. For example if we look at the dynamics of these models, we find that public health models replace the

[33] However, there are also key differences: public health models do not articulate a role for power and they also start with the individual rather than the society.

[34] The 'Tuskegee Study of Untreated Syphilis in the Negro Male' resulted in a class action and a payout of more than $9 million. Participants—all poor black men—were enticed and key information on the purpose and potential life-threatening consequences of the treatment for them, their partners and children was withheld. See http://www.tuskegee.edu/about_us/centers_of_excellence/bioethics_center/about_the_usphs_syphilis_study.aspx.

[35] G Rayner and T Lang, 'Ecological Public Health: Reshaping the Conditions for Good Health' (Abingdon, Routledge, 2012).

unidirectional continuum of structural stigma with multi-directional networks. The World Health Organisation (WHO) Commission model on social determinants of health posits a filtration process of inputs and outputs. Alternatively, sustainability scholars depict public health as a series of dynamic cogs, where everything is inter-connected and continually in motion making the health of the system as important as health as an outcome of the system.

Public health models also incorporate concepts of proximity that are absent from models of stigma. The above-mentioned WHO model includes proximal, distal and contextual determinants. *Proximal* determinants include health services, lifestyle and the physical living environment. *Distal* determinants include policy, economic development, knowledge and social interactions, ecosystem goods and services. Finally, *contextual* determinants include good governance structures, global markets, global communications and cross cultural interactions and global environmental change.

Finally, a third key difference is that public health models place the individual at the centre, as being subjected to different levels of environmental forces. For example, Dahlgren and Whitehead's heliocentric model places individuals at the centre of four concentric circles: individual lifestyle factors (age, sex, race); social and community networks; living and working conditions (including food production, education, work environment, unemployment, sanitation, health care and housing); and general socio-economic, cultural and environmental conditions. Bronfenbrenner's ecology of child health is also heliocentric, embedding the individual in three levels: a microsystem (comprising family, religion and peers); an exosystem (school, health agencies, community and mass media); and a macrosystem (political systems, culture, nationality, society and economics). Each level represents a different proximity to the individual, with the microsystem as the closest.

Models of stigma—and the anti-stigma principle—can benefit from these traits of public health models in two ways. First, public health models can contribute the use of concentric circles: Figure 1 depicts the public level as the power source of all stigma but presents this as the outer layer of the concentric circles so as to highlight containment, as per Dahlgren's model of public health. This is to show that public stigma envelopes and influences all other forms: structural, inter-personal and individual/internal stigma. The anti-stigma principle (ASP) therefore locates the origin of discrimination in the public level, from whence it filters through to the individual level.

Second, a heliocentric depiction can incorporate the zones of proximity used in models of public health, whereby internal stigma is the most intimate, experienced by an individual, and public stigma is the most distant form. Incorporation of the idea of proximity entrenches the inescapability of stigma, whether it be public or intimate: neither form is necessarily easier to escape than the other. The anti-stigma principle therefore incorporates recognition that discrimination is experienced by individuals at different intensities, whereby the most distant form at the public level maybe the least escapable as it is least within individual control.

Figure 1 depicts a model of stigma as per the anti-stigma principle.

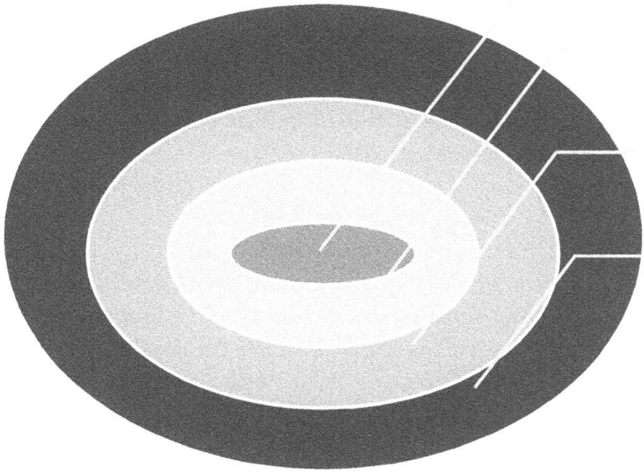

Figure 1: The Anti-stigma Principle and Spheres of Stigmatisation

The anti-stigma principle actively tackles stigmatisation/discrimination at four levels. At the individual level, stigmatisation is the consequence of interaction with oneself: it is the internal—probably intense—anticipation of stigma that is 'felt' rather than 'enacted'. An individual can feel stigmatised and fear stigmatisation even if their mark, status or condition is invisible or no longer exists. This experience can be described as 'stereotype threat' where, in order to pre-empt discrimination, 'marked' groups including women[36] and people of low socio-economic status[37] will adopt an external symbol, such as whistling Vivaldi,[38] to signify to the general public that they pose no danger. Using Goffman's terms, those who are 'discreditable' would experience stigma at this level. As depicted by the models of stigma discussed above, when stigmatised individuals internalise the general low expectations emanating from society, they thwart their own success. The anti-stigma principle imports this level of internal stigmatisation into anti-discrimination law.

[36] PB Carr and CM Steele, 'Stereotype Threat Affects Financial Decision Making' (2010) 21 *Psychological Science*, 1411.

[37] B Spencer and E Castano, 'Social Class is Dead! Long Live Social Class! Stereotype Threat Among Low Socio-Economic Status Individuals' (2007) 20 *Social Justice Research* 418.

[38] CM Steele, *Whistling Vivaldi: and Other Clues to How Stereotypes Affect Us* (Issues of Our Time) (WM Norton, London, 2010).

At the interpersonal level, stigmatisation is proximal. It occurs when a 'target' encounters a 'perceiver'[39]—a 'marked' or 'discredited' person comes across a 'normal' and is subjected to 'face-to-face' discriminatory treatment. The experience depends upon lifestyle, community networks and social capital—the extent to which one moves in homogenous circles and/or possesses resources to evade stigmatisation. At the interpersonal level, stigma is enacted in dyadic interactions. The anti-stigma principle therefore creates an anti-discrimination law that recognises discrimination that can be overt and direct.

At the structural level, stigmatisation is distal. It is not transmitted by any specific individual 'perceiver' but by rules, practices and procedures as, for example, via institutionalised discrimination—the norms by which an entity operates. It can include everyday living and working conditions. At this level stigma is enacted in neutral rules and institutionalised interactions. Discrimination can be indirect, that is seen only when its impact is examined. Here the anti-stigma principle creates an anti-discrimination law that can tackle indirect and institutional discrimination.

Finally, at the public level stigmatisation is contextual and environmental—it resides in the prevailing 'common sense' and is effectively transmitted by informal constituent sources, which are diffuse and abstract including the mass media, film, art and literature. At this level, the key mechanisms are symbols and representations. Discrimination is invisible. This is the level where the third dimension of power, or the potent and invisible mobilisation bias[40] operates. To address this, the anti-stigma principle creates an anti-discrimination law that can address narratives and discourses.

Although some forms of discrimination map directly onto modes of stigmatisation, the anti-stigma principle offers an original and broader way to think about anti-discrimination law. In most jurisdictions attention is focused on the interpersonal and structural levels but the anti-stigma principle also draws attention to the intimate and public levels. It should be noted that intersectional discrimination is not highlighted: this is because the complexity of intersectional discrimination is inherent in the model—stigma can be singular or synergistic. Under the anti-stigma principle, protection from intersectional discrimination is already embedded in the DNA of anti-discrimination law rather than accommodated as an afterthought.

The anti-stigma principle therefore offers a distinctive way to think about anti-discrimination law in general and furthermore, due to the origins of the principle, indirectly links anti-discrimination law to public health. What if ADL were directly linked to public health? What practical implication would this have? If critical

[39] Pryor and Reeder, 'HIV Related stigma' (n 15) 1.

[40] P Bachrach and MS Baratz, 'Two Faces of Power' (1962) 56 *The American Political Science Review* 947.

approaches to stigma are linked to public health, can a more critical approach to discrimination be developed by seeing it as a virus?

III. The Discrimination Virus

If stigma is linked to public health, can discrimination be approached this way too—can discrimination be approached as a virus? This idea has been advanced in a study of de-segregation by Morris and Morris.[41] They describe the 'discrimination virus' as similar to the flu:

> The cold virus has been around for centuries. Scientists have not found a cure for it, and it keeps passing from person to person, year after year. Medical science knows only how to treat the symptoms. Just as the cold virus affects the body and the spirit, the 'discrimination virus' poisons the mind and the spirit. Like the cold virus, the discrimination virus cannot be seen with the naked eye, yet it is highly infectious and can pass from one person to another very rapidly, often without recipients being aware that they have been infected. However, the discrimination virus, based on skin colour, differs from the cold virus in one very important way: the cold virus may be active in an individual's body for only one or two weeks per year, and maybe not even every year. But the discrimination virus has the potential for affecting the life of a victim everyday for a lifetime. You can't see the virus but victims can recognise how it sounds, how it feels and they experience the results of the infection in their lives.[42]

Although the authors focus on race discrimination, all forms of discrimination can be described as a virus. The virus afflicts perceivers as well as targets—none touched by it escape unscathed.

If discrimination can be appropriately described as a virus in society, why not explicitly treat it as one in law? The advantage is that this opens up a broader scope for different types of disciplines and other forms of action in addition to legal intervention. For example, discrimination could be located in other fields such as public health, where viruses are dealt with on a daily basis. Locating discrimination in public health gives it an additional anchoring in the academy—discrimination law is rarely taught outside of employment or labour law, but as a branch of public health it could be taught in schools of medicine and social studies as part of training on health and well-being.

This link would also enable public health methods to be adopted to tackle discrimination. As a virus, discrimination would have to be tackled not only at the interpersonal and structural levels, but also at the public and individual level. The problem takes on new dimensions and responses are required to address these

[41] VG Morris and CL Morris, 'They Paid the Price: Desegregation in an African American Community' (Teachers College Press, Columbia University, 2002) 80.

[42] Morris and Morris, 'They Paid the Price' (n 41) 80.

dimensions. Locating anti-discrimination law in public health can therefore add nuance to the analysis of discrimination and clarity to the design of measures to remedy it: if discrimination is a virus, public action is as important to address it as individual remedies.

There may therefore be some value in exploring more closely the extent to which discrimination can be approached in this way. If discrimination can per se be understood as a disease that invisibly 'rages through the public', what does the discrimination virus look, sound like and feel like? There may not be a single answer to this question—it is likely to differ, depending upon time and place. What is covert discrimination in one time and place may be overt in another. The virus may have a different appearance at each level.

At the public level, the discrimination virus might be most clearly manifested in social statistics. Data continues to show that women are paid less than men in all sectors and at all levels, Black men are more likely to be tasered, stopped and searched than white men, and disabled, overweight and transgender persons are disproportionately more likely to be unemployed than those who are not disabled, overweight or transgender. These disparities exist not due to anything done by the affected individuals, but because of a 'common sense' perception that women's work is worth less, that black men are more likely to be criminals and that those who do not conform to physical and gender stereotypes will be sub-standard workers. This is the level at which the virus is the most intractable because it is almost intangible, only visible in omissions, outcomes and patterns rather than action.

At the structural level, however, the virus lurks in rules, practices and procedures. The discrimination virus expresses itself, for example, in pan-homogeneity: in every sector of economic, social, political and artistic activity, Goffman's 'unblushing' white heterosexual male sits at the highest levels of decision-making. A white male heterosexual norm pervades sectors from academia to banking and the military. The more homogenous the professions, the more likely it will be to find the virus festering in that profession. However, the virus can fester even where there is diversity if that diversity is superficial or sectoral.

At the interpersonal level, the virus can be seen in acts of everyday discrimination between individuals: the iconic racist housing signs seen in England in the 1950s—'No Irish, No Blacks, No Dogs'—are an example of this, as are the 'discriminatory vacancies' of 1960s Britain, refusals of promotion or of entry to a disco. The more that individuals interact with homogenous environments and professional strata, the greater the chance of experiencing the virus at this level. Social power hierarchies inform and are played out at the interpersonal level:

> By virtue of their position in a social hierarchy, members of marginalized groups such as the uneducated, poor, or overweight have lower status than their more educated, wealthy, thin, or otherwise better socially situated counterparts. Status dynamics also play out in the interpersonal relations among people. The belief that others hold about whether someone possesses resources and/or personal characteristics that are important for the achievement of collective goals also influences perceptions of status. Members of

> stigmatized groups are unlikely to be viewed as contributors to these goals. Structural and interpersonal stigma, combining experiences of both a diminished control over resources and a devalued social identity, are defined by both low power and low status.[43]

Even at this level, the virus can be difficult to spot. It may take the form of stereotype threat. Sometimes marked groups 'perform' public acts to counter the popular image of them (the virus at the public level). Steele develops this theory to show the corrosive effects of a mark such as skin colour. In *Whistling Vivaldi*[44] he focuses on the position of black men in the social imaginary[45] of white Americans, where a young black man is per se presumed to be violent and dangerous. Steele suggests that in order to pre-empt this stereotype threat, young black men send out cues, such as whistling Vivaldi, to signal to white passers-by that will put them at ease. Emission of a strong cultural signal (familiarity with classical music) dispels the popular stereotype of criminality attached to young black men. It says 'I am like you and you do not need to be afraid of me. Your interests are my interests.' 'Whistling Vivaldi' is therefore a way to manage public stigma and negate the threat of being stereotyped.

Why would familiarity with classical music send a public signal that a young black man is cultured rather than criminal? Why would anybody automatically think otherwise? The expectation may arise from the virus at the public level—it is the images and narratives in the social imaginary that creates the norm of criminality for young black men. If it is the presence of the virus at the public level that gives rise to this expectation, it is at the public level that the virus is most effectively tackled. Thus negating the threat at the individual level does not necessarily impact upon the virus at the public level: there is no 'trickle-up'. This explains why the increase in the number of black businessmen or female mathematicians does little to change popular or common sense perceptions of those belonging to marked groups—inequality endures for marked groups even if some individuals from those groups are able to secure highly regarded roles and economic security.

Although the virus can be analysed at different levels, all levels interact and build upon each other to produce a cascade of effects for those who are 'marked' by society. As argued by Feagin,

> Today, unjustly inherited white resources and continuing discrimination restrict access of many Americans of colour to better jobs, quality education, healthy neighbourhoods, quality health care and political power. From the beginning, a white racial framing with its major elements being not only racial bias, but also racial ideologies, images, narratives, emotions and inclinations to discriminate, has aggressively defended this unequal and unjust society.[46]

[43] Richman and Lattamer, 'Self-regulatory Processes' (n 9).
[44] Steele, *Whistling Vivaldi* (n 38).
[45] Charles Taylor, *Modern Social Imaginaries* (Durham, Duke University Press, 2003).
[46] J Feagin and Z Bennefield, 'Systemic Racism and U.S. Health Care' (2014) 103(7) *Social Science & Medicine* 8.

A key requirement to tackle discrimination is therefore to know how the social environment becomes infected with this virus and how the infection spreads. This will be explored in Chapter 5.

There are many advantages to treating discrimination as a virus, or communicable disease (CD). The analytical sophistication of discrimination that becomes possible is one strong reason. It draws immediate attention to the environment is three specific and relevant ways—first, it highlights public impact: viruses are a danger to the public at large not just specific individuals. This is in contrast to the way in which discrimination is often seen—it is normally viewed as having narrow general relevance, being only of concern to those individuals whose lives are directly affected. Likewise, remedies are narrowly targeted.[47] However, like flu, discrimination affects everybody who lives within the environment in which it is at large. As with other threats to the public health, everybody is at risk. Thus treating discrimination as a virus makes it clear that its eradication is everybody's business.

Second, linked to this, it draws attention to the role of the public in addressing this risk—public action, including but not limited to education, is required to stem the progress of the virus. As with other CD's, public action becomes a norm of anti-discrimination law.

Third, equally importantly, it highlights the dynamism in the spread of discrimination. Communicable diseases (CD's) spread exponentially and surreptitiously: some are airborne, others transfer through contact with fluids, and others are transmitted by simple contact. The mode of transfer is what makes them so dangerous. Discrimination can be transmitted through education—as seen in the song 'Turning Point' discussed in Chapter 1, this can be at the interpersonal level from mother to child; at the institutional level through the educational curriculum; or at the environmental level via mass media. However, as with a medical virus, transmission may also be covert, unconscious and unintended—no mother deliberately passes the Ebola virus onto her child. Treating discrimination as a virus theresfore serves to keep in mind the varied modes and levels in and at which it can be transferred.

Thus to think of discrimination as a virus highlights its effect on the environment, not only its impact on the public but also the role of public action in containing its spread: public action can be both cause and cure. Multi-level focused intervention, which emphasises the role of public action in both perpetuation and resolution of discrimination, is required to check and contain the viral spread. The discussion moves away from solely focusing on individual or institutional behavioural change.

The anti-stigma principle thus approaches discrimination as a multi-level, dynamic social virus. This approach is not entirely new—it is similar to the social

[47] The Deregulation Act 2015, s 2 has removed the power of employment tribunals to make wider recommendations.

model of disability. The social model of disability focuses on the characteristics of the environment that make everyday activities and interactions difficult for persons with mobility or sensory limitations. For example, the difficulty of access into a building for a wheelchair bound person is caused not by the wheelchair but by the requirement to use stairs: the provision of a ramp would enable access for pedestrians as well as those in wheelchairs. The problem is, therefore, not the mobility impaired person or the wheelchair *per se*—the social model locates the problem in external physical structures rather than the person. The anti-stigma principle makes this social approach the norm for anti-discrimination law in general rather than disability discrimination alone. However, the anti-stigma principle builds upon the social model of disability by identifying multiple levels for intervention. It also explicitly understands discrimination as a virus.

The value of the anti-stigma principle lies in its clarification and illumination of the levels at which anti-discrimination law operates. Remedies currently contained in the UK Equality Act 2010 such as positive action and the public sector equality duty operate at the level of public stigma. Indirect and institutional discrimination, as is clear from the model, operate at the structural or distal level of stigmatisation while direct discrimination occurs at the level of interpersonal stigmatization. These are the three levels at which anti-discrimination law currently operates. It does little to tackle the virus at the individual level—there is no legal remedy for the psychological harm of discrimination, which is a significant omission. The anti-stigma principle also equalises these levels, making public action the norm alongside action to tackle structural and interpersonal stigma.

IV. Conclusion

When models of stigma are traced back to their origins, they lead to the field of public health. The idea of discrimination as stigma thus links discrimination to public health and provides an opportunity to identify an additional non-legal rationale for anti-discrimination law: the promotion of public health. This also gives anti-discrimination law an alternative home in the Academy. At present discrimination law is rarely taught outside of law and sociology, whereas as a branch of public health it could also be taught in schools of medicine and public policy. The anti-stigma principle thus makes action against discrimination a legal as well as a public health issue. It establishes discrimination as a key issue for well-being in general as well as equality in particular.

Imagining discrimination law from public health provides a different perview that can, first, invert the traditional approach and, second, broaden its perview. Rather than start with the individual attribute, the anti-stigma principle posits the public level as the source of discrimination—the pursuit of equality therefore flows from the public to individual level rather than vice versa. Furthermore, instead of focusing on the individual perpetrator, the anti-stigma principle shines a spotlight upon the context within which discrimination occurs. It embeds recognition of social responsibility, context and complexity into the DNA of anti-discrimination law and prioritises them. This changes the project and the practice of anti-discrimination law. Framing discrimination as a public health issue, similar to Ebola, flu or any other disease that rages through the public, presents it as a virus; in other words, as a preventable health risk requiring public action for successful eradication.

One consequence of this is to move the discussion away from solely focusing on individual or institutional behavioural change and emphasise the role of public action in both perpetuation and resolution of discrimination. This approach develops the idea of the social model promoted by disability discrimination activists and takes it further by making environmental action a key location for the solution as the norm for anti-discrimination law per se. From this position existing tools which are still marginalised in the battle against discrimination, such as positive action, are centralised—public action to tackle persistent inequality becomes the norm rather than the exception. Current measures described as 'positive' or 'affirmative' action could be renamed 'public' action measures. As public action measures they can also avoid the current confusion about 'positive discrimination'.

The anti-stigma principle does not necessarily change the tools of anti-discrimination law, but can change their prioritisation. First, it makes collective action to tackle discrimination the norm rather than the exception. Second, it embraces complexity rather than shunning it; and, finally, it is open to additional protected characteristics beyond immutability. It creates a new lens through which to view the current tools of anti-discrimination law. A focus on society rather than individuals creates the potential for more socially focused remedies, strengthening and even going beyond positive action and public sector equality duties. Thus stigma can update the twentieth century vision of anti-discrimination law: it can improve what (the social as well as individual level), how (intersectional and single dimension) and who (overweight, tattooed people etc) anti-discrimination law sees. A model of 'ecological anti-discrimination law' can replace the prevailing individual anti-discrimination law. The priority thus moves from individual attributes and behavioural deficits to social meanings and discourses, such as the stigma of obesity and the representation of fat in the media.[48]

These specific ways in which anti-discrimination law could be broadened will be discussed in the following chapters: modernisation of the narrative by democratisation of anti-discrimination law via public action; recognition of complexity and intersectionality; incorporation of flexibility; and a clear rationale for adding to the list of protected characteristics.

[48] K Holland, RW Blood, SL Thomas and S Lewis, 'Challenging Stereotypes and Legitimating Fat: An Analysis of Obese People's Views on News Media Reporting Guidelines and Promoting Body Diversity', 51 *Journal of Sociology* 431–445.

5

Public Action to Combat Discrimination

Following Goffman, classical studies of stigma focus on the individual and emphasise internal psychological factors. Following Link and Phelan, critical studies of stigma focus on power, emphasising society and external factors beyond the control of any single individual. As discussed in Chapter 4, the anti-stigma principle enables analysis of discrimination along four dimensions: a distal public sphere; a semi-proximate structural sphere; a proximate interpersonal sphere; and an intimate internal sphere. Recognition of these spheres of discrimination in the anti-stigma principle allows for development of an anti-discrimination law that can tackle discrimination at the collective and interpersonal levels.

According to the principle, the public level infuses and informs discrimination at all other levels. I understand the 'public' as the collective social domain. The anti-stigma principle therefore directs attention to the social as the source of discrimination. The principle does not ignore the public sphere: it forces anti-discrimination law to 'see' the social context. This theory of anti-discrimination law not only understands discrimination as a virus but also looks to the social environment as the source of this virus and thus as an important location for anti-discrimination law in action.

If the social environment is the source of discrimination, then anti-discrimination law must pay attention to the environment or context within which discriminatory behaviour occurs. It also follows from this that individual discriminators are influenced in their behaviour by cues contained in social norms and narratives. Arguably, persons who discriminate do so with some consciousness of a collective norm that will sanction their behaviour unless—and sometimes even if—they are caught. Public discourse acts as a resource and repository for discriminatory ideas and creates the context for face-to-face discriminatory behaviour. From the perspective of the anti-stigma principle, silencing these social origins leads to measures that tackle symptoms but overlook the source of discrimination. This chapter therefore focuses on the type of measures that arise from the anti-stigma principle to tackle the virus of discrimination permeating the social environment.

The idea of the 'public' in the anti-stigma principle is composed of conceptions from social psychology and public health. Public health models of stigma describe this level as comprising environmental and contextual phenomena. For Dahlgren and Whitehead the public level focuses on 'general socio-economic, cultural and environmental conditions';[1] Bronfenbrenner's ecology of child health includes an exosystem of 'school, health agencies, community and mass media' and a macrosystem of 'political systems, culture, nationality, society and economics'.[2] The public level is therefore broad and includes many locations of power in social life—it refers to those spaces and practices that are widely shared throughout a society. This can be, for example, a park, a doctor's surgery, a pub, an office, a place of worship, public transport, a cemetery, a shopping mall, a car park or a gym. The 'public' is that space where people meet for any range of activities and services. Even if privately owned, it is still to be available for public use, although owners can refuse to allow specific activities and entry.[3] Public stigma refers to the meanings that prevail in these spaces, that are given force and traction in these spheres. In social psychology, public stigma is understood as a collective negative reaction that confers lower social status and power to those who possess the stigmatised attribute. It is higly toxic and damaging—public stigma 'initiates a cascade of processes that ultimately lead to disparate outcomes among stigmatized and non-stigmatized individuals'.[4]

The power of stigma resides in this level: without society, there would be no social meaning affixed to attributes, statuses and conditions. These meanings are therefore prior to acts of discrimination and continue to exist after such acts. Stigma must be tackled at the public level if discrimination is to be effectively challenged. Arguably, if stigma is weakened at the public level, discrimination will reduce at this and the other levels. However, public stigma is like climate change: no single person is responsible for creating the damage to the ozone layer, yet everybody who heats their home, uses public transport or a car to get to work or takes holidays abroad contributes to this. Likewise no single person is responsible for public stigma, yet we all contribute to its existence. Another difficulty is that at the public level, stigma resides 'in the air', *invisibly* harming the environment for groups and individuals, who are invisible or due to stigma make themselves invisible. As put in the title of a research paper, in public life the stigmatised are 'belittled, avoided, ignored and denied'.[5]

[1] Goren Dahlgren and Margaret Whitehead, *European Strategies for Tackling Social Inequities in Health: Levelling Up Part 2* (WHO Collaborating Centre for Policy Research on Social Determinants of Health University of Liverpool, 2001).

[2] Geoff Rayner and Tim Lang, *Ecological Public Health – Reshaping the Conditions for Good Health* (Routledge, Abingdon, 2012) 28–35.

[3] BL Garrett, 'The privatisation of cities' public spaces is escalating. It is time to take a stand', available at http://www.theguardian.com/cities/2015/aug/04/pops-privately-owned-public-space-cities-direct-action. On POPS in New York, see http://apops.mas.org.

[4] SR Chaudoir, VA Earnshaw and S Andel, 'Discredited v Discreditable' in AER Bos, JB Pryor, GD Reeder and S Stutterheim, 'Stigma Advances in Theory and Research' (2013) 35 *Basic and Applied Social Psychology* 1.

[5] M Ilic, J Reinecke, G Bohner, HO Roettgers, T Beblo, M Driessen, U Frommberger and PW Corrigan, 'Belittled, Avoided, Ignored, Denied: Assessing Forms and Consequences of Stigma

Guinier and Torres use the image of a miner's canary to explain the unseen harm that lurks in the environment. Miners would send a canary into the mine to 'diagnose' the quality of the air, as the canary's fragile respiratory system would cause it to collapse from poisonous gases long before humans were affected. The distress of the canary thus alerted the miners to the need to leave the mine.[6] Stigma in the environment can be compared to these poisonous gases that hang 'in the air'—although invisible, they are damaging and deadly. Such stigma acts as an invisible backdrop to everyday discrimination. This invisibility makes stigma difficult, but not impossible, to tackle—public health viruses are also invisible but medics manage to tackle them. If discrimination can be tackled as a virus, then experience from public health can contain useful suggestions on how to defeat it successfully. It is therefore instructive to consider how a public health virus was effectively tackled. There may be lessons that can be useful to anti-discrimination law.

This chapter begins with discussion of a public health crisis, the Ebola epidemic of 2014. The purpose is to consider what can be learnt from the public action taken to combat this virus. The goal is identification of lessons arising from combating viral epidemics in public health that can be transferred to tackling the virus of discrimination using anti-discrimination law. As will be seen, one of the key ways to tackle a virus is to identify its modes of transmission. In section II, I therefore discuss the 'mechanics' of public stigma, the techniques by which common meanings are created and maintained in this collective space. I consider the use of language and images as constituent forces of the public and their contribution to the creation, sustenance and transmission of stigma. This section highlights in particular the role of the media in giving attributes concrete social meaning.

Section III then uses the lessons identified in the study of Ebola as a lens through which to evaluate the current tools in the UK Equality Act 2010 to tackle discrimination at the public level: positive action and the public sector equality duty (PSED). Positive action refers to a category of measures designed to remedy past discrimination. These type of measures have been subject to sustained attack, in particular in the USA, where the US Supreme Court has repeatedly had to respond to questions on the constitutionality of affirmative action in education and employment.[7] Such action does not have the same profile in Canada or

Experiences of People with Mental Illness' in Pryor and Bos (eds), *Social Psychological Perspectives on Stigma* 31.

[6] L Guinier and G Torrres, *The Miners Canary: Enlisting Race, Resisting Power and Transforming Democracy* (Cambridge, Harvard University Press, 2002) 11–12. They argue that persons 'who are racially marginalized are like the miner's canary: their distress is the first sign of a danger that threatens us all'.

[7] Such as *University of California v Bakke* 438 US 265 (1978); *United Steel-workers of America v Weber* 99 S Ct 272 (1979); *Fullilove v Klutznick*, 448 US 448 (1980); *Mississippi University for Women v Hogan* 458 US 718 (1982); *Wygant v Jackson Board of Education*, 476 US 267 (1986); *United States v Paradise* (1987); *Johnson v Transportation Agency* 480 US 616 (1987); *City of Richmond v J.A. Croson Co*, 488 US 469 (1989); *Adarand Constructors, Inc v Peña*, 515 US 200 (1995); *Hopwood v Texas*, 78 F.3d 932 (5th Cir. 1996); *Gratz et al v Bollinger et al* No 02-516, 539 US (23 June 2003); *Grutter et al v Bollinger et al* 123 S Ct 2325, 2341 (2003)/ No 02-241, 539 US (23 June 2003); *Meredith v Jefferson County Board of Education* 548 US 938 (2006); *Parents Involved in Community Schools v Seattle School Dist No 1*, 551 US—Supreme Court (2007); *Fisher v University of Texas at Austin*, 133 S Ct 2411.

Australia and although sanctioned by the European Union (EU),[8] positive action remains marginal in the EU member states. A review through the lens of public health raises the question of whether these legal tools for tackling non-individual specific discrimination are being used as effectively as possible. This examination is followed by the exploration in section IV of how the anti-stigma principle can improve their effectiveness. I suggest that the anti-stigma principle can do this because it changes the way we think about collective action: first, by prioritising the public level, the anti-stigma principle foregrounds social responsibility and, second, in so doing it makes 'public action' a norm rather than an exception.

Finally in section V, I suggest that the anti-stigma principle provides a logic for the creation of new legal action to tackle the public level of discrimination. I propose a simple initiative which applies the key lessons from public health: monitored desk-based equality e-training in the workplace. Just as online packages have been developed to promote collective responsibility for health and safety at work, there is also scope to create similar packages focusing on discrimination. Such programmes are an example of public action in action.

I. Tackling a Public Health Virus: The Ebola Outbreak of 2014

Ebola was apparently brought into Nigeria on 20 July 2014 by Patrick Sawyer, a Liberian-American financial consultant. Sawyer initially denied exposure to the disease and demanded to be allowed to leave the hospital where he was being treated.[9] He was forced to stay in confinement by Dr Ameyo Adadevoh at the First Consultants Hospital in Lagos.[10] Sawyer died five days after his arrival. Dr Adadevoh also eventually died of the disease.

Scientists first detected the Ebola virus in 1976 in Sudan and the Democratic Republic of Congo, and researchers named the disease after the Ebola River that flows in the Congo. Although the virus has been present for more than 35 years, the outbreak in 2014 was the largest in history—it affected people in Sierra Leone, Guinea and Liberia as well as Nigeria, the UK, the USA, Italy, Scotland, Spain, Senegal and Mali. The most severely affected countries were Guinea, Liberia and Sierra Leone, nations with histories of conflict and instability resulting in under-developed health systems, limited health personnel and weak infrastructural resources.[11]

[8] Case C-319/03 *Serge Briheche v Ministre de l'Intérieur, Ministre de l'Éducation Nationale and Ministre de la Justice* [2005] 1 CMLR 4.

[9] F Ogunsola, 'Nipping it in the Bud: How Nigeria Beat The Ebola Virus in Three Months', available at http://digg.com/2015/how-nigeria-beat-the-ebola-virus-in-three-months.

[10] See M Burke and C Freeman, 'How Nigeria beat the Ebola virus' *The Telegraph* (20 October 2014), available at http://www.telegraph.co.uk/news/worldnews/ebola/11174554/How-Nigeria-beat-the-Ebola-virus.html.

[11] See http://www.who.int/mediacentre/factsheets/fs103/en/.

Of the 27,000 cases reported more than 11,000 people—including children—died.[12] The survivors endure debilitating joint and muscle pain, deep fatigue, hearing loss and even loss of sight.[13] Victims in addition become susceptible to other illnesses, such as meningitis.

Ebola is particularly dangerous during outbreaks because it is not confined to any specific space but can be found anywhere where people gather. It spreads as quickly in society as in clinics and hospitals. Experts identified the various ways in which Ebola permeated society: human-to-human transmission occurred in two main ways: first via direct contact (through broken skin or mucous membranes) with the blood, secretions, organs or other bodily fluids of infected people, and second by contact with surfaces and materials (for example bedding or clothing) contaminated with these fluids.[14] Thus combating Ebola required a variety of interventions and changes, some of which were harder than others.

Anthropologists identified that a key source of transmission in Sierra Leone was an important custom: burial practices. In this country, preparation of the corpse and last respects include washing the body, crying and praying over it. Not touching the body went against custom. However, the corpse of an Ebola victim is highly contagious because the level of the virus is at its peak in the body at precisely this time, thus touching the corpse contributes to the spread. Cruelly, saying goodbye according to cultural norms spread the virus. As funerals were a major source of transmission, Sierra Leoneans had to learn to abandon this custom. This one reform contributed greatly to control of the disease.[15]

Healthcare professionals also had to change their practices. Effective outbreak control required multi-level interventions, from short-term responses such as wearing personal protective equipment, using and discarding dedicated medical equipment properly, to longer term measures including case management, surveillance, contact tracing, creating a strong laboratory service and in particular, social mobilisation. Community engagement was identified as key to successfully controlling outbreaks by raising awareness of risk factors for infection and of protective measures to reduce human transmission. The World Health Organisation (WHO) prevention of Ebola included all of these elements: surveillance; community engagement; case management; laboratory services; contact tracing; infection control; logistical support; and training and assistance with safe burial practices.[16]

[12] See http://www.cdc.gov/vhf/ebola/outbreaks/history/chronology.html.

[13] D Grady, 'After Nearly Claiming His Life, Ebola Lurked in a Doctor's Eye' 7 May 2015, available at http://www.nytimes.com/2015/05/08/health/weeks-after-his-recovery-ebola-lurked-in-a-doctors-eye.html?_r=0.

[14] See http://www.cdc.gov/vhf/ebola/transmission/.

[15] JB Bien, 'Ebola is a Deadly Virus—But Doctors Say It Can Be Beaten' 2 July 2014, available at http://www.npr.org/sections/goatsandsoda/2014/07/22/333628899/ebola-is-a-deadly-virus-but-doctors-say-it-can-be-beat.

[16] See http://www.who.int/mediacentre/factsheets/fs103/en/.

These aspects played a part in the successful handling of Ebola in Nigeria. An emergency operation centre was set up; a co-ordinating team of 40 epidemiologists and 150 contact tracers was created to supervise house-to-house surveillance. Hot spots were identified and 26,000 households were visited. The team also managed data, communications—from infection alerts to the 'rumour mill'—and conducted community-based surveillance. Five units supported their work: strategy (responsible for coordination with the health ministries and the international agencies, funding, educating the media and managing rumours, administration and logistics); case management and infection control (treatment and management of all cases, confirmed or suspected, prevention of transmission through training health care workers in precaution and prevention as well as constructing screening centres and safe burials); social mobilisation (advocacy, well-being of contacts, tackling stigma and community reintegration of discharged patients); laboratory services; and points of entry (all air, sea and land borders were monitored and the temperature of every person passing through an entry point was checked for potential exposure).[17] Nigeria prevented the spread due to a rapid co-ordinated response with a unified plan, backed up with expertise, manpower and a health system with effective infection controls. But most importantly for this book was the level of co-operation between the Nigerian public and private sectors, teaching hospitals, universities and volunteers. It was described as an 'unprecedented' team effort led by Nigerians assisted by the international agencies[18] As important, was the initial determination by Dr Adadevoh, even though exposure to this disease would ultimately take her life.[19]

Although Ebola is an interpersonal disease, in that it spreads from person to person, the above story illustrates that it was impossible to combat it by focusing on individual carriers alone. Infection control was just one prong of action: while infected individuals needed life-saving treatment, it was equally vital to take social action to halt the spread of the disease. Social action was also essential to stop new infection and re-infection—the public or social aspects of the epidemic had to be addressed in order to break the cycle of infection. Thus in order to eliminate ebola from society, society needed to take responsibility for it and act. This included changing cultural practices such as long-held burial practices, thus forcing families to say goodbye to their loved ones in a manner which was alien to them. Songs were also written to educate people on the dangers of the disease.[20] The two-pronged approach of individual and collective action eventually worked. There was a will, thus a way was found even where this required relinquishing customs.

[17] Ogunsola, 'Nipping it in the Bud' (n 9).

[18] ibid.

[19] Burke and Freeman (n 10).

[20] See J Poole, '"Shadow" and "D-12" Sing an Infectious Song About Ebola' *goats and soda* (19 August 2014), available at http://www.npr.org/sections/goatsandsoda/2014/08/19/341412011/shadow-and-d-12-sing-an-infectious-song-about-ebola.

From the perspective of public health, tackling the social source of a disease is as essential as treating the individual manifestations of that disease.

This also applies to discrimination. Routing out the stigmas that have had centuries to sink in and hook themselves in the public consciousness requires equally decisive treatment and united action. Anti-discrimination law must tackle not only individual acts of discrimination but also the social sources of discrimination. The social source is as, or arguably more,[21] important than the individual perpetration of discrimination—if the environment is the source of all stigma then this is the main place where discrimination must be tackled. As with a medical virus, social action is therefore a priority rather than an exception and should be a norm in anti-discrimination law. As with Ebola, the task is to heal society as well as individuals.

The actions taken to combat Ebola indicates the potential breadth of social intervention. Ebola was contained by actions taken internally and externally. Internal actions included those taken by individuals as well as institutions. The former included adaptation of public cultural practices; the latter included reform of public institutional medical practices. Old ways had to be abandoned and new ones adopted. In Nigeria there was national and sectoral unity in the commitment to combat Ebola. A unified plan was adopted and implemented via co-operation between the public and private sectors, teaching institutions, universities and volunteers. Externally, international support was provided by the World Health Organisation and the United Nations. It is also clear from the Nigerian experience that the quicker and more committed the reaction to a public virus, the more effective it is. It may help to attack discrimination in a similar way.

Clearly women and men dressed in yellow suits wearing goggles and wellington boots will not combat discrimination, and house-to-house visits cannot be made, but there are other actions that can be taken and practices that can be reformed in relation to tackling discrimination. Three key lessons can be drawn from observation of how this epidemic was tackled. First, there was a commitment to change public cultural and institutional practices, even where this required abandoning traditions if those contributed to the problem. Second, adoption of a unified plan that was implemented via wide-spread co-operation between public and private actors, educational institutions and volunteers allowing for a co-ordinated response. Third, where possible internal action was undertaken in co-operation with external bodies that could contribute expertise and best practice.

However, there are challenges in transferring these lessons to tackling discrimination. First, while there may be official agreement that discrimination is a problem and/or that it is dangerous and should be eradicated, many in society do not agree. Second, and linked to this is the fact that although discrimination does affect everybody in society most people do not live with an active everyday

[21] CR Lawrence, 'Listening for Stories in All the Right Places: Narrative and Racial Formation Theory' (2012) 46(2) *Law and Society Review* 247.

fear of discrimination in the same way that everybody feared Ebola. Third, there are many different types of discrimination and each has a different impact—there is only one type of Ebola virus, and one impact which befalls all but the fortunate: death. These differences notwithstanding, if discrimination is viewed as a virus, these lessons can perhaps help to tackle discrimination.

Before addressing this, however, it is worth reflecting upon the mechanics of stigma—just as ebola has a mode of transmission, so too does stigma. To tackle public stigma effectively, it is important to think about how language and images can construct and convey meanings that stick to certain attributes.

II. The Transmission of Stigma

The previous section focused on the eradication of a virus; in contrast this section looks at how a virus spreads. Every virus has its own mode of transmission. As mentioned above, for Ebola it was contact with bodily fluids which contained the virus. There is no clear answer as to who is responsible for the creation and maintenance of stigma in society. Yet it cannot be denied that stigma exists and that any environment can become poisonous to the extent that certain individuals and groups feel constantly under threat or, alternatively, empowered to mistreat others. Chaudoir et al argue that stigmas are sneaky and insidious because there are many mechanisms that help them to spread, to enter the psyche and entrench themselves there[22]—this is as true for the individual psyche as for the public psyche. The means can be both formal and informal: the latter are more powerful than the former because, even if formally tackled and negated, stigma can continue to exert informal influence in the environment.

The transmission of stigma—or stigmatisation—is not benign: it has 'purpose, direction, and consequence'.[23] There are many ways of using stigma to achieve discriminatory outcomes. Power is essential to the social production of stigma, but as stigma is invisible—and can be unconscious—is not easy to illustrate the way in which power accrues to social meanings that stigmatise individuals. Loury argues that there is little evidence of stigma other than the stigmatisation itself:

> We will not necessarily find evidence of racial stigma by searching government statistics for instances of racial discrimination. The effects of stigma are more subtle, and they are deeply embedded in the symbolic and expressive life of the nation and our narratives about its origins and destiny. America, for example, is often said to be a nation of immigrants and a land of opportunity. But one of the first things new immigrants to

[22] SR Chaudoir, VA Earnshaw and S Andel, 'Discredited v Discreditable' in Bos et al, 'Stigma Advances' (n 4).

[23] Lawrence, 'Listening for Stories in All the Right Places' (n 21) 253.

America discover about their adopted country is that African Americans are a stigmatized group.[24]

He suggests that stigma operates invisibly and furthermore makes the individual invisible: in a double move, the stigma simultaneously magnifies the 'mark' and hides the person.[25]

Lawrence uses ideas of cognitive psychology to develop a theory of 'unconscious bias' that acts as the source of racism. He argues that stigma, in particular racial stigma, is not only invisible in society but also operates unconsciously in the American mind. According to cognitive psychology, values, beliefs and preferences transmitted by culture (for example by the media, an individual's parents, peers and authority figures) are entrenched in symbols and expressions, so that they are no longer experienced as overt lessons but as implicit understandings. They become common sense truths that order the world. As common sense they are unchallengeable. He argues that because racism is so deeply ingrained in American culture, it is likely to be transmitted by tacit understandings so that even if a child is not told directly that black people are inferior, she learns that lesson by observing the behaviour of others,[26] just as in the song Turning Point discussed in Chapter 1, Wendy learns this from her mother. Informal observation or 'tacit understandings' that remain hinted at but never clearly articulated can never be experienced at a conscious level—this makes them all the more powerful. Stigma residing in the unconscious can explain what Loury calls the 'durable racial inequality with which the United States is still encumbered'.[27] Law often overlooks the role of the unconscious on individual or collective behaviour but Lawrence argues that 'where the goal is the eradication of invidious racial discrimination, the law must recognize racism's primary source'.[28] For both Loury and Lawrence, racial inequality will continue until racial stigma is tackled.

Inaction is also an effective mechanism for stigmatisation. Inaction can be as meaningful as action, and the same inaction/action can transmit messages to both targets and perceivers. The targets of stigma can be encouraged 'to believe that they should not enjoy full and equal participation in social and economic life'.[29] Conversely, perceivers can be surreptitiously informed by inaction that targets do not have a right to regard. For example, take police inaction in the face of right-wing violence in 1970s Britain: by doing nothing to protect Asian communities terrorised by skinheads, the police simultaneously sent out a message to this community and

[24] GC Loury, 'Racial Stigma and Its Consequences' (2005) 24(1) *Focus* 2. See also GC Loury, *The Anatomy of Racial Inequality* (Cambridge, MA: Harvard University Press, 2002); GC Loury, 'The Anatomy of Racial Inequality: The Author's Account' (2004) *Review of Black Political Economy* 75.

[25] Loury, 'Racial Stigma and Its Consequences' (n 24).

[26] CR Lawrence, 'The Id, the Ego, and Equal Protection: Reckoning with Unconscious Racism' (1987) 39(2) *Stanford Law Review* 317, 323.

[27] Loury, 'Racial Stigma and Its Consequences' (n 24) 5.

[28] Lawrence, 'The Id' (n 26) 323.

[29] B Link and J. Phelan, 'Conceptualising Stigma' (2001) 27 *Annual Review of Sociology* 378.

to the British community at large—in particular skinheads—that Asians lacked the right to regard. Abandonment by the enforcement arm of the state stigmatised these communities. This abdication of official responsibility was the social backdrop to the killing of two Asian men.[30] Likewise, it is argued that the grooming of vulnerable young girls in parts of Britain, such as that in Rochdale which resulted in prosecutions in 2012 and 2016, could only take place because of official inaction.[31] The girls were stigmatised as 'runaways', 'loose' or 'wild' tear-aways making poor lifestyle choices. Arguably, social services and the local police actively ignored the abuse when it was reported to them because the girls were poor, white and working-class. The failure of social services to protect girls as young as 14 from sexual predators gave the groomers a green light to prostitute, rape and abuse these children.

Beyond inaction, images and language in the media, film, art and literature can be constituent forces of stigma in society. The public space is flooded with sounds and images—on billboards, smartphones, newspapers, radio, buses and bus shelters, sports fields and television. We hear sounds and see colours, shapes, letters and words, and often unconsciously soak in subliminal messages without bothering to think about them. The power of images is emphasised in cultivation theory. Cultivation theory posits the media as the most powerful storyteller in Western culture, 'continually repeating the myths, ideologies, and patterns of relationships that legitimize the social order'. The main argument is that images depicted in the media 'act like the pull of gravity toward an imagined center. This pull results in a shared set of social conceptions and expectations such that media portrayals become ideal representations of reality.'[32] The common sense conveyed provides subtle encouragement to perceivers—or discriminators—and discouragement to targets. The images that we don't see bear as much meaning as those that we do—where, for example, are positive images of black men or fat women? An example of this pull is Operation Vaken, discussed below.

[30] C Webster, *Understanding Race and Crime* (Maidenhead, Open University Press, 2007) 70.

[31] BBC News Online, 'Rochdale grooming: "Shocking" failure over sex abuse' (20 December 2013), available at http://www.bbc.co.uk/news/uk-england-manchester-25450512.

[32] Discussed in TA Judge and DM Cable, 'When It Comes to Pay, Do the Thin Win? The Effect of Weight on Pay for Men and Women' (2010) *Journal of Applied Psychology* 1; JD Brown, 'Mass Media Influences on Sexuality' (2002) 39 *Journal of Sex Research* 42; G Gerbner, L Gross and M Morgan, 'Growing Up with Television: Cultivation Processes' in J Bryant and D Zillman (eds), *Media Effects: Advances in Theory and Research* (Mahwah, NJ: Erlbaum, 2002) 43.

A. 'Go Home or Face Arrest'

Figure 2: A Van Displaying the Operation Vaken Message

Operation Vaken began in 2013, when the Conservative-Liberal Democrat Coalition government set out to reverse the loss of some Conservative supporters to the UK Independence Party (UKIP) by declaring an intention to take strong action on immigration. Prime Minister David Cameron stated

> My government will bring forward a bill that further reforms Britain's immigration system. The bill will ensure that this country attracts people who will contribute and deters those who will not.[33]

In disgust at the stated policy of making Britain hostile to immigrants, London MP Sarah Teather, once a rising star of the Liberal Democrats, resigned.[34] Her resignation did not change the policy; instead the Home Office embarked upon the first of many pilot projects[35] to put this plan into action, Operation Vaken. In this project, vans were driven around the streets of the London boroughs of Hounslow, Barking and Dagenham, Ealing, Barnet, Brent and Redbridge carrying billboards that declared:

> In the UK illegally? Go home or face arrest. Text HOME to 78070 for free advice, and help with travel documents. We can help you to return home voluntarily without fear of arrest or detention.

[33] The Queens Speech 2013, https://www.gov.uk/government/speeches/the-queens-speech-2013.

[34] D Aitkenhead, 'Sarah Teather: "I'm angry there are no alternative voices on immigration"' *The Guardian* (12 July 2013), available at http://www.theguardian.com/theguardian/2013/jul/12/sarah-teather-angry-voices-immigration.

[35] See RAMFEL website for details of similar subsequent campaigns: http://ramfelspeaksout.blogspot.co.uk/2014/07/ramfels-adventures-at-home-office-and.html.

The billboards purported to show residents how many illegal migrants had recently been arrested in their local area and gave a text number for overstayers to use to arrange their return home. The vans were part of a £10,000 pilot: if deemed successful, the intention of the Home Office was to use them across the country.

The campaign had three prongs. Alongside the use of the vans, leaflets were distributed in the same areas with the same message, and random identity checks were also carried out in these areas. Officials from the UK Border Agency (UKBA) wearing protective vests and carrying walkie-talkies[36] conducted spot checks at London Underground stations in areas with large black and minority ethnic populations such as Walthamstow, Kensal Green, Stratford and Cricklewood. The checks, shown on the news programmes of the day, clearly focused on black and brown people: the officials 'were only stopping people who looked Asian or African and not anyone who was white'.[37] Many of those stopped were not immigrants but British citizens.

The mobile billboard campaign was greeted with outrage and anger, and the spot checks were described as 'racial profiling' by Baroness Doreen Lawrence,[38] mother of murdered black Londoner Stephen Lawrence. Complaints came from within Westminster and from academics, non-governmental agencies and clergymen. MP Diane Abbott described it as tantamount to 'scrawling "Paki go home" on the side of buildings'.[39] Bishop Patrick Lynch, of the Catholic Bishops' Conference described it as 'a very inappropriate way to discourage illegal immigrants from staying in the UK, not least because the message that is often received is that all immigrants and foreigners are unwelcome in the UK'.[40] Even Home Office staff opposed the campaign. The PCS wrote to permanent secretary, Mark Sedwill describing the action as 'exactly the thing rightwing racist and fascist organisations such as the BNP, EDL, EVF and others feed off' to 'stir up racial tension and hatred in these very same London boroughs'.[41] However, the Home Office defended the initiative as positive, describing it as providing an 'opportunity to

[36] M Kelcher, 'What was the border agency doing at Kensal Green station?' *New Statesman* (31 July 2013), available at http://www.newstatesman.com/voices/2013/07/what-was-border-agency-doing-kensal-green-station.

[37] O Wright and A Withnall, 'Doreen Lawrence pledges to condemn "racial profiling" spot checks in the House of Lords' *The Independent* (2 August 2013), available at http://www.independent.co.uk/news/uk/politics/exclusive-doreen-lawrence-pledges-to-condemn-racial-profiling-spot-checks-in-the-house-of-lords-8742754.html.

[38] J Lyons, '"Racist" immigration spot checks probe after new Labour peer Doreen Lawrence condemns operations' *The Mirror* (3 August 2013), available at http://www.mirror.co.uk/news/uk-news/racist-immigration-spot-checks-probe-2119337.

[39] M Taylor, M Gidda and R Syal, '"Go Home" ad campaign targeting illegal immigrants faces court challenge' The Guardian (26 July 2013), available at https://www.theguardian.com/uk-news/2013/jul/26/go-home-ad-campaign-court-challenge

[40] Ibid.

[41] ibid.

leave the country voluntarily and with dignity, rather than be arrested, detained and removed'.[42]

Immigration Officer Mark Harper insisted that the visa checks were based on behaviour not skin colour,[43] but the Equality and Human Rights Commission (EHRC) announced that it would investigate the legality of the visa spot checks.[44] In addition, legal action was initiated against the mobile billboard vans. As a result the campaign was ended after one week. The government was forced by the legal action to provide 'an assurance that if the Home Office were to carry out any further campaigns of this nature it would have due regard to the effect this would have on migrants living in those communities and in so doing would carry out a consultation. Any such consultation would of course have to be meaningful.' The whole action took on an air of farce when in February 2014 Harper was forced to resign after it emerged that he had employed a cleaner who was working in the UK illegally.[45] The Home Secretary Theresa May subsequently informed the House of Commons that the vans were too blunt an instrument and would not be used again.[46]

It can be argued that the media campaign was neutral, since after all, there were no images of people on the posters. However, the random checking of people of colour made it clear who the targets were. The main victims were black men—an easy target because, as will be discussed below, black men are actively stigmatised in everyday media discourse. Nelson Mandela may be internationally lauded as a great freedom fighter and leader; Barack Obama may be feted as the first black President of the United States; Lewis Hamilton may be thriving, basking in the glory of his racing triumphs, but this is not the experience of most black men in Europe and the Americas.

In the UK and USA, there are more black men in prison than in higher education, and black men are absent in most public spheres save the criminal justice system, sport and entertainment. Even in sport, black athletes are only represented in a handful of events such as football, boxing and athletics (in particular the 100m sprint). *Playing* sport is often seen as the limit of their abilities—the shortage of

[42] M Taylor, M Gidda and R Syal, '"Go home" ad campaign targeting illegal immigrants faces court challenge' *The Guardian* (26 July 2013), available at http://www.theguardian.com/uk-news/2013/jul/26/go-home-ad-campaign-court-challenge.

[43] M Molloy, 'Immigration spot checks "not based on skin colour", government insists, *Metro* (3 August 2013), available at http://metro.co.uk/2013/08/03/mark-harper-immigration-spot-checks-not-based-on-skin-colour-3909915/.

[44] L King, 'Equality watchdog to investigate immigration checks in Brent' *Brent & Kilburn Times* (2 August 2013), available at http://www.kilburntimes.co.uk/news/equality_watchdog_to_investigate_immigration_checks_in_brent_1_2314680.

[45] 'Immigration minister Mark Harper quits over cleaner's visa', available at http://www.bbc.co.uk/news/uk-politics-26101442; Mark Townsend, 'Immigration minister Mark Harper resigns over illegal immigrant cleaner', available at http://www.theguardian.com/uk-news/2014/feb/09/mark-harper-immigration-minister-resigns.

[46] Mark Harper, Written Statement to Parliament 'Immigration enforcement: Operation Vaken' 31 October 2013.

black coaches in the world of football is remarkable given their prevalence in this game. In music, they may be visible in genres originating from black culture, such as hiphop or rap, but not as composers or conductors, even though many memorable pieces of music were penned by black musicians including Bobby Womack and Lamont Dozier. In all sectors, the privileges of manhood—leadership, responsibility and general deference—enjoyed by white men are narrowly circumscribed for black men.

This is because black men belong to a group that remains actively stigmatised. The social imaginary surrounding them is blinkered by the narratives—words and images—surrounding their bodies.[47] The media plays a central role in this. One of the first major studies on the news presentation of race, undertaken by Unesco in 1974,[48] highlighted the influence of the media in associating certain types of behaviour with certain groups and conferring approval or disapproval on both persons and values. The study asserted that the media has power to 'select issues, define problems, legitimise behaviour, label persons, places and things, draw up the agenda and structure the whole debate in any given area'.[49] A more targeted empirical UNESCO study, *Race as News*,[50] investigated the impact on race in society as reported in quality newspapers (for example, *The Times* and *The Guardian*) and the tabloids (for example, *The Daily Express* and *The Daily Mirror*). This survey concluded that while there was significant coverage of race in the newspapers, rarely was this good news.[51] Between 1963 and 1970, race appeared in the British press in ever more negative terms, predominantly about immigration, in particular comments about the number of black people in the country and keeping them out.[52] Black people in Britain were increasingly framed by a news perspective in which they appeared as a problem[53] and thus became stigmatised in the public mind as a problem.

Decades later, all that has changed is the scope of the stigmatisation: whereas in the 1960s, all black people were the target of stigma, in the twenty-first century this is now focused on black boys and men. The REACH survey of 2011 concluded that in the media construction of black men and boys, these images are overwhelmingly negative. The study found that the dominant discourse surrounding black young men and boys in the news media links them with violent crime, in particular murders involving knives and/or gangs: seven out of 10 stories of black young men and boys related in some form to crime. This figure was high when compared with coverage of young men and boys in general. Thus in the mainstream news, young black men and boys are overwhelmingly associated with

[47] Tate makes this point in relation to women in SA Tate, *Black Women's Bodies and the Nation—Race, Gender and Culture* (Palgrave Macmillan, 2015).
[48] UNESCO, 'Statement on Race and Racial Prejudice' (1968) 9(4) *Current Anthropology* 270.
[49] UNESCO, *Race as News* (Paris, UNESCO, 1974), 14.
[50] UNESCO, *Race as News* (n 49).
[51] UNESCO, *Race as News* (n 49) 128 and 147.
[52] UNESCO, *Race as News* (n 49) 139.
[53] UNESCO, *Race as News* (n 49) 159.

violent crime, murders, gun and knife crime. Furthermore, in some tabloids, articles reported the black identity of young male perpetrators as if this was in some way relevant to the criminal activities.'[54]

Interestingly, the report noted that 'no clear or explicit stereotype of black young men or boys was constructed across news reports'.[55] Thus the media uses the power of suggestion, implicitly, conveying stigma in the images served to the mainstream. This stigma provides a powerful and unquestioned general justification for not only racial profiling, as in Operation Vaken, but also the casual slaughter—by police and by ordinary citizens—of black boys and men such as Stephen Lawrence, Rohit Duggal, Michael Duggan, Smiley Culture[56] and Michael Duggan[57] in the UK, or 12-year-old Tamir Rice and 18-year-old Michael Brown in the USA.

III. Positive Action and the Public Sector Equality Duty (PSED)

What tools exist to tackle this transmission at the public level? Moral agency[58] is no shield against these pervasive mechanics of stigmatisation. As this section will show, anti-discrimination law does provide for social action to address stigmatisation. It focuses on two specific tools in the Equality Act 2010 designed to address discrimination beyond the individual level: sections 158 and 159 on positive action and section 149 on the public sector equality duty. I begin by briefly explaining these provisions and then discuss how they tackle stigmatising narratives and the extent to which they apply the lessons from public health. This section will bring together the previous two sections by reviewing how the Equality Act tackles the virus of discrimination at the public level through the lens of the lessons highlighted in the battle to contain the spread of Ebola.

[54] S Cushion, K Moore and J Jewell, 'Media representations of black young men and boys—Report of the REACH media monitoring project', available at http://www.cardiff.ac.uk/jomec/resources/media_representations_of_black_young_men_and_boys.pdf.

[55] ibid.

[56] See the Institute of Race Relations (IRR) website: http://www.irr.org.uk/news/deaths-with-a-known-or-suspected-racial-element-1991-1999/

[57] See http://killedbypolice.net; The Counted http://www.theguardian.com/us-news/ng-interactive/2015/jun/01/the-counted-police-killings-us-database; http://www.buzzfeed.com/nicholasquah/heres-a-timeline-of-unarmed-black-men-killed-by-police-over#.egqEO4NkX.

[58] TC Williams, '"Loaded Dice"—Review of *Between the World and Me* by Ta-Nehisi Coates' (3 December 2015) 37(23) *London Review of Books* 2, http://www.lrb.co.uk/v37/n23/adam-shatz/magical-thinking-about-isis?utm_source=newsletter&utm_medium=email&utm_campaign=3723&utm_content=ukrw_nonsubs&hq_e=el&hq_m=4046615&hq_l=9&hq_v=4a1976d511.

A. Positive Action in the Equality Act 2010

Positive action is group focused. In general, positive action measures include a range of interventions designed to benefit a specific targeted disadvantaged group. There is no set pattern for these measures—positive action includes a range of policies and initiatives such as special welfare assistance, using specific channels for recruitment, outreach work in schools, organisational change to accommodate needs of specific groups, introduction of stronger sanctions to punish prejudice and time-limited preferential treatment. They are always measures introduced to eliminate prohibited discrimination. Because they focus on providing a remedy for groups facing persistent inequality, positive action measures tend to be asymmetrical—only groups in need benefit from them. Such measures therefore go beyond formal symmetrical equality and are often seen as controversial for this reason. They prioritise substantive change and use law to improve society.

Bamforth et al describe positive action as 'measures which go beyond the prohibition of discrimination and seek by means of positive steps to alter existing social practices as to eliminate patterns of group exclusion and disadvantage'.[59] The Government Equalities Office describes it as necessary where some groups need more help or encouragement than others because they are disadvantaged, under-represented or have different needs from the population as a whole 'due to past or present discrimination or exclusion or particular experiences'. In such circumstances, the Equality Act allows action that may 'involve treating one group more favourably where this is a proportionate way to help members of that group overcome a disadvantage or participate more fully, or in order to meet needs they have that are different from the population as a whole'. It can also be defined as 'proportionate measures undertaken with the purpose of achieving full and effective equality in practice for members of groups that are socially or economically disadvantaged, or otherwise face the consequences of past or present discrimination or disadvantage'.[60]

Although sometimes controversial, positive action is a traditional concept in anti-discrimination law—it was included in the International Convention on the Elimination of All Forms of Racial Discrimination (ICERD) 1965,[61] the first non-discrimination Convention to be adopted after World War II. The ICERD set out a broad definition of 'racial discrimination', covering any 'distinction, exclusion, restriction or preference based on race, colour, descent, or national or ethnic origin which has the purpose or effect of nullifying or impairing the recognition,

[59] N Bamforth, M Malik and C O'Cinneide, *Discrimination Law: Theory and Context: Text and Materials* (Sweet & Maxwell, 2008) 345.

[60] European Commission, DG Employment, *International Perspectives on Positive Action Measures—A Comparative Analysis in the European Union, Canada, the United States and South Africa*, 6.

[61] International Convention on the Elimination of All Forms of Racial Discrimination (ICERD). Adopted and opened for signature and ratification by General Assembly resolution 2106 (XX) of 21 December 1965 entry into force 4 January 1969, in accordance with Art 19.

enjoyment or exercise, on an equal footing, of human rights and fundamental freedoms in the political, economic, social, cultural or any other field of public life'. Article 1(4) specifically provides for positive action, stating that

> Special measures taken for the sole purpose of securing adequate advancement of certain racial or ethnic groups or individuals requiring such protection as may be necessary in order to ensure such groups or individuals equal enjoyment or exercise of human rights and fundamental freedoms shall not be deemed racial discrimination.

Such actions are however subject to two conditions. First, they must be temporary and, second, they may not lead to any system of separate rights being established and maintained. Article 2(2) further stresses the obligation upon signatories to the Convention to take 'special and concrete measures' in the social, economic, cultural and other fields to ensure the adequate development and protection of certain racial groups and individuals belonging to them, so as to guarantee such persons both full and equal enjoyment of human rights and fundamental freedoms.

Positive Action is set out in EU equality law as well as international law. Article 5 of Race Directive 2000/43 includes a provision allowing both remedial and non-remedial positive action: 'With a view to ensuring full equality in practice, the principle of equal treatment shall not prevent any Member State from maintaining or adopting specific measures to prevent or compensate for disadvantages linked to racial or ethnic origin.' Article 7 Equal Treatment Directive 2000/78 uses the same wording and in addition allows, with regard to disabled persons, measures to:

> 2. … to maintain or adopt provisions on the protection of health and safety at work or to measures aimed at creating or maintaining provisions or facilities for safeguarding or promoting their integration into the working environment.

Positive action was not included in the first anti-discrimination statute created in the UK: the Race Relations Act 1965 (RRA 1965). This has now been replaced by the Equality Act 2010, which contains a general and specific provision for positive action. Section 158(1) of the Act sets out the context for positive action, that is, the circumstances under which it can lawfully be used. Positive action can be used to tackle disadvantage experienced by persons who share a protected characteristic, where the disadvantage is 'connected to the characteristic'; or to address the specific needs of such persons that arise from the characteristic and differ from those without the characteristic; and, finally, to promote inclusion in an activity by persons sharing a protected characteristic where their participation is disproportionately low.

Section 158(2) clarifies that the Act allows a decision-maker to take 'any action which is a proportionate means of achieving the aim of' first, enabling or encouraging persons who share the protected characteristic to overcome or minimise that disadvantage; second, meeting those needs; or, finally, enabling or encouraging persons who share the protected characteristic to participate in that activity. For example, an organisation was created to address the under-representation of black and minority ethnic (BME) parliamentarians—Operation Black Vote (OBV) exists to enable and encourage BME groups to participate in local and national politics[62] and ultimately in the House of Commons. Positive action has also been undertaken to improve the presence of women in Parliament. This has been significantly more successful, with the number of women in national politics outstripping the number of BME politicians.

There are only few examples of positive action being used by the media. However, one good example of how Article 158 can be used is the initiative introduced by *The Guardian* newspaper. One strategy to address the presentation of black men and race generally in the media has been to tackle the issue of racially homogenous newsrooms. *The Guardian* newspaper has taken this seriously—it believes there should be a better representation of our diverse society in journalism. Thus in 2001, this newspaper introduced a scheme to give budding journalists from BME groups the chance to experience life in the newsroom of a daily national paper. Each summer, students and graduates are offered a placement of up to two weeks to learn about different aspects of the profession and gain an insight into the newspaper and website.

Beyond the media, British Telecom introduced an initiative targeting both women and ethnic minorities. Realising that the overwhelming number of staff employed in a key part of its rapidly developing business—Open Reach, providing broadband services—were white and male, the company adopted the goal to increase representation of BME staff from 6% to 15% and women from 2% to 10% as it recruited 1,500 new engineers to improve its broadband services. The project involved provision of mentoring to BME applicants by guiding them through the application process as well as reaching out to these communities by using a different range of imagery in advertisements and placing adverts in a broader range of media, such as *The Voice* and *The Asian Times*.

Section 159 of the Equality Act 2010 focuses specifically on recruitment and promotion. It allows a recruiter who reasonably thinks that a group of persons who share a protected characteristic suffer a disadvantage connected to the characteristic, or that the participation of this group in an activity is disproportionately low, to also take 'action' so as to enable or encourage persons who share the protected characteristic to overcome or minimise that disadvantage, or participate in that activity. That 'action' is treating a person with the protected characteristic more favourably in recruitment or promotion processes than another person without that protected characteristic.[63]

This provision for positive action is often confused with 'positive discrimination', that is, the decision to recruit and promote persons who are unqualified or under-qualified. Positive discrimination is specifically ruled out in section 159(4) which makes clear that the 'action' applies only if the person to be recruited or promoted

[62] See the Operation Black Vote website: http://www.obv.org.uk.
[63] Section 159(5) of the Equality Act 2010.

is as qualified for the position as the alternative person. In addition, the decision-maker must not have an automatic policy of preference and must be able to show that the action taken is a proportionate means of achieving the aim. Positive action in recruitment and promotion can therefore only be used where it is merit-based,[64] non-discriminatory and respects the principle of proportionality.

The difference between lawful positive action and unlawful positive discrimination can be illustrated by two examples. Imagine a department store which employs nine senior managers but only two of them are women. When a vacancy arises, it seeks to address this under-representation by only interviewing women applicants, regardless of whether they meet the criteria for the post. This action would be discriminatory and therefore unlawful. Likewise, if a call centre located in an area with a large Indian population wished to diversify the ethnicity of its predominantly white workforce, it would not be permitted to overlook the top two candidates merely because they were white, in order to hire the third placed Indian candidate.

For positive action to be lawful, the protected characteristic can only be used as a criterion of merit in a tie-break situation. For example: a health and fitness club has two applicants for a job as the manager of a leisure facility. One is a woman, with a Leisure Management Foundation Degree but little practical experience; the second is a man with no formal qualifications but several years' relevant experience. Having interviewed both candidates, the employer decides that both could do the job to the same standard but in different ways as each would bring a different set of skills and experiences to the job. As the candidates are of equal merit the manager could voluntarily use the positive action provisions when choosing between the candidates and opt to employ the man because all of the other senior positions at the leisure complex were held by women.

Positive action is rarely used in the UK. Employers remain wary and are unsure how to use it without breaking the law.[65] However, recently it has been called upon to assist in the task of diversifying the judiciary. According to data from the Judicial Appointments Commission (JAC), lawyers from BME groups are nearly four times less likely to be appointed as judges than white candidates.[66] In order to improve the diversity of the judiciary, the Crime and Courts Act 2013 (CCA 2013) allows the JAC to apply a tie-break clause when making recommendations for judicial appointment. The CCA 2013[67] implemented recommendations arising

[64] FJ Crosby and C VandeVeer (eds), *Sex, Race and Merit* (Ann Arbor, University of Michigan Press, 2000).

[65] Unlike in the USA, there are hardly any cases. Examples include: *McGowan v Omagh District Council* [2009] NIIT 38_08IT where a scheme was upheld as lawful positive action; *Kenney v Ministry of Defence* (2008) 152(34) SJLB 30 on positive action plan in the navy; *Arnold v Barnfield College* Appeal No. UKEAT/0544 0545/03/SM where an allegation of unlawful positive action was rejected.

[66] P Gallagher, 'Ethnic minority lawyers nearly four times less likely to be appointed as judges' *The Independent* (7 December 2014), available at http://www.independent.co.uk/news/uk/home-news/ethnic-minority-lawyers-nearly-four-times-less-likely-to-be-appointed-as-judges-9908451.html.

[67] Received Royal Assent on 25 April 2013.

from the Lord Chancellor's Advisory Panel on Judicial Diversity, in particular the 'Equal Merit Provision',[68] a measure designed to enable consideration of diversity in the appointments process. The Equal Merit Provision complements the merit principle,[69] allowing for a candidate to be chosen on the basis of improving diversity when there are two candidates of equal merit. A new subsection, added to section 63, states that neither selection 'solely on merit', nor Part 5 of the Equality Act 2010,

> prevents the selecting body, where two persons are of equal merit, from preferring one of them over the other for the purpose of increasing diversity within (a) the group of persons who hold offices for which there is selection under this Part, or (b) a sub-group of that group.

The JAC applies the Equal Merit Provision only at the final selection decision-making stage and only in relation to gender and race. Lawful application of the provision requires that there be clear under-representation on the basis of race or gender, as determined by reference to national census data and data published by the Judicial Office showing the self-declared diversity of the courts and tribunals judiciary.[70] In such circumstances, the Equal Merit Provision raises race and gender to criteria of merit. Its use is closely circumscribed—the candidates must be otherwise equally qualified, as assessed against the advertised requirements, for a specific post. The policy has applied to all selection exercises launched since 1 July 2014. According to the JAC activity report of 2015, it has been applied in just seven out of the 305 recommendations made between October 2014 and March 2015.[71]

These examples illustrate how positive action can be used in the public and private sector—Operation Black Vote and the JAC tie-break provision focus on the public sector, while *The Guardian* and British Telecom schemes are examples of positive action in the private sector.

B. The Public Sector Equality Duty (PSED) in the Equality Act 2010

The focused voluntary approach of positive action can be contrasted with the obligatory general approach expected of decision-makers in the public sector. The creation of the PSED introduced what has been described as the 'fifth generation' of anti-discrimination law in the UK. The PSED has attempted to incorporate 'mainstreaming' into UK anti-discrimination law. It first appeared in the Race Relations Act 2000 to

[68] Schedule 13, Part 2, of the CCA.

[69] As set out in s 63(2) of the Constitutional Reform Act 2005 (CRA 2005). See also para 10 of Sch 13 to the CCA.

[70] https://jac.judiciary.gov.uk/equal-merit-provision.

[71] Judicial Appointments Commission, 'Judicial Selection and Recommendations for Appointment Statistics, October 2014 to March 2015' 4 June 2015, reissued November 2015, pp 4 and 7.

tackle racism lingering 'in the air' or 'institutional racism' which was identified in the MacPherson Report[72] as a key reason for the sub-standard police response to the killing of a young black teenager, Stephen Lawrence.[73]

Stephen Lawrence was murdered in an unprovoked racist attack by a gang of white youths at a bus stop in South London. After two failed private prosecutions brought by his family, the Labour Government commissioned a public enquiry. The ensuing MacPherson Report defined institutional racism as

> The collective failure of an organisation to provide an appropriate and professional service to people because of their colour, culture, or ethnic origin. It can be seen or detected in processes, attitudes and behaviour which amount to discrimination through unwitting prejudice, ignorance, thoughtlessness and racist stereotyping which disadvantage minority ethnic people.[74]

In order to address this, the Race Relations (Amendment) Act 2000 (RRA 2000) inserted section 19(b) into the RRA 1976 which made it unlawful 'for a public authority in carrying out any functions of the authority to do any act which constitutes discrimination.' In addition, section 71 of the RRA 1976 created a new general statutory duty upon the police and specific public authorities to have 'due regard to the need (a) to eliminate unlawful racial discrimination and (b) to promote equality of opportunity and good race relations between persons of different racial groups' whilst carrying out their functions. Parallel duties were subsequently introduced into the Disability Discrimination Act (DDA) 1995[75] and the Sex Discrimination Act (SDA) 1975.[76]

The essence of the duty was a requirement upon the public authority to conduct an 'Equality Impact Assessment' wherein they considered all relevant and available information in order to anticipate any likely negative impact on people from different racial groups, on disabled people, or on men and women. The authority was to seek to avoid that negative impact by taking alternative courses of action wherever possible. Thus in *Elias*[77] the compensation scheme breached the duty because the Ministry of Defence had not carried out a race equality impact assessment. There had been no careful attempt to assess whether the scheme raised issues relevant to racial equality nor to assess the extent of any adverse impact, or to find ways of eliminating or minimising such impact. The scheme had therefore resulted in indirect discrimination on grounds of national origins and was unlawful. Likewise in *Kaur*[78] Ealing Council breached the duty because it had carried out the

[72] W MacPherson, *The Stephen Lawrence Inquiry* (London, Stationery Office, 1999); *MacPherson Report—Ten Years On*, available at http://www.publications.parliament.uk/pa/cm200809/cmselect/cmhaff/427/42703.htm.

[73] See http://www.stephenlawrence.org.uk/about-us/stephens-story.

[74] Sir William MacPherson of Cluny, 'The Stephen Lawrence Inquiry' February 1999, Cm 4262-I, para 6.34.

[75] Section 49A.

[76] Section 76A.

[77] *R (Elias) v Secretary of State for Defence* [2005] IRLR 788.

[78] *R (Kaur) v London Borough of Ealing* [2008] EWHC 2062 (Admin).

impact assessment after formulating the policy rather than during the development period. Moses LJ stressed that the duty was not a 'rearguard' action.

The Equality Act 2010 brought these duties together into a single provision which now applies to all protected characteristics set out in the Act. Section 149 of the Equality Act 2010 imposes a triple-fold general duty upon public bodies to have 'due regard to the need to' eliminate conduct prohibited by Act, advance equality of opportunity (by removing and/or reducing disadvantages, taking steps to meet needs and encouraging participation where this is low) and, finally, foster good relations by tackling prejudice and promoting understanding. In addition, specific duties[79] exist for organisations with more than 150 employees, which these must produce an annual compliance report (employees and others) and publish 'SMART'[80] objectives. Under section 156 any claim based on the PSED must be brought by way of judicial review.

Guidance produced by the Equalities and Human Rights Commission (EHRC) has stressed that there is no one point of compliance: as a fully integrated core task, the duty arises prior to policy formation, during policy consideration, during decision-making and of course during application. It is also a duty to be met by central authority not delegated bodies. In relation to how the duty should be met, the EHRC suggests that organisations should prioritise their policies, gather and analyse information, and where necessary conduct an impact assessment to address the key question: has 'due regard' been exercised?

However, principles arising from the case-law suggest a lighter duty. Judicial review has contributed ad hoc guidance, focusing more on what the PSED *does not* require than setting out clearly what it *does*. An impact assessment may not always be required.[81] Collection of equality data providing a reliable base of information and adequate documentation has instead been stressed. The duty also does not call for assessment of equality issues where they are not relevant, or for disproportionate action (such as the translation of material into all 300 languages spoken in London). Nor does it impose an obligation to overlook differences or treat everyone the same. Single sex services remain legitimate and there is no call for equal treatment, for example, of all religious ceremonies. Group appropriate services (for example services for the elderly or facilities delivered by faith groups) remain acceptable. The courts have suggested that organisations begin with establishment of the relevance of the duty to its core functions: which part of the duty is, for example, relevant to providing an IT service—fostering good relations, advancement of equality or the elimination of certain conduct? Organisations need to engage with affected groups and maintain oversight over procurement and contractors.

79 Equality Act 2010 (Specific Duties) Regulations 2011 (SI 2011/2260).
80 Specific, Measurable, Achievable, Realistic, Time-bound.
81 *CPAG v SSWP* [2011] EWHC 2616 (Admin) [76].

This approach has resulted in a somewhat ineffective duty. Over the last five years, the judicial interpretation of 'due regard' has transformed the PSED into a vague action with low potential to change thinking and cultural practices. The courts have emphasised that the PSED is an obligation to demonstrate *consideration* rather than achievement of any particular result. For example, in *Baker*, LJ Dyson stated:

> In my judgment, it is important to emphasise that the section 71(1) duty is not a duty to achieve a result, namely to eliminate racial discrimination or to promote equality of opportunity and good relations between persons of different racial groups. It is a duty to have due regard to the need to achieve these goals. The distinction is vital ... What is due regard? In my view, it is the regard that is appropriate in all the circumstances. These include on the one hand the importance of the areas of life of the members of the disadvantaged racial group that are affected by the inequality of opportunity and the extent of the inequality; and on the other hand, such countervailing factors as are relevant to the function which the decision-maker is performing.[82]

In *Brown*,[83] a set of guiding principles were laid out to explain the parameters of the duty in decision-making procedures. The duty begins with awareness: decision-makers must know about the duty and those bound by it may not delegate it to others. The temporal element stresses when it arises: the duty is continuing, and must be fulfilled before and at the time when a particular policy which might affect relevant persons is being formulated, as well as during application of policies. Thus the duty is to be integrated within the discharge of every[84] public function of the authority and is to be exercised in substance, with rigour and with an open mind. However, the duty does not include an 'ad infinitum'[85] investigation but rather 'regard' to what have been described as 'material considerations',[86] or equality goals 'that is appropriate in all the circumstances.'[87] The statute therefore does not require any exhaustive 'forensic analysis' but rather action which can be used to demonstrate to a court that there has been a 'proper and conscientious focus on the statutory criteria'.[88] So, for example, while making

> homelessness determinations in areas in which a person's disability could be of relevance, a local authority would need to have due regard to ... the need to take steps to take account of disabled persons' disabilities'. This would be relevant in relation to three areas in particular: the priority of need, the intentionality of homelessness and the suitability of accommodation.[89]

[82] *R (Baker) v Secretary of State for Communities and Local Government* [2008] EWCA Civ 141, [31].
[83] *R (Brown) v Work and Pensions Secretary* [2008] EWHC 3158 (Admin), [2009] PTSR 1506, [89].
[84] *Pieretti v Enfield LBC* [2010] EWCA Civ 1104, [2011] HLR 3.
[85] *Bailey & Ors, R (on the application of) v London Borough of Brent Council & Ors* [2011] EWCA Civ 1586.
[86] Ryder J in *R (D) v Manchester City Council* [2011] EWHC 17 (Admin) [52].
[87] *Greenwich Community Law Centre* [2012] EWCA Civ 496 [48]; *R (Baker) v Secretary of State for Communities and Local Government* [2008] EWCA Civ 141, [2009] PTSR 809, [31].
[88] *Hurley and Moore v Secretary of State for Business* [2012] EWHC 201 (Admin).
[89] *Pieretti v Enfield LBC* [2010] EWCA Civ 1104, [2011] HLR 3.

As stated in *Hurley*, the decision maker must be able demonstrate in court that she is clear on the equality implications, recognises their importance, and has taken a balanced approach. The court will only 'review what the authority did to ascertain whether what it did or did not do was something no reasonable authority could have done in the circumstances'.[90] The substance of the duty seems therefore to be a combination of the Wednesbury and proportionality tests, setting non-discrimination goals alongside other objectives. While paying due regard is 'an integral part of the mechanisms for ensuring the fulfilment and aims of anti discrimination legislation'[91] and an essential preliminary to any decision,[92] the equality implications do not thereby become a priority. It is for the decision-maker to determine 'what weight they should be given in the light of all relevant factors'.[93]

The legal challenge to Operation Vaken was based upon the PSED. No equality impact assessment had been conducted prior to the pilot. RAMFEL argued an assessment should have been carried out given the impact of the campaign on race relations. They argued that the duty applied to the decision to launch an 'anti-migrant campaign'. The failure to conduct an impact assessment, or even consult with the community groups and local authorities likely to be affected by the campaign, was therefore a breach of the PSED—the Home Secretary failed to have 'due regard to the needs to eliminate discrimination and promote equality of opportunity in terms of race and religion and belief'. The Secretary of State questioned whether an impact assessment was at all necessary.

According to case-law, it may indeed have been the case that no impact assessment was necessary. The PSED therefore, despite being a duty, is not a guarantee of consideration. Officials retain significant discretion to determine when it arises and what must be done to fulfil it. The judicial review is to ensure that an impact assessment is conducted per se rather than how it is conducted. However, officials would be wrong to be blasé in their approach: in the absence of evidence of a conscious, rigorous and structured reflection upon equality issues a breach of the PSED will be found, making the decision unlawful.[94] This happened in a case[95] concerning the allocation of EU structural funds, where a decision had been taken depriving Rotherham and Liverpool of a regional allocation. LJ Stewart found an absence of 'due regard':

> I reject these contentions by the Defendant. The Defendant's decisions fixed the individual allocation for each region. Those allocations are in no sense preliminary or provisional. The fact that the individual regions would themselves have to consider the PSED when

[90] *R (D) v Manchester City Council* [2011] EWHC 17 (Admin) [52].

[91] Wilkie LJ in *Williams & Dorrington v Surrey CC* [2012] EWHC 867 (QB) (libraries) [16]–[17].

[92] *R (BAPIO) v Secretary of State for the Home Department* [2007] EWCA Civ 1139 [3].

[93] *Hurley and Moore* [78].

[94] *Bracking v SSWP* [2013] EWCA Civ 1345 (closure of ILF) [61]–[69]. See also *R (on the application of JM and others) v Isle of Wight Council* [2011] EWHC 2911 (Admin), per Lang J at [95]–[108].

[95] *Rotherham and Liverpool v SS for Business* [2014] EWHC 232 (Admin) [91]–[93].

deciding how to use the funds allocated to them cannot absolve the Defendant from the PSED. Given that the Claimants are, according to the Defendant 'hard cases' in terms of the allocation given to them for 2014—2020, it seems clear to me that the Defendant should have had 'due regard' to the s149(1)(a) and (b) objectives. I therefore find that the Defendant breached the PSED.[96]

IV. Public Action to Tackle the Virus of Discrimination

To what extent do these tools apply the lessons of public health? It will be remembered that the three key lessons that can be drawn from the public action to combat the Ebola epidemic include first, a commitment to change public cultural and institutional practices, even where this requires abandoning traditions if these contribute to the problem; second, adoption of a unified plan that is implemented via widespread cooperation between public and private actors, educational institutions and volunteers, allowing for a coordinated response; and, third, the support of international agencies that can contribute expertise and best practice. There is little in the application of the positive action and PSED provisions that apply these lessons. I suggest that if these lessons were applied, they would transform these tools into more rigorous forms of public action to tackle the virus of discrimination.

The positive action and equality duty provisions develop anti-discrimination law from the reactive, individual enforcement that is the norm, but neither of them completely apply the lessons required to tackle a virus at the environmental level. Each of the above examples applies the lessons from tackling Ebola to a different extent. There is clearly some commitment to change public cultural and institutional practices—the JAC, OBV and *The Guardian* schemes are long term and their potential for institutional and cultural impact is significant. OBV can claim some credit for changing the complexion of Parliament—in 2015, 16 BME MPs entered the House of Commons, taking the total number of BME MPs to 41, up from 27 in 2010 and just 15 in 2005. Likewise, *The Guardian* must be applauded for its contribution towards increasing the number of BME journalists working on daily newspapers. However, as concluded by the REACH study of 2011, black men are still demonised in news stories. There are still too few BME journalists in newsrooms to make a significant difference to the way in which black men are portrayed in the media.

The BT scheme was also successful, and it did enable future employment for a number of persons in the targeted groups. Yet this success was only within the

[96] ibid [91]–[93].

context of a single recruitment drive—the scheme was one-off, thus shortlived—and it remains questionable whether it changed cultural practices within the organisation as a whole so as to, for example, preclude the dominance of white male employees in other parts of the organisation.

It is perhaps too soon to evaluate the JAC tie-break provision but taken together with other initiatives, it may be the best example of public action to address discrimination. The tie-break provision is embedded within a range of other actions taken by public and private actors, including the professional regulatory bodies, the Judicial Office, educational institutions and private firms. Thus the provision itself is just one aspect of a broad programme of action to diversify the judiciary and change the culture in the courts.

These are all voluntary measures targeted at carefully identified groups. They must be focused and are envisaged as temporary. Measures can be applied by any organisation in the public or private sectors. By contrast, the PSED imposes a general duty, but only upon public sector organisations. Unlike positive action, the nature of the duty does not extend to results nor to the private sector. However, the PSED imposes a permanent duty that is ongoing and non-delegable. In theory, the PSED is a concept through which the lessons arising from public health could be applied. When approached as a core principle, it could be used to change both public and institutional practices from the inside out. However, the obligatory PSED accommodates a huge amount of discretion as regards application. In practice the duty has been given limited substance—'due regard' requires demonstration of reflection upon equality rather than a commitment to change. In addition, a duty that applies only to public sector organisations is not robust enough to support a plan that encourages and co-ordinates action throughout the private sector.

It is therefore worth considering how the anti-stigma principle can strengthen these existing tools. The ASP would improve them by aligning them more closely with the lessons from public health. The priorities would be to make them clear; anticipatory; sustainable; long term; and multi-level. For example, under the anti-stigma principle, the use of positive action would be actively promoted rather than simply permitted. Equality aims would also countenance a greater use of time-restricted quotas and the tie-break: at present quotas are controversial and the tie-break is carefully circumscribed. It could be more widely used if informed by the anti-stigma principle. There would also be greater scope for non-remedial action—as seen in the USA—but without the controversy. As *public* rather than *positive* action, the link would be to stigma rather than to group identity per se. Being linked to stigma, the reason for the action would be clear and indisputable. *Public* action to address social stigma would be seen to help society as a whole rather than specific individuals or groups in particular. The arguments from *Grutter* would support this: as the prize is high, the price must be paid.

Second, the PSED could be improved. The idea of 'due regard' at present permits only limited judicial enforcement. From the perspective of the anti-stigma principle, the PSED would have a firmer meaning necessitating more rigorous action to ensure that the virus of discrimination is not being allowed to fester. The anti-stigma principle would also provide guidance on the use of the other strands of the PSED. As yet, little attention has been paid to the need to 'foster good relations' by tackling prejudice and promoting understanding.

However, the PSED may be short-lived: despite its light touch, it has been described as 'unnecessary bureaucracy'.[97] A review created to assess the effectiveness of the general and specific duties under the PSED, concluded that 'in far too many cases, we have uncovered useless bureaucratic practices which do nothing for equality'.[98] The EHRC responded with observation that the study supporting this conclusion was highly questionable. It was, first, light on evidence ('more definite conclusions drawn than the fairly light evidence presented justifies'); second, light on solutions ('the best way to reduce bureaucracy and over-engineering of compliance with the PSED would be to publish a statutory Code'); and, third, light on coherence ('we are concerned that the current proposals are not clear').[99]

Theresa May is no longer at the Home Office but the future of the PSED remains questionable. Thus it is also worth considering whether the anti-stigma principle could create stronger tools that align more closely with practice in public health to address stigma at the public level. Such a tool would create opportunities for regular social confrontation with the 'common sense' that allows stigma to survive and discrimination to continue. The anti-stigma principle could provide the rationale for a simple and yet potentially effective alternative that could take equality law beyond the current approaches to collective action.

One such tool that could be introduced as a norm of anti-discrimination law when informed by an anti-stigma principle is unconscious bias testing. Unconscious bias testing makes people aware of the biases they hold. It does not tell people how to think. By making people aware of the biases they harbour, the test encourages participants to reflect and change their way of thinking and perhaps behaving. This test has already been designed thus only a mode of administration would have to be introduced. It could be made mandatory for all, administered in schools, training and job centres, and workplaces throughout the country.

Unconscious bias testing could be introduced into the workplace as part of monitored online training on equality. E-training is already widely used. For example it is a means by which organisations fulfil their obligations in relation to Health and Safety at work—in leading Universities, e-learning enables all staff and students to access this important training on compliance with health and safety and risk assessment without leaving their desks. The training can in fact be completed anywhere internet access is available, thus at a time, place—and pace—determined by the individual.

[97] Former Home Secretary Theresa May, HC Debate, 15 May 2012, Column 29WS.

[98] Government Equalities Office 'Review of the Public Sector Equality Duty: Report of the Independent Steering Group', 6 September 2013, 6.

[99] See: http://www.equalityhumanrights.com/news/2013/october/commission-responds-to-psed-review-report.

E-learning on Health and Safety is delivered in regular short bursts. It takes no more than 20 minutes and is designed to create a simple, consistent foundation that can be built upon. It therefore ensures that every member of the University has a basic knowledge of health and safety law and practice which complements more comprehensive training workshops. However, this e-learning is mandatory. For example, all staff must complete e-training on four separate modules—'Risk Assessment for DSE Users', 'Fire Safety Training', 'Manual Handling Training' and 'Health and Safety Training for DSE Users'—this latter in particular is obligatory in order to gain access to certain benefits such as free eye tests and reduced price spectacles.

This obligation would be non-existent in the absence of monitoring and enforcement. Monitoring is conducted electronically, and upon completion of the test a certificate is produced with a score. Each module contains a series of statements and culminates in a Q&A which generates a score. A record is then kept on the individual training file by the Human Resources department. As soon as this date is registered, a 24-month countdown begins. At the end of two years, a reminder is sent to repeat the training, and thus the basis of knowledge is refreshed at least once every two years. Where the two-year time frame is exceeded, more regular reminders are sent: these begin as electronically generated messages, but as time goes on the matter is escalated: general computer generated reminders become emails addressed to a named individual written by a human health and safety manager. The e-learning is therefore actively enforced.

This e-learning does not exist in isolation but is part of a multi-layered and multi-level health and safety policy which is delivered by management, consultation and professional support at four different levels: by the University Council and Vice Chancellor through responsibility for strategy and policy; by the University Executive Group and Faculty Deans through responsibility for resourcing and monitoring; by Heads of School through responsibility for implementation; and by all staff and students via responsibility for compliance. In addition, short reminder leaflets on the importance of health and safety are both posted around all parts of the University as well as sent to each employee. These are individually addressed to the employee, suggesting use of payroll information.

Respect for health and safety therefore cascades throughout the organisation. Just as with the campaign against Ebola, it is taken so seriously that it must be everybody's business. There is a clear top-level commitment to changing institutional culture and individual practices; there is a unified plan to ensure that this commitment is co-ordinated and penetrates the organisation; there is external professional action to support internal organisational action.

The health and safety policy is a good example of what public action in discrimination law can be. The policy, designed in response to a statutory health and safety law, works to create a safe environment by engaging all in the organisation, and some beyond the University. It uses a multi-level approach to create a general culture of concern for health and safety at all levels in the organisation. The policy is embedded from top to bottom with active compliance enforced at the lower level. The e-learning tools ensure a minimum level of awareness and regular monitoring ensures that this minimum level of awareness is maintained. Compliance is further encouraged by linking compliance to access to key benefits. It is a policy designed with a clear commitment to change institutional culture from the inside over the long term.

This multi-layered integrated model should also be applied to tackling discrimination. The policy on equality and diversity is also designed to respond to a statutory obligation—the public sector equality duty. There are some similarities with the regime for health and safety: for example it has a detailed horizontal and vertical structure for strategic policy development and approval, operational monitoring and implementation, and engagement, stretching from Council to students. Some elements are, however, missing: for example, it lacks the professional support seen in the health and safety policy, which includes human resources, occupational services and the University Physician. In addition, there is no similar entrenchment of ongoing compliance—there are no mandatory short, repeated modules for e-learning that are monitored and enforced, or indeed leaflets individually addressed to each member of the organisation. The action therefore suffers from a key deficit in relation to the commitment to long-term change. However, this omission is easily reversible: online equality training is currently obligatory for those involved in recruitment thus it is simply a matter of extending this obligation throughout the organisation. The anti-stigma principle provides the rationale for this. With the will and resources, the current policy can therefore be strengthened with the inclusion of e-learning, pushed through to the computer screens of all members of the University and linked to key benefits. Leaflets can also be delivered to individual pigeonholes. The E-quality Training Module could also be designed to allow stigmatised groups to tell their own stories. This is important because as put by Charles Lawrence,

> When outsider racial groups tell stories, when we engage in the project of racial reconstruction, we seek not only to change the pejorative meanings assigned to our races, but also to transform the communal narrative that defines the nomos of the larger social world in which we live.[100]

Beyond this, a key way to allow stigmatised groups to tell their own stories is to ensure that the curriculum is inclusive—movements like 'why is my curriculum white?' therefore play an important role in tackling stigma at the public level.

V. Conclusion

The anti-stigma principle encourages us to listen for the stories that are told in the public sphere about groups. By listening to the public discourse, individuals are

[100] Lawrence, 'Listening for Stories in All the Right Places' (n 21) 252.

set in the context from which discrimination arises. Stigmatisation is not a benign project thus the tools used to fight against it and its consequences must be sharp. Under the anti-stigma principle, action focused on the environment would become a norm as the public level is identified as the source of discriminatory behaviour. Anti-discrimination law created using this principle would speak of 'public' rather than 'positive' action. Public action to combat discrimination is more than positive action: it is action that is designed to affect society by obliging every individual to confront stigma. The goal of public action would be to challenge public stigma so that this ceases to exist as a resource for structural and interpersonal discrimination. The rationale for public action therefore changes significantly if viewed where anti-discrimination law is informed by the anti-stigma principle and used to promote public health. Likewise the remedies are broader—as no single person is responsible, punishment of individuals is insufficient. Instead, action is required to change the environment rather than chastise a perceiver.

6

Stigma, Synergy and Intersectionality

The previous chapter considered how the anti-stigma principle could inform the design of public action to tackle discrimination. It was shown that tools already exist in the Equality Act 2010 to tackle social stigma, namely positive action and the public sector equality duty. However, I argued that these could be more effectively used. I also suggested that the principle could justify introduction of a more effective form of action, in the shape of unconscious bias testing and online equality training. This chapter focuses on the second important contribution that the anti-stigma principle can make to anti-discrimination law: the improvement of how it sees—and in particular its ability to tackle—structural or intersectional discrimination.

Traditionally, anti-discrimination law adopts a zero-sum perspective. It sees in the singular—race *or* gender *or* disability—and requires separate proof for every ground in a complaint. Yet it is increasingly recognised that discrimination is not always experienced in this way. At the 58th Session of the UN Commission on Human Rights, the Resolution on the Human Rights of Women recognised 'the importance of examining the intersection of multiple forms of discrimination, including their root causes from a gender perspective'.[1] In 2001, at the World Conference Against Racism, Racial Discrimination, Xenophobia and Related Intolerance ('WCAR'), Mary Robinson also emphasised that intersectional discrimination needs to be addressed. Intersectionality was also mentioned when the UN CERD Committee 2000 adopted General Recommendation 25 on gender aspects of racial discrimination. In 2000, the European Union also introduced two Directives that explicitly call for recognition of 'multiple discrimination'[2]—Directive 2000/43 and Directive 2000/78.[3]

The difficulty has been in finding a method to incorporate intersectionality into a legal framework premised upon the single dimension and zero sum logic. While there is clearly a will, a way has yet to be found. There are two specific challenges.

[1] Resolution E/CN.4/2002/L.59 in MT Berger and K Guidroz (eds), *The Intersectional Approach—Transforming the Academy through Race, Class, and Gender* (Chapel Hill, UNC Press, 2010) 44–45.

[2] Multiple discrimination is the over-arching term for different types of pluralist approaches to anti-discrimination law introduced in S Hannett, 'Equality at the Intersections: The Legislative and Judicial Failure to Tackle Multiple Discrimination' (2003) 23 *Oxford Journal of Legal Studies* 65.

[3] European Commission, 'Communication from the Commission to the Council and the European Parliament: The Application of Directive 2000/43/EC of 29 June 2000 Implementing the Principle of Equal Treatment Between Persons Irrespective of Racial or Ethnic Origin'(COM (2006) 643 Final).

First, intersectionality has given rise to confusion because it is not about identity in the particularist tradition of Hegel and Taylor; rather, it is about the impact of social structures on specific groups. This becomes clear with exploration of the intellectual tradition to which it belongs. Second, tackling intersectional discrimination within the dominant paradigm of the single-dimension approach is impossible. Its complexity is unsuited to the logic of traditional anti-discrimination law.

However, it is important to find a method for intersectional discrimination, for addressing this flaw in the structure of anti-discrimination law will also enable it to effectively tackle structural stigma, which is embedded in social organisation. Structural stigma is damaging because it creates a discriminatory environment of 'increased threat, punishment, lack of resources, and other social constraints'[4] for some groups in society.

The anti-stigma principle is well suited to respond to the complexity of intersectionality. As stigmas travel alone and in groups, the concept of stigma can provide categories that go beyond the single-dimension logic. The anti-stigma principle therefore accommodates both single-dimension discrimination and intersectional discrimination without having to prioritise or choose. It would therefore enable anti-discrimination law to tackle intersectional discrimination without undermining its ability to tackle single dimension discrimination.

This chapter begins with a brief explanation of intersectionality and the qualitative difference of this form of discrimination. It continues with an explanation of categorisation in anti-discrimination law and its consequences. It then explores the contours of the current legal dilemma before finally clarifying how the anti-stigma principle can create a remedy in anti-discrimination law for intersectional discrimination.

I. Understanding Intersectional Discrimination

> Wherever one looks in women's and gender studies … intersectionality is being theorized, applied or debated.[5]

When spoken of in this way, it is easy to think of intersectionality[6] as an abstract theory looking for a home in reality. The opposite is the case—the theory emerged to describe a form of discrimination experienced in reality but not covered by the legal framework set out in discrimination law. The theory is based in the

[4] LS Richman and MR Lattanner, 'Self Regulatory Processes of Stigma' (2014) 103 *Social Science and Medicine* 95.

[5] MT Berger and K Guidroz (eds), *The Intersectional Approach: Transforming the Academy Through Race, Class and Gender* (Chapel Hill, UNC Press, 2009) 1.

[6] K Crenshaw, 'Demarginalizing the Intersection of Race and Sex: A Black Feminist Critique of Antidiscrimination Doctrine, Feminist Theory and Antiracist Politics' (1989) 140 *University of Chicago Legal Forum* 139.

employment experiences of black women workers.[7] The section below will discuss just two ways in which intersectional discrimination had an impact upon black women workers: job security and professional progress.

A. Job Security

Intersectional discrimination arose when the entry and retention of African American women on the labour market was undermined by organisational traditions, such as systems of seniority. Seniority systems are premised upon the belief that those in position for the longest time are the most productive and therefore of most value to the organisation. This establishes a hierarchy based on longevity of service, according to which those who were the first to be hired have the highest salaries, enjoy privileges and the greatest job security while those who are the last to be hired have lower salaries and are the first to be fired.

Due to the lingering impact of slavery on the American labour market, African American women workers always fell into the latter category—they were inevitably the last to be hired in jobs beyond domestic service and thus seen by the employer as the least important workers, despite the importance of their earnings to their household income. In an economic downturn, the combination of the seniority system and the after-effects of slavery meant that African American women were always the first to lose their jobs. Five women fired by General Motors (GM) in St Louis claimed this was intersectional discrimination.[8] In 1977, 22% of the city's population were black women, yet prior to 1970, GM—one of the largest employers in the city—employed only one black woman, as a janitor. GM admitted in court that until May 1970, all women at its St Louis plant were excluded from any assembly line work that required shifts longer than nine hours, but the company did employ only white women in the cushion room producing automobile seats and upholstery.

Five women who were employed for around six months charged GM of intersectional (sex and race) discrimination. Emma DeGraffenreid applied for employment with GM in 1968 and in 1973; she was hired in June 1973 but due to recession was fired in January 1974. Brenda Hines applied for employment twice in 1971 and 1973; eventually hired in June 1973, she went on sick leave in September and was eventually made redundant in January 1974. Alberta Chapman applied for employment with GM in 1971, was hired in 1973 and by January 1974 was made redundant. Brenda Hollis and Patricia Bell both applied for employment in November 1970 and were hired by December 1970. However Hollis was made redundant by December 1971; Bell was fired in May 1972, re-hired in May 1973 and fired again in January 1974. In total, GM hired just 6 black female

[7] JA Winston, 'Mirror, Mirror on the Wall: Title VII, Section 1981 and the Intersection of Race and Gender in the Civil Rights Act of 1990' (1991) 79 *Calif Law Rev* 775.

[8] *DeGraffenreid v General Motors Assembly Division*, St Louis, 413 F.Supp. 142, 143 (E.D.Mo. 1976).

workers in 1970, 11 in 1971, none in 1972, and 137 in 1973. By late 1973, GM had 155 black women workers out of a total workforce of 8,500. Yet by January 1974, all of GM's black women workers had been made redundant: only the black female janitor remained.

All five women claimed that were it not for GM's past discriminatory policies, they would have applied and been hired in the mid-1960s. They also claimed that the seniority system and 'last hired-first fired' termination rule (agreed by the Union) was in breach of Title VII of the Civil Rights Act 1964 and 1981, because it perpetuated the effect of GM's past race and sex discrimination. They sought seniority benefits retroactive to the dates when they would have applied for employment at GM but for the discriminatory employment policy.

B. Professional Progress

Even if African American female workers did manage to get and hold on to a good job, progress could be withheld and treatment could be less favourable due to race and gender stigma. A second form of intersectional discrimination was experienced when employers decided that black women workers did not 'fit' into specific roles. These tended to be roles that involved management duties or were client facing. Thus situations arose where due to the combination of the history of slavery and the role of black women within it, employers refused to give a black woman a role granted to a white woman or a black man. This scenario was at the heart of the case of *Jeffries v HCCAA*.[9]

From 1967, Dafro Jeffries worked as a Secretary to the Director of Programs at Harris County Community Action Association (HCCAA). After three years, she was promoted to Personnel Interviewer. However her progress then stalled: between 1970 and 1974 she made several unsuccessful applications for promotions to various positions within the agency. Jeffries was a union steward from 1970 until her termination, and during her seven years with HCCAA, she filed many grievances on her own behalf and on the behalf of union members. In 1974 Jeffries applied for one of two vacancies announced for Field Representative position. These positions had previously been held by a white female and a black male. On the day of her application for the vacant position, Jeffries saw a confidential document confirming that a black male colleague had already been hired for the position of Acting Field Representative.

Jeffries complained to the Personnel Manager and the Executive Director of HCCAA (Silva). Believing she was a victim of discrimination, Jeffries also copied the confidential form and sent it with other materials to the Chair of the HCCAA personnel committee and a member of the HCCAA Board of Directors. Rather

[9] See *Jeffries v Harris Cty Community Action Association* 615 F.2nd 1025 (5th Cir. 1980); *Lam v University of Hawaii* 40 F. 3d 1551, 1561 (9th Cir. 1994); *Hicks v Gates Rubber Co* 833 F.2d 1406 (10th Cir. 1987) and *Lewis v Bloomsburg Mills Inc* 773 F.2d 561 (4th Cir. 1985).

than addressing the complaint made, the Chair expressed a concern to Silva about the use of confidential agency documents. Silva commenced an investigation on April 23 and subsequently (three days later) decided to dismiss Jeffries for 'conduct prejudicial to the interest of HCCAA'. In June the personnel committee conducted a hearing on the Jones promotion and on Jeffries' discharge. The committee approved the dismissal.

In court, Jeffries confirmed that 'every position for which she had applied had been filled by males or non-black females'. As the position for which she had applied (Field Representative) had previously been held by a white female and was given to a black male, a straightforward race or gender complaint would have been unsuccessful. In her complaint she therefore argued that HCCAA discriminated against her in promotion 'because she is a woman, up in age and because she is Black' (the age discrimination claim was subsequently dropped).

African American women in academia have had similar problems with promotion.[10] In one case a black female Associate Professor who had received the highest accolades for her teaching and research fell swiftly out of favour when she reported concerns about unlawful discriminatory behaviour by her colleagues. She was ultimately forced to resign[11] and her pursuit of an academic career was blocked. She brought a total of 14 claims against her employer, the University of Florida and its Law School, one of which alleged unlawful intersectional discrimination and harassment under Title VII. She argued that she had been denied equal terms and conditions of employment as employees who were white and/or male.[12] She also claimed intersectional discrimination in relation to incentive pay awards, arguing that she had had to do more to secure these than a white and/or male colleague.[13]

The women at General Motors, Jeffries and Russell-Brown argued that as black women they experienced discrimination as a 'synergistic' combination of two degraded statuses: 'the disabilities of blacks and the disabilities which inhere in their status as women'.[14] They highlighted the synergy between race and gender that had been overlooked in the past, asserting that the combination left them in a condition 'more terrible than the sum of their two constituent parts'.[15] Although

[10] N Kitroeff, 'Denied Tenure, Professors Sue over Discrimination' *Business Week* (23 December 2014), available at http://www.businessweek.com/articles/2014-12-23/denied-tenure-professors-sue-over-discrimination.

[11] *Russell-Brown v The University of Florida Board of Trustees et al*, No. 2:2009cv02479—Document 28 (D.N.J. 2009). After accusing her of 'vexatious conduct and impermissible forum-shopping' the case was voluntarily withdrawn conditional upon payment of the law school's costs. See *Sherrie Russell-Brown v Robert H Jerry, II, Levin College of Law, The University of Florida, The University of Florida Board of Trustees*, Case No. 1:2009cv00257, available at https://Cases.Justia.Com/Federal/District-Courts/Florida/Flndce/1:2009cv00257/56567/141/0.pdf

[12] *Russell-Brown v Board of Trustees* at para [105]. No. 2:2009cv02479.

[13] ibid, at paras [159/60]. The case was withdrawn in 2010—having lost her job, she was unable to settle her legal bills and was left without a legal team.

[14] J Scales-Trent, 'Black Women in the Constitution: Finding Our Place and Asserting Our Rights' (1989) 24 *Harvard Civil Rights-Civil Liberties Law Review* 10.

[15] Scales-Trent, 'Black Women in the Constitution' (n 14).

the law saw race and sex separately, they argued that in their existence as black women, racism and sexism converged. There was no 'either-or proposition' giving them a choice over which one would haunt their lives and which one they would be free of. They had to manage both.[16] They therefore asked the courts to recognise them as Black women per se, as an 'integrated, undifferentiated, complete whole',[17] who lived in society as 'twice-stigmatised … twice kin to the despised majority of all the human life that there is'.[18]

II. Categorisation in Anti-discrimination Law

The idea of being 'twice-stigmatised' only makes sense in light of the single dimension structure of anti-discrimination law. As discussed in Chapter 2, the anti-discrimination principle has been anchored in laws focusing on specific attributes—race or gender or disability in isolation but not together. There is no inherent reason why legal protection from discrimination is organised on the basis of categories. It may be that the law was designed and operates in this way because political campaigns for equality were organised in this way. Campaigns were not overlapping, and one group that fell into a social and political vortex was black women.[19] The Suffragettes did not include voting rights for black or poor women[20] and campaigns for racial equality did not take gender into account.

Historically, black women have never been the focus of equality campaigns, even though during the trans-Atlantic slave trade, women from Africa were also captured to work in North America, parts of Latin America, Europe and the Caribbean. It was not only the labour of enslaved women that was expropriated and exploited but also their capacity for procreation: they were owned and so their offspring belonged to and contributed to the wealth of their owner. Women slaves were beaten, maimed and killed at whim, just like the men, but unlike men they were also sexually mutilated through rape and tortured as mothers by being forced to breed slaves for the owner to keep or sell.[21] Both their labour and their bodies were property—they were workers who owned nothing and had no rights. As described by Fanon, they were the 'wretched of the earth'.[22] Patsy, the slave girl

[16] C Jones and K Shorter-Gooden, *Shifting: The Double Lives of Black Women in America* (New York, Harper Collins, 2003) 59.

[17] R Austin, 'Sapphire Bound!' (1989) 3 *Wisconsin Law Review* 540.

[18] J Jordan, 'Where is the Love?' in J Jordan, *Civil Wars* (New York, Simon and Schuster, 1981).

[19] GT Hull, P Bell Scott and B Smith, *But Some of Us Are Brave: All the Women Are White, All the Blacks Are Men: Black Women's Studies* (New York, The Feminist Press, 1982).

[20] A Brah and A Phoenix, 'Ain't I a Woman? Revisiting Intersectionality' (2004) 5(3) *Journal of International Women's Studies* 76.

[21] Toni Morrison's *Beloved* (New York, Knopf, 1987) tells the story of a slave woman who would rather kill her children than see them enslaved.

[22] F Fanon, *The Wretched of the Earth* (London, Penguin, 1967).

in Solomon Northup's haunting tale of his 12 years living as a slave, provides an example of precisely how wretched life could be for the female slave. Pretty, hard working and keen to please, she was repeatedly raped and whipped by the 'Master' and mutilated by his frustrated wife out of bitter jealousy. According to the narrative by Northup, so wretched was her life that she begged him to take it from her.[23]

Slave women like preacher-activist Sojourner Truth[24] who managed to escape these horrific conditions and secure their liberty—by fleeing to the North like Harriet Tubman or joining communities of Maroons—could be enslaved again if they happened to find themselves in the wrong state (like Northup),[25] or their state changed political hands.[26] Many who did remain in slavery resisted as best they could through revolts and midnight education classes.[27] Few succumbed placidly like the character of Eliza in the well known story of *Uncle Tom's Cabin*: there were as many—if not more—'Harriet Tubmans' than 'Elizas'.[28]

The fight for formal equality by enslaved black women is inter-twined with action for gender equality but the relationship is littered with paradoxes. When white working women went on strike to protest the 'double oppression they suffered as women and as industrial workers'[29] they used enslaved black workers as the foil against which to assert their political and legal autonomy. Striking mill-workers in Massachusetts sang: 'Oh, I cannot be a slave, I will not be a slave. Oh, I am so fond of liberty, I will not be a slave.'[30] Although middle-class white women, such as Lucretia Mott, were abolitionists active in female anti-slavery movements, they excluded all black women from the gender equality movement that arose from it. While black abolitionist Frederick Douglass was invited by Elizabeth Cady Stanton to the 1848 Seneca Falls Convention to promote equal rights for women, not a single black woman was present. It was at a subsequent Women's Rights convention in Akron, Ohio in 1851 that Sojourner Truth stood up to ask white feminists 'Ain't I a woman?'[31]

There were two brief periods when black men and women worked alongside white women. The first was between 1867 and 1869 in an organisation known as the Equal Rights Association.[32] This organisation, however, framed emancipation in dichotomous terms: for the black man or white woman. Its campaigns eclipsed black women and consequently the specific nature of their oppression

[23] S Northup, *Twelve Years a Slave* (London, Harper Collins, 2014), subsequently made into a critically acclaimed period drama film '12 Years a Slave'.

[24] S Truth, *Narrative of Sojourner Truth* (New York, Dover Publications, 1997).

[25] Northup, *Twelve Years a Slave* (n 23).

[26] When the USA bought Louisiana from Napoleon (the Louisiana Purchase of 1803) free women in that state became slaves again.

[27] AY Davis, *Women, Race and Class* (Vintage Books, 1983) 22.

[28] Eliza in Harriet Beecher Stowe's *Uncle Tom's Cabin* (John P Jewett, 1852) was a depiction of contented servility.

[29] Davis, *Women, Race and Class* (n 27) 54–55.

[30] Davis, *Women, Race and Class* (n 27) 33.

[31] Truth, *Narrative* (n 24) v.

[32] Davis, *Women, Race and Class* (n 27) ch 4.

was written out of law in favour of white female and black male narratives of domination. Where this organisation failed because it was under-inclusive, the second (discussed below) failed because it was over-inclusive.

The second period was over 100 years later when the Combahee River Collective (CRC) was created. 2014 marked the fortieth anniversary[33] of the Combahee River Collective;[34] named after the Combahee River Raid of June 1863 where Harriet Tubman liberated hundreds of slaves.[35] The CRC was a social movement created in the 1970s to establish a political narrative for the lives of Black women. Meeting under the leadership of Barbara Smith,[36] it took on the ambitious goal of developing emancipatory projects that were explicitly pluralist in nature, addressing simultaneously the multiple challenges of race, gender, class and sexuality.[37] As set out in its political philosophy, the CRC was

> actively committed to struggling against racial, sexual, heterosexual, and class oppression, and see as our particular task the development of integrated analysis and practice based upon the fact that the major systems of oppression are interlocking. The synthesis of these oppressions creates the conditions of our lives.[38]

The plurality of the CRC emerged due to four separate sources of discontent. The first was dissatisfaction with the focus of the predominantly white feminist movement—as noted by Anna Julia Cooper: white women may have been 'The Angel in the House'[39] but 'could at least plead for her own emancipation; the Black woman, doubly enslaved, could but suffer and struggle and be silent'.[40] This led to the creation of the National Black Feminist Organisation in 1973.[41] The second was disappointment with the middle-class focus of NBFO. Although it was created to highlight the different type of sexism experienced by black women—while white feminists focused on abortion rights, Black feminists fought to prevent forced sterilisation of Black girls and women[42]—its emancipatory projects, however, neglected the plight of poor women and the everyday racism they had

[33] K Price, 'Black, Feminist, Revolutionary: Remembering the Combahee River Collective', available at http://www.ebony.com/news-views/the-combahee-river-collective-405#axzz3NqFwdcPf.

[34] Formally disbanded in 1980.

[35] See http://womenshistory.about.com/od/timelines19501999/a/combahee_river.htm.

[36] Price, 'Black, Feminist, Revolutionary' (n 33).

[37] Davis, *Women, Race and Class* (n 27) 216.

[38] The statement was released in 1977 and printed in Z Eisenstein, *Capitalist Patriarchy and the Case for Social Feminism* (New York, Monthly Review Press, 1978).

[39] In this narrative poem, Coventry Patmore describes his ideal woman. His docile depiction of femininity came to represent the Victorian ideal. Virginia Woolf explores its impact on her professional development in her essay 'Professions for Women' (1931). Available in JD Lester (ed), *Daughters of the Revolution: Classic Essays by Women* (NTC, 2001) 36.

[40] AJ Cooper, *A Voice from the South: By a Woman from the South* (New York, Oxford University Press, 1988 [1892]).

[41] The German women's movement similarly promoted the rights of women, but did not recognise the needs of black German women. They were 'für Gleichberechtigung' but 'nicht jedoch gegen Rassismus'. See I Hügel-Marshall, *Daheim Unterwegs. Ein deutsches Leben; Die Frau in der Gesellschaft* (Frankfurt am Main, Fischer Verlag, 2008) 82.

[42] Davis, *Women, Race and Class* (n 27) 216.

to face. The NBFO ignored economic stratification: some members joined white women in judging poor women for having too many children and supported forced sterilisations.[43]

Third, the CRC had its origins in disillusionment with movements for racial equality. Civil rights activists, Black nationalists and the Black Panther Party did not take gender into account: black women were discouraged from taking an independent stance and disappeared into a political vacuum.[44] Yet speaking up for black women was not a rejection of solidarity with Black men but a call for Black women to struggle alongside their fathers, brothers and sons against racism, even while fighting 'with Black men about sexism'. This linked to the rejection of 'lesbian separatism' which demanded an exclusion of Black men, as well as heterosexual women and children. In addition, it ignored race and class, suggesting that female oppression came solely from sex: the CRC declared that 'as Black women we find any type of biological determinism a particularly dangerous and reactionary basis upon which to build a politic'. This led to a broad political philosophy and an ambitious goal, highlighting 'multiple interlocking oppressions':

> The most general statement of our politics at the present time would be that we are actively committed to struggling against racial, sexual, heterosexual, and class oppression, and see as our particular task the development of integrated analysis and practice based upon the fact that the major systems of oppression are interlocking. The synthesis of these oppressions creates the conditions of our lives. As Black women we see Black feminism as the logical political movement to combat the manifold and simultaneous oppressions that all women of color face [...] We might use our position at the bottom, however, to make a clear leap into revolutionary action. If Black women were free, it would mean that everyone else would have to be free since our freedom would necessitate the destruction of all the systems of oppression.[45]

The CRC therefore established a Black feminism that was an inclusive movement to challenge oppressive political relationships. The pursuit of rights for all women and men started from recognition of the experiences of African American women, in particular their 'extremely negative relationship' to the political structure in the USA, but ended with general liberation.

Black feminism was also established as a movement recognising the simultaneous experience of race and class and sex oppression, that was neither one nor the other. Sexual politics were as pervasive and damaging as class and race politics. All three were intertwined and acknowledged as being experienced simultaneously. When put together, this perspective called for a complete reform of social, political and economic organisation:

> We realize that the liberation of all oppressed peoples necessitates the destruction of the political-economic systems of capitalism and imperialism as well as patriarchy.

[43] AP Harris, 'Foreword: The Unbearable Lightness of Identity' (1996) 2 *African-American Law & Policy Report* 207, 214.
[44] Hull et al, *But Some of Us Are Brave* (n 19).
[45] See n 38 above.

> We are socialists because we believe that work must be organized for the collective benefit of those who do the work and create the products, and not for the profit of the bosses. Material resources must be equally distributed among those who create these resources. We are not convinced, however, that a socialist revolution that is not also a feminist and anti-racist revolution will guarantee our liberation.[46]

The CRC can therefore be described as a social movement that sought to question fundamental norms in the structure of everyday life from the perspective of black women. Although race was central to its starting point, it was not the sum of the CRC vision for liberation—the absence of any 'racial, sexual, heterosexual, or class privilege' was the focus of debate and discussion. Its vision of Black feminism was inclusive: Black feminism was both the starting point 'to combat the manifold and simultaneous oppressions that all women of color face' and the position from which to free all women because '[i]f Black women were free, it would mean that everyone else would have to be free since our freedom would necessitate the destruction of all the systems of oppression'.[47]

The CRC inherited this approach to equality and liberty from enslaved black women workers. Black feminism was seen as 'the outgrowth of countless generations of personal sacrifice, militancy, and work by our mothers and sisters'. It consciously located itself in the intellectual thought of enslaved black women activists such as Sojourner Truth, Harriet Tubman, Frances EW Harper,[48] Ida B Wells[49] and Mary Church Terrell.[50] These women shared an 'awareness of how their sexual identity combined with their racial identity to make their whole life situation and the focus of their political struggles unique'. They examined the slave plantation economy through their own eyes: the eyes of enslaved women at its centre, women denied bodily integrity and autonomy, economic or social power and political voice. They recognised that their social position was not the same as white women, who enjoyed racial superiority and could at least fight for sexual equality, nor black men who despite their racial oppression could enjoy some of the privileges of patriarchy. They established the intellectual legacy called upon by Black feminists in the CRC and the philosophy of structural inequality from which intersectionality drew in the twentieth century.

[46] ibid.

[47] ibid.

[48] Frances EW Harper created the first African-American heroine, Iola Leroy, in her novel *Iola Leroy or Shadows Uplifted* published in 1892.

[49] Daughter of slaves, she was orphaned as a teenager and founded a newspaper in Memphis. An anti-lynching campaigner, she was also a founder of the first Back Woman's Suffrage Club (Davis, *Women, Race and Class* (n 27) 111) and friend of Susan B Anthony.

[50] Daughter of a slave, third black woman college graduate in the USA, University Professor, first President of the National Association of Colored Women's Clubs' created in 1896, and first black woman appointed to the Board of Education of the District of Columbia (Davis, *Women, Race and Class* (n 27) 134–35).

III. Addressing Intersectional Discrimination

The link with slavery and the CRC clarifies that the emphasis in intersectionality is not identity per se but structural stigma that gives rise to discrimination. To overlook this inherent critique of political, economic and social structures is to misunderstand the philosophy of intersectionality and the task of intersectional discrimination. Set within the intellectual tradition of critical race feminism,[51] the goal of intersectional discrimination is therefore not to create a new hierarchy of mutually exclusive categories but to improve protection from discrimination by exposing the structural blindnesses inherent in the design of anti-discrimination law. The aim of intersectionality is to 'disrupt' dominant narratives in anti-discrimination law, to make power visible and thereby certain forms of discrimination experienced by groups at the cusps of categories. Intersectionality was designed to be inclusive: black women were the immediate—but not exclusive—'physical and material representation of the intersection of race and gender'.[52] Any group demonstrating that it is discrete, insular and powerless can potentially claim similar protection.[53] It is perhaps stating the obvious to say that 'black people can be old, that old people can suffer gender discrimination, and that women can be discriminated against because they are Latinas'.[54] For example, Asian women experience discrimination on the grounds of gender and national origin[55] and young black men experience discrimination on the grounds of race, age and gender. As recently reiterated by Crenshaw:

> The metaphor upon which intersectionality is scaffolded acknowledges a wide variety of encounters as well as relationships. In this sense, intersectionality applies to everyone—no one exists outside of the matrix of power, but the implications of this matrix—when certain features are activated and relevant and when they are not—are contextual. Intersectionality represents a structural and dynamic arrangement; power marks these relationships among and between categories of experiences that vary in their complexity. To map intersectionality from instance to instance both confirms the relevance of categories and provides the impetus for disrupting dominant discourses that regard these categories as fixed and mutually exclusive. Intersectionality then was an attempt to create a prism that revealed the confluence of structure and identity and to highlight vectors in which discrimination was rendered invisible by the prevailing frameworks that were deployed to identify and intervene against it. Intersectionality was not the only attempt …[56]

[51] AK Wing, *Critical Race Feminism—A Reader* (New York, New York University Press, 1997).

[52] P Caldwell, 'A Hair Piece: Perspectives on the Intersection of Race and Gender' (1991) *Duke Law Journal* 365, 372.

[53] Scales-Trent, 'Black Women in the Constitution' (n 14).

[54] J Scales-Trent, *Notes of a White Black Woman: Race, Colour, Community* (University Park, PA: Pennsylvania University Press, 1995) 173.

[55] V Wei, 'Asian Women and Employment Discrimination' (1996) 37 *Boston College Law Review* 771.

[56] H Lutz, MT Herrera Vivar and L Supik, *Framing Intersectionality: Debates on a Multi-faceted Concept in Gender Studies* (Farnham, Ashgate Publishing, 2011) 230.

The legal challenge is therefore to create a remedy for intersectional discrimination that reflects this goal.

In both the UK and USA, intersectionality has no clear legal remedy, as anti-discrimination law was not designed to tackle it. It has been difficult to translate the goal of intersectionality into a legal remedy because of the structure of anti-discrimination law. As discussed above, the legal prohibition of discrimination is premised on single dimension attributes, whether race or gender or disability or age; there is no precedent for a legal response to discrimination triggered by a synergistic combination of attributes. Thus initially the women at GM were unable to access a legal remedy due to the structure of anti-discrimination law: the first response was rejection, the second was accommodation. As will be discussed below, attempts to date do not disrupt prevailing frameworks of discrimination law but, rather, re-invent intersectionality so that it can be accommodated within them. Neither the single attribute nor the 'sex-plus' theories of discrimination respect synergy or disrupt. However, it will be argued that the anti-stigma principle can do so.

A. Rejection: Adherence to the Single Dimension Theory

In *Degraffenreid*, the District Court refused to consider the existence of a 'super-remedy' for black women, reasoning that to find race and sex discrimination would create a new sub-category within Title VII and would generate a new protected 'class of minorities'. It decided that there was no indication that Title VII envisaged creation of a new classification of 'black women' who would have greater standing than, for example, a black male. Furthermore, to create a sub-category was described as 'opening the hackneyed Pandora's box' that would unleash 'new classes of protected minorities, governed only by the mathematical principles of permutation and combination'.[57] It thus applied the existing single-dimension logic of discrimination. The claims were divided into separate complaints of race and sex: the sex claim was dismissed and the race claim was consolidated with a complaint brought by African American men against GM.[58] Upon appeal, the seniority system was upheld: a neutral, legitimate seniority system did not become unlawful under Title VII simply because it perpetuated discrimination.[59] The consolidation focused on race alone, and the women lost.

This approach was also adopted in the case of *Bahl v The Law Society*,[60] the first intersectional case in the UK. It was brought against the Law Society, the representative body for solicitors in England and Wales. Kamlesh Bahl, a former

[57] District Court, *DeGraffenreid v General Motors Assembly Division*, St. Louis, 413 F.Supp. 142, 143 (E.D.Mo. 1976).
[58] *Moseley v General Motors*, 497 F. Supp. 583 (E. D. Mo. 1980).
[59] United States Court of Appeals, Eighth Circuit—*DeGraffenreid v. General Motors Assembly Division*, St Louis, 558 F.2d 480.
[60] See also *Network Rail v Griffiths-Henry* [2006] IRLR 865.

Commissioner at the Equal Opportunities Commission, was appointed as the new Vice-President at the Law Society. Her role was to drive forward reforms. However, staff complained of bullying and in 2000 an internal inquiry was conducted to investigate the allegations. Bahl eventually resigned, and complained of discrimination. Her case raised the question of whether black women could form a synergistic category in anti-discrimination law.

Bahl was successful at the first instance. Using a white man as a hypothetical comparator, the employment tribunal upheld some of her allegations of race and sex discrimination against the two defendants (Mr Sayer and Ms Betts) and the Law Society. The Tribunal found that a white man would not have been treated as Ms Bahl was treated, that Mr Sayer and Ms Betts had committed unconscious direct sex and race discrimination, and that the Law Society was liable for their actions. In coming to this conclusion, the tribunal looked at race and sex together:

> We do not distinguish between the race or sex of the Applicant in reaching this conclusion. Our reason for that is simple. The claim was advanced on the basis that Kamlesh Bahl was treated in the way she was because she is a black woman. Kamlesh Bahl was the first office holder that the Law Society had ever had who was not both white and male. There was no basis in the evidence for comparing her treatment with that of a white female, or a black male, office holder. We can only draw inferences. We do not know what was in the minds of Robert Sayer and Jane Betts at any particular point. It is sufficient for our purposes to find, where appropriate, that in each case they would not have treated a white person or a man less favourably.[61]

However, this decision was reversed upon appeal. The EAT reversal was upheld in the Court of Appeal where Gibson LJ described the above passage as 'puzzling'.[62] The EAT did not understand why the tribunal decided against the use of a white female or black male office holder as a comparator for Bahl. Elias LJ stated that, while a finding of discrimination on the grounds of race and sex was possible after consideration of the evidence in relation to each ground,

> If the evidence does not satisfy the tribunal that there is discrimination on grounds of race or on grounds of sex considered independently, then it is not open to a tribunal to find either claim satisfied on the basis that there is nonetheless discrimination on grounds of race and sex when both are taken together … Nor can the tribunal properly conclude, if it is uncertain about whether it is race or sex, that it will find both.[63]

As in *Degraffenreid*, the senior judges held that it was not possible for Bahl to claim race and gender as a single combined ground of discrimination: these two aspects had to be treated separately and independent evidence in support of each brought forward. Elias LJ concluded that the employment tribunal erred in law by failing to distinguish between the elements of alleged race and sex discrimination, with the result that it was hasty to conclude that Bahl had proven that discrimination had occurred in respect of either ground.

[61] *Bahl v The Law Society* [2004] EWCA Civ 1070 [135].
[62] ibid [136].
[63] *The Law Society v Kamlesh Bahl* [2003] IRLR 640 [158].

B. Accommodation: The Sex Plus Theory

In *Jeffries*, the claim was also dismissed by the District Court—it held that she did not prove that HCCAA's failure to promote her was based on race or sex discrimination. However, in its rejection, the District Court did not address the complaint that HCCAA discriminated against her on the basis of *both* race and sex—it was silent in relation to intersectional discrimination. This was picked up by the Federal Court, which upheld the District Court's findings that Jeffries had failed to prove race discrimination regarding promotion, but instructed the District Court to re-consider the question of sex discrimination.[64]

The race discrimination complaint failed because her colleague who was promoted (albeit in an acting capacity) to the job that Jeffries sought, was black. This finding drew upon a similar sex discrimination case, *Adams v Reed*, where both the person seeking promotion and the person achieving promotion were women, thus sex discrimination was ruled out as a plausible explanation for the decision.[65] Yet the Federal Court agreed with Jeffries that the district court was wrong to ignore her claim of discrimination on the basis of both race and sex. It held that 'discrimination against black females can exist even in the absence of discrimination against black men or white women'.

Using a textual analysis, it found that a category of black women was potentially within the language of Title VII—first, the use of the word 'or' in the Title VII[66] remedy against employment discrimination ('race, color, religion, sex, or national origin') indicated a Congressional intention to prohibit employment discrimination based on any or all of the listed characteristics. Support for this conclusion was found in examination of the legislative history of Title VII, where the House of Representatives had rejected an amendment to add the word 'solely' so that the Act would read 'solely sex'.[67]

Second, the Appeal Court noted the significant number of black women in the workforce: it refused to condone a result which left these women without a viable Title VII remedy 'in the absence of a clear expression by Congress that it did not intend to provide protection against discrimination directed especially toward black women as a class separate and distinct from the class of women and the class of blacks'.[68] Recognising the need for intersectional discrimination, it found that Title VII[69] was capable of 'prohibiting employment discrimination based on any or all of the listed characteristics' thus 'discrimination against black females can

64 *Jeffries* [12]–[21].

65 Paragraph 11. *Adams v Reed*, 567 F.2d 1283, 1287 (5th Cir. 1978). See also *Jenkins v Caddo-Bossier Ass'n*, 570 F.2d 1227, 1228–29 (5th Cir. 1978).

66 Title VII 42 U.S.C. § 2000e-2(a).

67 110 Congressional Records 2728 (1964).

68 *Jeffries* (n 66) [23]–[24].

69 110 Congessional Records 2728 (1964).

exist even in the absence of discrimination against black men or white women'.[70] The claim, dismissed by the District Court with no consideration of the complaint of intersectional race and sex discrimination, was thus supported by the US Federal Court of Appeal.

Yet the approach adopted by the Appeal Court was additive rather than intersectional: it used a 'sex-plus' analysis that had been established in the *Phillips* case.[71] Mrs Phillips had applied for a job with Martin Marietta Corporation in 1966. However, Martin had informed Phillips that it was not accepting job applications from women with pre-school-age children. Phillips thereupon brought a claim of sex discrimination as Martin employed men with pre-school-age children. The difficulty was that at the time Phillips applied, 70–75% of the applicants for the position she sought were women; and 75–80% of those hired for the position of assembly trainee were women, thus there was clearly no bias against women per se.

The case was decided using the idea of pre-school age children as a neutral criterion that could be 'added' to the discriminatory criterion of sex. The court determined that under Title VII of the Civil Rights Act of 1964, an employer may not discriminate against women with children as this equates to unlawful discrimination based on *sex plus* the neutral factor of having children. In the absence of business necessity, a refusal to hire women with pre-school-age children while hiring men with such children would constitute unlawful discrimination. Applying this 'sex plus' analysis to Jeffries, the court approached the claim as gender discrimination plus discrimination based on race.

The 'additive' approach is also used in Britain. In the case of *Ali v North East Centre for Diversity and Racial Equality*,[72] a tribunal found that a Pakistani Muslim woman had been harassed because of her sex and race. A co-worker, Mr B, had humiliated in front of her colleagues and family, had subjected her to unsubstantiated complaints about her work, had drawn her into questionable financial dealings, and expected her to cook for him. The tribunal found that she had been subjected to such treatment because she was a Muslim woman who had grown up in Pakistan: a male employee, a white female employee or a Muslim woman who had been brought up in Britain would not have been treated in the same way.

This analysis was also used in *Nwoke v Government Legal Service*[73] where a British court held that a Nigerian woman was discriminated against because of her race and her sex. Nwoke had applied for a post in the Government Legal Service. Her ranking after the interview was 'E', which was the lowest grade, with 'A' being

[70] *Jeffries* (n 66) [23]–[24]. These claims were brought under Title VII 42 U.S.C 2000e-2(a) (2004) which prohibits workplace discrimination.

[71] *Phillips v Martin Marietta Corp* 400 US 542 (1971).

[72] *Ali v North East Centre for Diversity and Racial Equality* Case: 2504529/03. Discussed in N Bamforth, M Malik and C O'Cinneide, *Discrimination Law: Theory and Context* (London, Sweet and Maxwell, 2008) 526–27.

[73] *Nwoke v Government Legal Service and Civil Service Commissioners* (1996) 28 *Equal Opportunities Review* 6. Discussed in A McColgan, *Discrimination Law: Texts, Cases and Materials* (Oxford, Hart, 2005) 34.

the highest. However, it was discovered that all white applicants—both male and female—were graded higher than Nwoke, even if they had a lower degree class. The court found that the only reason for her low grading was her race, which meant she had suffered unlawful racial discrimination. In addition, however, even those white women who were graded higher than Nwoke were unlikely to be offered a job, and if appointed they were paid less. There was therefore also separate evidence of sex discrimination—all women were at a disadvantage when compared to men—and the court accordingly held that the Government Legal Service was discriminating on the grounds of sex. Nwoke successfully alleged race and sex discrimination. She was able to provide separate evidence to prove that she had suffered discrimination because she was black, and also because she was female.

The additive approach was incorporated into the Equality Act 2010 in an attempt to create a legal remedy for intersectional discrimination. The Equality Act 2010, section 14 states that:

> A person (A) discriminates against another (B) if, because of a combination of two relevant protected characteristics, A treats B less favourably than A treats or would treat a person who does not share either of those characteristics.

The provision does go beyond the additive approach as it releases claimants from the burden of producing separate evidence when claiming more than one type of discrimination. The Act specifically stated that 'B need not show that A's treatment of B is direct discrimination because of each of the characteristics in the combination (taken separately)'. However, the restriction to combinations of two protected characteristics make clear that it is premised on aggregation and the legislative background confirms that a mathematical approach lurks behind this Section. The Peers Briefing explains that

> If, for example a black disabled woman is discriminated against, it is likely that the discrimination she experienced was because of any one of the three strands, or because of a combination of any two of these protected characteristics, but less likely to only be because of the particular combination of the three. Evidence shows that enabling claims combining two protected characteristics addresses most (90%) of the cases of intersectional discrimination.[74]

Section 14 also sets out that a claim will fail if discrimination is lawful by virtue of another provision in the EqA 2010, such as a genuine occupational requirement:[75]

> if a man who is denied a job in a domestic violence refuge alleges this denial is because he is a disabled man, but in fact it is because being a woman is an occupational requirement for the post, a multiple discrimination claim combining sex and disability would not succeed—because, based on the facts, there was no disability discrimination and the sex discrimination was not unlawful.[76]

[74] Government Equalities Office (2009) 'Peers Briefing' (PB), 15.

[75] Under section 14.4, '... B cannot establish a contravention of this Act by virtue of subsection (1) if, in reliance on another provision of this Act or any other enactment, A shows that A's treatment of B is not direct discrimination because of either or both of the characteristics in the combination.'

[76] Government Equalities Office (2009) 'Peers Briefing' (PB), 15.

Thus if a justification or any other kind of exception is applicable, the less favourable treatment would not be unlawful under the multiple discrimination provision.

It is clear that s 14 was not intended to replace the single dimension approach: it was to be a remedy of last resort:

> It is not intended that this provision should be a panacea for all forms of discrimination; rather, it provides a specific legal remedy for those who have experienced less favourable treatment because of a combination of protected characteristics, where currently it may difficult, complicated and sometimes impossible to get a legal remedy. Just as multiple single strand claims are often necessary now, multiple claims may be necessary in the future, even with the advent of dual discrimination.[77]

It is therefore questionable whether the new provision corrects the eclipse highlighted by the theory of intersectional discrimination.

There are two major problems with section 14. First, there is no sense in the provision or the accompanying explanatory notes of the synergy that underlies intersectional discrimination, and differentiates it from additive discrimination. Synergy highlights 'co-operative effects', the effects produced by two or more elements, parts or individuals … that operate together. Synergistic effects are always co-determined and interdependent; the elements work together so that if one is removed it becomes something else.[78] Just as oxygen and hydrogen produces water not 'oxydrogen', or tin and copper together make bronze, not 'tinper', intersectional discrimination creates a new whole subject. In the absence of synergy, the idea of intersectional discrimination loses its social and political context. It is reduced to the first stage of identity politics[79] and the prospect of potentially unlimited 'combination' of characteristics—as indeed feared by the Court in *DeGraffenreid*—emerges. Both black women workers and the systemic critique are lost.

Second, the idea of 'combination' prevents any shift of perspective: it does not change the way anti-discrimination law sees—there is no alternative experience centred. It is synergy that facilitates this shift of perspective centralising those whose lives are blighted by stigmatised characteristics. Without synergy these voices return to the margins and the white male norm returns to dominate. Its absence indicates a fundamental misunderstanding of the problem that the concept of intersectionality was conceived to address. An intersectional approach must take into account the 'historical, social and political context'[80] and recognise

[77] ibid (n 76).

[78] P Corning, 'Synergy and the Systems Sciences', available at http://www.isss.org/primer/corning.htm.

[79] Harris, 'The Unbearable Lightness of Identity' (n 45) 217: 'In the first stage of identity theory, scholars chronicle the harms visited on subordinated groups, arguing that they are neither trivial nor inevitable but the result of systemic injustice. In the second stage, scholars bring their critical attention to the source of injustice, showing the bias and nonrepresentativeness of formerly dominant and unquestioned ways of speaking, thinking, and acting. And in the third stage of identity theory, the task becomes reconstruction: imagining a future without these forms of subordination, and inventing ways to get there from here.'

[80] CA Aylward, 'Intersectionality: Crossing the Theoretical and Praxis Divide' (Paper Distributed at Transforming Women's Future: Equality Rights in the New Century: A National Forum on

the unique position of the individual based on the interaction of attributes; history and contingency are both important elements in synergy.[81] Synergy is at the core of intersectional discrimination, and without it intersectionality becomes just another name for 'sex-plus' or additive discrimination.

It therefore seems that intersectional discrimination has been made to fit into the current legal framework—the Equality Act has multiplied its vision (that is, what it sees), without shifting its perspective (that is, the way it sees). However, in the USA 'sex-plus' no longer has credibility: in *Lam*[82] the Federal Court of Appeal (9th Circuit) explicitly stated that this form of 'mathematical' approach or dissection of a person into distinct components would distort or ignore the particular nature of intersectional discrimination.[83] Lam, a woman of Vietnamese descent, alleged discrimination on the basis of race, sex and national origin following her unsuccessful application for the post of Director of the Law School's Pacific Asian Legal Studies Program. The District Court again analysed the racism and sexism claims as distinct but the Appeal Court found this approach to be incorrect and stated that 'where two bases for discrimination exist, they cannot be neatly reduced to distinct components' because 'attempt[ing] to bisect a person's identity at the intersection of race and gender often distorts or ignores the particular nature of their experiences'.[84] The Court recognised that refusing the claim would leave migrant women without a remedy in the face of discrimination. It is also time for the UK to revise its approach.

C. Disruption: The Anti-stigma Theory

How then to disrupt the anti-discrimination legal framework? The goal is not to destroy this framework but to improve how it sees. Put simply, plural vision must become a norm for anti-discrimination law rather than the exception. The anti-stigma principle could perform this task. It could be the starting point for the creation of categories 'founded not on an ideal of neutrality, but on the reality of oppression'[85] both historical and contemporary. The use of stigma would place social structures clearly in the spotlight and make anti-discrimination law contextual; by contextualising discrimination 'we shed light on the historical, social, cultural and political processes and developments which have significance for the occurrence of discrimination'[86] in society.

Equality Rights presented by West Coast Leaf, 4 November 1999) [unpublished]. Cited in Ontario Human Rights Commission, 'An Intersectional Approach to Discrimination—Addressing Multiple Grounds in Human Rights Claims', fn 7, available at http://www.ohrc.on.ca.

[81] See n 80 above.
[82] *Lam v University of Hawaii* 40 F. 3d 1551, 1561 (9th Cir. 1994).
[83] ibid [1562].
[84] ibid [1562].
[85] M Matsuda, 'When the First Quail Calls' (1989) 11(7) *Women's Rights Law Reporter* 10.
[86] European Commission, 2007, 31 (n3).

It can be argued that stigma is an imprecise concept: this is true to an extent but even a child—such as Wendy in the song 'Turning Point' discussed in Chapter 1—understands what a stigma is. She may not use the word stigma, but after speaking with her Mom, in addition to not wanting to play with Beatrice, Wendy will also not want to *be* or *be like* Beatrice. Beatrice now has an attribute which is denigrated[87] and 'deeply discrediting'[88] to an extent that 'tarnishes'[89] her whole identity. Stigmatisation is the social imposition of a negative relationship to a personal attribute which permits the 'doubting of the person's worthiness'.[90] All other traits, including abilities, 'are subordinated to or negated by this trait, which is immediately felt to be more central to the "actual" identity of the individual'.[91] They exist independently of individual merit.[92] Stigmatisation has been described as 'the mechanism by which a person's humanity is reduced and justifies the reduction or removal of civility, opportunities and life chances'.

If the creation of 'protected characteristics' or 'grounds' were informed by the logic of stigma—in place of or in addition to dignity and immutability—discrimination law could move beyond the current single dimension logic. Stigma can rectify the vision of anti-discrimination by addressing the blind spot identified by Crenshaw. It facilitates synergy because stigmas can occur alone or in groups, which means that individuals can be seen as complete beings. Furthermore, stigma would keep the law in this area grounded in the reality of those requiring its protection.[93] I am not suggesting that all stigmas be brought within the scope of discrimination law. Using the anti-stigma principle, discrimination law would focus on stigmas that are arbitrary, to which the public response is always punitive[94] rather than just negative; which therefore make a significant difference in relation to access to and acquisition of resources in key areas, such as health, housing, education, training and employment; and which, finally, are difficult to escape.[95]

Anti-discrimination law could therefore offer a remedy for single and intersectional forms of discrimination: it would disrupt the current framework without destroying it and address the gap in the current protection in a deep rather than superficial way. At the same time, it would address concerns about the limits of anti-discrimination law. There would be no need to revise the existing protected

[87] A Dijker and W Koomen, *Stigmatization, Tolerance and Repair* (Cambridge, Cambridge University Press, 2007) 8.

[88] E. Goffman (1990) *Stigma: Notes on the Management of Spoiled Identity.* London: Penguin, 12.

[89] R Page, *Stigma* (London, Routledge and Kegan Paul, 1984) 19.

[90] G C Loury (2002) *The Anatomy of Racial Inequality.* Cambridge, Mass.: Harvard University Press, 61.

[91] Page, *Stigma* (n 89) 10.

[92] In *Chagger,* the successful complainant in a race discrimination case was subsequently unable to find work because he was 'stigmatised' on the job market (*Chagger v Abbey National Plc and Another* [2009] EWCA Civ 1202, [2010] IRLR 47).

[93] PR Smith, 'Separate Identities: Black Women, Work and Title VII' (1991) 14 *Harvard Women's Law Journal* 74.

[94] Page, *Stigma* (n 89) 3.

[95] S Levin and C van Laar, *Stigma and Group Inequality* (2006), London: Lawrence Erblaum Associates, 4.

characteristics, although these could be renamed 'stigmatised characteristics'. The anti-stigma principle would correct how anti-discrimination law sees, and bring socially relevant characteristics within its vision.

Intersectional discrimination would apply only where there is synergy. This does not require the 'elements' or characteristics of intersectional discrimination to be pre-determined—the synergy arises from the effects of their combination—but in the absence of this effect, there is no intersectional discrimination. In order to ensure that there is a qualitative difference to intersectional discrimination, intersectional discrimination should only be used where synergy is evident. It is synergy that makes intersectional discrimination qualitatively different to a case of single-dimension discrimination.[96]

This point was powerfully made by the Ontario Human Rights Commission in *Baylis-Flannery*.[97] The Court decided to find intersectional discrimination, even though a single dimension approach would have been successful, in order to demonstrate legal acknowledgement that Baylis-Flannery 'is not a woman who happens to be Black, or a Black person who happens to be female, but a Black woman'. This was because in terms of the impact of the discrimination 'on her psyche, the whole is more than the sum of the parts: the impact of these highly discriminatory acts on her personhood is serious'—according to Scales-Trent, 'more terrible than the sum of their two constituent parts'.[98] The Commission wanted to make a point about the discrimination that she experienced and therefore held that:

> the serious forms of discrimination Ms Baylis-Flannery endured, with respect to her race and her sex, were intersectional in nature. The Respondent, in his role as her employer, sexually solicited her, sexually harassed her, racially harassed her, engaged in discriminatory treatment toward her within her employment, and poisoned her workplace with pornography that mirrored both her race and gender. He did so because she is an attractive, young Black woman, and all the evidence heard about his views about Blacks and Africans, his comments about dating, his visits to strip clubs in Detroit, about his fixation with Malina, about the Black female escort he found attractive on the internet, and about his hiring practices indicate that he has a stereotypical view of attractive, young, Black women over whom he can assert economic power and control.[99]

IV. Applying Intersectional Discrimination

There are perhaps two issues that may need to be approached differently under cases of intersectional discrimination. The first concerns the comparator: who

[96] Solanke (2009) 'Putting Race and Gender Together: A New Approach to Intersectionality'. 72 *Modern Law Review* 723–49.

[97] *Ontario Human Rights Commission and Rachael Baylis-Flannery v Walter DeWilde (cob. Tri Community Physiotherapy)* [2003] OHRTD No 20.

[98] Scales-Trent, 'Black Women in the Constitution' (n 14).

[99] *Baylis-Flannery vs. Walter DeWilde* [146].

would the comparator be in cases of intersectional discrimination? This question has now been answered in a few cases. In relation to indirect discrimination, as stated in *Burnip*, statistical evidence is no longer a prerequisite where a group is recognised as in need of protection against discrimination.[100] The second issue concerns sanctions: what could compensate a target and should the perceiver be punished? This is not the only reason why intersectional discrimination matters, but it is relevant.

A. The Comparator

In *Jeffries*, the Federal Appeal Court held that both black males and white females, as persons outside Jeffries's class, could be used as comparators. The fact that her promoted colleague was also black did not bring him within her class.[101] In some cases, such as *Lewis*, *Mackie* and *Hewage*, white men have been used as comparators in complaints brought by black women.

Lewis v Tabard Gardens[102] concerned Ms Lewis, a black woman, who worked for Tabard Gardens as an administrator. She criticised a colleague, Mr Otite, a Nigerian man, in front of her line manager, Mr Dunne, a white man. Dunne subsequently told Lewis that she should not speak to Otite like that because as a Nigerian man he could not take instructions from women. At a subsequent meeting, Dunne continued to make strong criticisms of Lewis and told her to resign or negotiate a compromise agreement. She agreed to consider the latter and was placed on 'garden leave'.[103] However, before she could respond to an offer, one of the directors, Ms Pauliszky, contacted her to say that Dunne had behaved improperly and that she could return to a new position where she would have limited contact with him. The case came before an employment tribunal, which found that Lewis had been treated less favourably by Dunne: he had not criticised others in the organisation in such an unconstructive way or told to them resign or accept a compromise agreement. His remarks about Nigerian men together with his unreasonable treatment of Lewis led the tribunal to find that his treatment of her was partially influenced by her sex and race—he would not have treated a white male employee with whom he had performance issues in this way. Likewise in *Mackie v G & N Car Sales*,[104] a tribunal held that an Indian woman had been summarily dismissed because of her sex and racial origin: had she been a white

[100] *Burnip v Birmingham CC and Others* [2012] EWCA Civ 629 [13].
[101] *Jeffries* (n 66) [34].
[102] *Lewis v Tabard Gardens TMC Ltd* [2005] ET/2303327/04.
[103] 'Garden leave' is the term given to the period during which an employee who leaves the employer is required to serve out a period of notice at home (or 'in the garden'). The employee continues to receive all salary and benefits and is prohibited from commencing employment with new employers until the garden leave period has expired. It is a common practice in relation to employees with access to confidential information or customers. See S Bone, *Osborn's Concise Law Dictionary* (London, Sweet and Maxwell, 2001).
[104] *Mackie v G & N Car Sales Ltd t/a Britannia Motor Co* Case: 1806128/03.

man possessing identical qualities, she would not have been subjected to the less favourable treatment.

Another example is provided in *Hewage.*[105] Mrs Hewage, a British citizen born in Sri Lanka was employed as a consultant orthodontist by the Grampian Health Board in 1993. In 1996 she became Head of Service for the Orthodontic Department. However, she resigned from her position in 2003 and had left the Health Board by March 2005. She brought a claim against her employer for unfair dismissal and race and sex discrimination on three issues relating to her predecessor and her successor in the post. First, when she resigned as Head of Service due to the problematic conduct of the Service Manager, the Board immediately hired another consultant to replace her. However, when her predecessor—a white man—had resigned as Head of Service for the same reason, the Board not only re-instated him but re-organised the department to minimise his contact with the Service Manager.

In relation to this complaint, the employment tribunal found 'marked similarities' between the case of Professor Forrester and Mrs Hewage:

> 32 ... It was satisfied that there was a like for like comparison between them. It found that when Professor Forrester resigned as Head of Service because of Mrs Strachan's conduct, Mrs Strachan was relieved of responsibility in his department; whereas when the appellant resigned as Head of Service for the same reason, the respondent allowed Mrs Strachan to retain her responsibilities in the appellant's department and appointed another consultant, Mr Larmour, to succeed the appellant on a temporary basis, thereby preventing her from seeking re-appointment as Head of Service. It found the respondent's explanation unconvincing. It concluded that the appellant' complaints of sexual and racial discrimination in this respect should be upheld.[106]

Second, it also transpired that she had consistently been given a significantly lower level of support by her colleagues: her suggestion to include a consultant on interviewing panels was repeatedly rejected by her colleagues, but they agreed to this 'within days' of her white male replacement becoming Head of Service. The tribunal described the change in attitude as 'astounding and inexplicable' and in the absence of an adequate explanation found both sex and race discrimination. Third, whereas her successor had been offered support to deal with the Service Manager as soon as he was in post, no such help was offered to Mrs Hewage. She was only told to take time off. The tribunal again found both sex and race discrimination. Although the EAT overturned these findings, they were upheld upon appeal by the UK Supreme Court: as a black woman Hewage could rely upon a white male comparator.

A final example is the case of Carol Howard where an employment tribunal found race and sex discrimination in the Metropolitan Police Service. Carol

[105] *Hewage v Grampian Health Board* 2012 GWD 25-521, [2012] IRLR 870, [2012] WLR(D) 235, [2012] Eq LR 884, [2012] ICR 1054, [2012] UKSC 37, [2012] 4 All ER 447; *Hewage v Grampian Health Board* [2011] CSIH 4, 2011 GWD 4-127, 2011 SLT 319, [2011] ScotCS CSIH_4.

[106] *Hewage v Grampian Health Board* [2011] ScotCS CSIH_4 (14 January 2011) [32].

Howard was the only black woman in her firearms unit, which remains almost exclusively male and white. The tribunal concluded that her manager had formed a negative conclusion of her because she was a black woman, and that he targeted her for over a year 'because she was black and because she was a woman'.[107] The tribunal found that he had not treated any white male or black male colleague as he had treated her.

Likewise in the USA, a white male comparator has been used in a case brought by a black female law professor who complained of intersectional discrimination at the University of the District of Columbia School of Law (DCSL). Stephanie Brown taught at DCSL for 20 years and submitted an application for tenure and a promotion to full professor in January 2009. The DCSL Faculty Handbook lists three qualifications for tenure: teaching, scholarship and service. The scholarship component requires three published articles. Brown's application was refused on the basis of insufficient publications. At the same time, however, her white male colleague who had no publications was awarded tenure and promotion to full professor.

Brown brought a claim of *inter alia* race and gender discrimination in violation of the Civil Rights Act 1866 (CRA)[108] and D.C. Human Rights Act (DCHRA).[109] She argued that the University had applied less stringent criteria to the tenure application of her white colleague, McLain: his tenure submission was as deficient as her own yet he was credited for 'various and sundry legal contributions' to address this lack of scholarship, while she was given no similar credit for her 'academic accomplishments and a record of selfless and thankless contributions to the law school'.

While she failed before the District Court, upon appeal her two claims of discrimination under the CRA and the DCHRA, were upheld.[110] The Appeal Court reversed the District Court dismissal and remanded them for further proceedings.[111] The Appeal Court stated that Brown had a *prima facie* case, as she had identified a similarly situated employee outside of her protected class and explained why she held equivalent qualifications. Neither she nor McLain

[107] *Howard v Metropolitan Police Service* ET Case No 2200184/2013 and 2202916/2013 [157]–[158].

[108] 42 US Code, Section 1981.

[109] Code of the District of Columbia (D.C. CODE) Section 2–1401.01 states: 'It is the intent of the Council of the District of Columbia, in enacting this chapter, to secure an end in the District of Columbia to discrimination for any reason other than that of individual merit, including, but not limited to, discrimination by reason of race, color, religion, national origin, sex, age, marital status, personal appearance, sexual orientation, gender identity or expression, familial status, family responsibilities, matriculation, political affiliation, genetic information, disability, source of income, status as a victim of an intra-family offense, and place of residence or business.' NB 2-1401.02 Definitions: '9) "Employee" means any individual employed by or seeking employment from an employer; provided, that the term "employee" shall include an unpaid intern.'

[110] Case No 13-7027 *Stephanie Y. Brown (Appellant) v Allen L. Sessoms, President, University District of Columbia, et al., (Appellees)* (No. 1:12-cv-00799), 19 December 2014.

[111] Civil Case No. 12–799 (RJL) *Brown v District of Columbia*, United States District Court, District of Columbia 919 F.Supp.2d 105 (D.D.C. 2013).

submitted three published law review articles with their tenure applications yet only Brown was not awarded a tenure. Drawing all inferences in her favour, the Appeal Court stated that

> … we believe that Brown's complaint sufficiently makes out that she and McLain had similar records with regard to teaching and service. Because both also failed to meet the publication requirement, their tenure applications appear, from the complaint, to be on comparable footing. The fact that McLain won tenure and Brown did not allows us 'to draw the reasonable inference that the defendant is liable for the misconduct alleged.'[112]

Ultimately, however, the anti-stigma principle could free claimants from the need to identify a comparator at all—stigma is, after all, an objective phenomenon.

B. Sanctions

Secondly, there is a question on what procedures and sanctions should be made available for intersectional discrimination? If it is agreed that this form of discrimination is qualitatively different to single dimension discrimination, then the process for trying and remedying such cases should also be different. There are examples of a different approach to compensation in countries that have addressed additive discrimination. These include financial remedies or hearings in larger courts. For example, in Sweden compensation increases with each ground of discrimination but this depends upon a finding that the discrimination also occurs at different times. In a case where discrimination was alleged on the basis of sex and age, the court required evidence to support both grounds and decided that as both grounds occurred at the same time, it was a single offence thus no higher award was made.[113] Article 6(2) of the Croatian Anti-Discrimination Act also requires a court to take multiple discrimination into account when determining the level of compensation.[114] No higher sanctions exist in Bulgaria but a different procedure is used—multiple discrimination cases are heard by a five-person panel instead of the usual three.

The Czech Republic provides an interesting example of how the sanction for intersectional discrimination could be approached. In response to cases of involuntary sterilisation of Roma women during the Communist period, the Czech courts provided a monetary award, importantly also stressing that such financial compensation was only symbolic. CZK 200,000 (approx €8,000) was awarded in one case and just CZK 150,000 (approx €6,000) in a second case where a woman's ovaries were unnecessarily surgically removed by doctors without her informed consent. More significant was the response of the Czech Government, which issued

[112] *Brown v District of Columbia* Case No 12-799 11.
[113] AD 2011 No 13 AD 2011 No 13, *The Equality Ombudsman v Municipality of Helsingborg*, Judgement 16 of February 2011.
[114] Croatia Anti-Discrimination Act 2008, Reg. No.: 71-05-03/1-08-2.

official apologies for the sterilisations and in 2009 passed a Decree[115] expressing deep concern at these unlawful sterilisations. These actions were based on recommendations by the Committee against Torture of the Governmental Council for Human Rights.[116] Such a multi-level response may be the correct approach to remedy intersectional discrimination. The state response is an acceptance of social responsibility that challenges the stigmatisation of Roma and begins the process for the creation of a new norm.

It is hard to think of a sanction that would be appropriate in the case of *Baylis-Flannery*.[117] As in Sweden, damages were awarded for each violated protected ground, despite the fact that the case was intersectional. She was awarded $25,000 in general damages for sex discrimination, sexual solicitation and harassment, and reprisal, and $10,000 in general damages for racial discrimination and racial harassment. Is this enough? It would be reasonable for her to not return to work for at least six months, thus as a practical matter compensation to at least cover her salary during this timeframe would be appropriate. However, she was only awarded $3,384 for lost wages and an additional $10,000 for mental anguish.

Beyond this, what should happen to the perceiver, in this case her employer who subjected her to such demeaning treatment? He was ordered to fulfil a series of public interest remedies but should he in addition be forced to give a public apology, perhaps paying for a full page spread in a daily newspaper, setting out his behaviour and acknowledging that it was discriminatory? This would at least force him to experience some amount of the humiliation that he caused Baylis-Flannery to feel. A public apology would also be appropriate in the cases of *Brown* and *Hewage*. A decision has to be made in each case as to whether the priority is punishment, rehabilitation or a combination of the two.

V. Conclusion

Throughout history, campaigns for racial and gender equality each incorporated a blindness—strategic or unconscious—to the other. As noted by Crenshaw, feminists, civil rights activists, legislators and courts shared a 'blind spot'.[118] This chapter considered the way in which the anti-stigma principle can help to create an anti-discrimination law that can address forms of intersectional discrimination that go beyond the single-dimension logic of anti-discrimination law.

115 Decree No 1424 of 23 November 2009.

116 Human Rights Council, Committee for Human Rights, motion on the unlawful sterilisations of women, available at http://www.vlada.cz/cz/ppov/rlp/cinnost-rady/zasedani-rady/zasedani-rady-dne-9--kvetna-2011-86162/.

117 n 97 above.

118 Crenshaw, 'Demarginalising the Intersection of Race and Sex' (n 6) 150.

Intersectionality is not only being interrogated in women's studies. The idea has taken root in academia and can now be found in disciplines across the natural and social sciences. For example, Irazabal and Huerta use intersectionality theory to investigate the multiple axes of disenfranchisements making young, black LGBTQ people invisible to urban planners in New York[119] or Bauer suggests that intersectionality theory has the potential to enrich population health research through improved attention to health and disease at different intersections of identity, social position, processes of oppression or privilege, and policies or institutional practices.[120]

One way of thinking about intersectionality is as a demand to recognise the sovereignty of black women.[121] Traditionally, equality law did not envisage a form of discrimination that could befall black women per se—it saw all women as one group and all blacks as one group: to use the well known phrase, all the women were white and all the blacks were male. It was to address this total eclipse of black women in anti-discrimination law that the idea of intersectional discrimination was conceived. However, intersectionality goes beyond claims for sovereignty. More importantly, it is an invitation to rethink our approach to understanding and tackling discrimination. It is an attempt to recognise the social complexity of discrimination in anti-discrimination law. Its articulation by critical race feminists working in the legal academy was not designed to create (as feared by the District Court in *Degraffenreid*) a never-ending new hierarchy of mutually exclusive categories nor to reify identity, but rather to disrupt dominant discourses, especially those that make certain forms of discrimination invisible. Intersectional discrimination is a challenge to move outside of the established paradigms to address the treatment of individuals and groups at the cusps of the current categories who are subject to structural discrimination, that is, discrimination arising from institutionalised norms and patterns of relations.

Synergy is at the core of intersectionality. Synergy emphasises the effects produced when two or more elements work together, just as red and yellow must work together to make the colour orange. It is therefore the central element that differentiates intersectionality from other forms of multiple discrimination—without it intersectionality becomes just another name for additive discrimination. The current structure of anti-discrimination law in the UK (and elsewhere) does not accommodate this synergy. The difficulty is epitomised in the response of senior judges in the Employment Appeal Tribunal in *Bahl*, the first intersectional case in the UK, which resembled sentiments expressed in 1977 by the US Court of Appeal in *Degraffenreid*–the possibility of combining two separate grounds would not be

[119] C Irazábal and C Huerta, 'Intersectionality and Planning at the Margins: LGBTQ Youth of Color in New York' (2015) *Gender, Place & Culture: A Journal of Feminist Geography*, DOI: 10.1080/0966369X.2015.1058755.

[120] GR Bauer, 'Incorporating Intersectionality Theory into Population Health Research Methodology: Challenges and the Potential to Advance Health Equity' (2014) 110 *Social Science & Medicine* 10.

[121] P Markell, *Bound by Recognition* (Oxford, Oxford University Press, 2003).

countenanced: the complainant could not sue for discrimination on two grounds *put together*. The single dimension approach has created silos which stand alone. Any attempt to combine them must begin with one and 'add' the other, leading inevitably to the 'mathematical' approach ultimately rejected by the US District Court in *Lam*.

The additive approach remains the most visible legal response to intersectional discrimination. Paradoxically, intersectionality has made the least progress in the discipline in which it first appeared—there is still no remedy for intersectional discrimination in anti-discrimination law. This is because synergy is hard to accommodate in the single dimension logic embedded in traditional anti-discrimination law. It is difficult to re-design anti-discrimination law with synergy as the norm rather than the exception. Statutory reorganisation and textual modification, as seen in the Equality Act 2010, are insufficient to address this. In order to change how it 'sees', anti-discrimination law needs a new rationale that centralises and normalises complexity and context.

If intersectional discrimination is an invitation to rethink the premises of anti-discrimination law to prioritise synergy, the anti-stigma principle offers a way to do this. This principle could provide the necessary amount of disruption to the current categories. The logic of stigma explains how a variety of individual attributes become impairments, not only disability.[122] Stigma also offers a way to address intersectional discrimination without slipping into additive discrimination, as it focuses on social systems that have demeaning outcomes for specific groups. Also, stigma helps anti-discrimination law see the complexity inherent in intersectional discrimination as the rule rather than the exception.

The anti-stigma principle could be useful in the UK, where the legislator is searching for a way to address intersectional discrimination in the new single equality framework. In addition, a stigma-based approach to discrimination law could be of use in European anti-discrimination law as it would accommodate the diverse empirical realities of discrimination in the different member states. Finally, disruption by the anti-stigma principle allows anti-discrimination law to tackle new forms of discrimination. This is the focus of the next chapter.

[122] SR Bagenstos, 'Subordination, stigma and "disability"' (2000) 86(3) *Virginia Law Review* 397, 436.

7

Legal Protection Against 'Fattism'

Anti-discrimination law has found greater public acceptance as social understanding of and support for the pursuit of equality has grown. The principle of equality for all is a popular idea in modern democracies. Thus there has in recent years been public support for the introduction of legal protection against discrimination for groups united, for example, by religious or political belief, sexual orientation and age. Most recently, the principle of non-discrimination has resulted in the possibility of same sex marriage. However, the situation is not perfect. First, there has been backlash, such as the law introduced in North Carolina to permit discrimination against persons identifying as LGBT.[1] Second, anti-discrimination law still does not protect all groups who face disadvantageous treatment: it says nothing for example in relation to discrimination because of appearance, such as weight or height, or social conditions such as class, or possession of a spent criminal conviction. The caring responsibilities of parents may be recognised, but those who care for elderly or other relatives are not protected from discrimination.[2]

A very important question is therefore who anti-discrimination law should protect—which groups and individuals should be the subjects of anti-discrimination law? As argued in Chapter 2, this question can no longer be answered by recourse to the idea of immutability: of the protected characteristics in the Equality Act 2010, some are immutable but others are mutable, and change over time. Dignity is also too vague: dignity can be impaired for a number of reasons, but should all of those reasons be covered by anti-discrimination law? A clear answer to this question is important because anti-discrimination law may lose credibility if it is unclear why some forms of different treatment are not protected as unlawful discrimination. Likewise, it may lose its purpose if coverage is extended to make it universal. It is therefore important to the continued success of this form of law for protection to be selective and for the public to understand what informs that selection.

This chapter will discuss the extent to which the anti-stigma principle can fulfil this task. It will argue that the anti-stigma principle can provide a logic for identifying legitimate beneficiaries of anti-discrimination law. The principle can be used to determine what anti-discrimination law sees, that is, to identify where anti-discrimination should be active. Individuals and groups that are demeaned

[1] JM Katz and E Eckholm, 'Anti-Gay Laws Bring Backlash in Mississippi and North Carolina', *New York Times* (5 April 2016, online edition).

[2] *Hainsworth v Ministry of Defence* [2014] EWCA Civ 763.

due to a single or a set of characteristics can become visible through this principle. This principle, it will be argued, will allow anti-discrimination law to address forms of discriminatory behaviour that were far from the minds of the diplomats at the United Nations in 1946. Furthermore, the anti-stigma principle can provide a rationale to explain to current and future generations why some forms of demeaning treatment remain beyond the bounds of anti-discrimination law.

Use of the anti-stigma principle would not incorporate a completely new approach to discrimination law—immutability is, after all, a part of stigma—but on the contrary it would provide a rationale for its expansion which disrupts but does not destroy the existing framework. Not all stigma should be protected—as will be seen, being stigmatised per se is not enough to warrant protection under anti-discrimination law—thus additional factors would have to be considered to determine which stigma warrant legal protection.

This chapter begins with an explanation of how the anti-stigma principle can be applied to guide legislators when deciding whether a trait, condition or attribute should be protected by anti-discrimination law. The principle focuses on stigmatisation as a process and application of this process can guide legislators to the decision as to whether legal protection should be applied. In addition to context, the principle pays attention to the character and consequences of stigmatisation. It does not therefore offer ready-made categories, but rather a series of questions which will guide the creation of categories in anti-discrimination law that are meaningful to the context in which the law is set. This process is then applied to a stigmatised attribute—weight—to demonstrate how it works by considering whether legal protection in the Equality Act 2010 should be extended to make this the tenth protected characteristic.

I. The Application of the Anti-stigma Principle

The anti-stigma principle offers a simple and sustainable way to explain why law is used to prevent and protect some individuals from discrimination yet not others. It can be used to determine when a particular trait, attribute or condition is protected by anti-discrimination law, offering a practical method that is flexible without being flaccid: it allows the law to reflect upon discrimination in the twenty-first century but also to reject frivolous ideas regarding discrimination. It does this in a way that has many advantages over the current rationales for anti-discrimination law.

First, the principle takes anti-discrimination law beyond identity and individualism. Stigmas are by definition contextual: they are socially determined and maintained, and to focus on them is to prioritise social meanings.[3] The anti-stigma principle therefore necessitates reflection upon the role of society in discrimination. It widens the view of discrimination law to situate the

[3] E Goffman, *Stigma: Notes on the Management of Spoiled Identity* (London, Penguin, 1990) 14.

individual in society and analyse the role of society in everyday discrimination. The anti-stigma principle shifts attention to social responsibility as well as individual responsibility. Restoration of the link between discrimination and society is important because it firmly anchors discrimination law: discrimination law separated from society can lose its rationale, and measures to remedy past injustice or secure future equality are easy to attack as 'reverse discrimination'.

Second, it highlights the idea of discrimination as the consequence of a process. There is nothing natural about stigma—a 'mark' is given meaning rather than having any inherent meaning of its own. This process reminds us that meanings are made and thus can be unmade. Third, it legitimates the use of law beyond the permanent/produced dichotomy: it includes immutable characteristics but is not limited to them. Fourth, it is flexible enough to facilitate both single dimension and intersectional discrimination: stigma can travel alone, but also in company, hence the anti-stigma principle accommodates intersectional as well as single dimension discrimination. It therefore reconstructs two aspects of the vision of anti-discrimination law—*who* it sees as well as *how* it sees. Fifth, it enables provision of legal protection for both historical and contemporary injustices, to support remedial goals as well as tackling current discrimination. Finally, as it is also sensitive to context, the anti-stigma principle can be applied in many places (for example throughout the EU) without needing to be uniform.

The process of stigmatisation draws upon the work of critical stigma scholars discussed in earlier chapters. The sociology of stigmatisation put forward by Link and Phelan[4] lists a series of components that converge: an arbitrary element and deliberate labelling by powerful parties in society, followed by stereotyping that separates persons with the element from others, and reduces their status making them targets of discrimination. Herek[5] lists key characteristics of stigma such as embeddedness, endurance and negative evaluation by the powerful who have means of control over the powerless (who have no access to such means). Hannem and Bruckert[6] stress not only low social power but also low interpersonal status: stigmatisation is not just a process of what people do to each other (interpersonal power) but also what society entertains and allows people to do (institutional power). It cannot be 'wished away',[7] thus is inescapable through individual action alone.

Putting together the ideas of these scholars, the following ten questions would be used to determine the stigmatised characteristics protected in antidiscrimination law:

1. Is the 'mark' arbitrary or does it have some meaning in and of itself?
2. Is the mark used as a social label?

[4] BG Link and JC Phelan, 'Conceptualizing Stigma' (2001) 27 *Annual Review of Sociology* 377.

[5] GM Herek, 'Thinking About AIDS and Stigma—A Psychologists Perspective' (2002) 30 *Journal of Law, Medicine and Ethics* 595.

[6] S Hannem and C Bruckert (eds), *Stigma Re-visited: Re-examining the Mark* (University of Ottowa Press, 2012), 12.

[7] K Plummer, *Sexual Stigma* (London, Routledge and Kegan Paul, 1975) 26.

3. Does this label have a long history? How embedded is it in society?
4. Can the label be 'wished away'?
5. Is the label used to stereotype those possessing it?
6. Does the stereotype reduce the humanity of those who are its targets? Does it evoke a punitive response?
7. Do these targets have low social power and low interpersonal status?
8. Do these targets suffer discrimination as a result?
9. Do the targets suffer exclusion?
10. Is their access to key resources blocked?

These 10 questions can be a useful guide to identify those stigmas that should be protected by law. Stigma-based anti-discrimination law would therefore focus on the deepest, longest, punitive stigmas that have a corrosive impact on social relations by constructing and imposing dominant negative beliefs on weaker groups and punishing those stigmatised by exclusion from key resources such as employment, education, healthcare and housing as well as political power. In order to illustrate the type of stigmas that might therefore be included in anti-discrimination law according to the anti-stigma principle, this test will now be applied to the example of weight discrimination.

II. Weight-based Stigma and Discrimination

The next time you are in a restaurant or waiting room, cinema or concert hall, airport or bus terminal, train, car or airplane, think for a moment about entrances and checkpoints where there are turnstiles, or 'attached seating' (where the seat is attached at a fixed distance from the table, or to the seat next to it)—these are very difficult to use comfortably if you are larger than the 'norm'. Many of these are too small for bigger or fat bodies. 'Fat' is relative, but can be determined according to the Body Mass Index (BMI).[8] Overweight and obese people have a number of difficulties with public accommodations. Airline seating is notoriously small, often with neither adequate leg room nor sufficiently large seats, even for people of 'normal' size. South West Airlines[9]—has a long-standing policy that 'people of size' have to pay for an additional seat. No guidelines are given to determine when

[8] The Body Mass Index (BMI) was created in 1830s by Belgian Adolphe Quetelet. It has four categories—underweight (below 18.5), normal (18.5–24.9), overweight (25–29.9), and obese (30 and over). These standards to evaluate body weight were developed by the International Obesity Task Force (IOTF) of the WHO, supported by funds from major pharmaceutical companies.

[9] See B Higginbotham, 'A Super-sized Problem' (2003) *International Travel Law Journal* 84; B Bolton, 'The Battle For The Armrest Reaches New Heights: The Air Carriers Access Act and the Issues Surrounding the Airlines' Policy of Requiring Obese Passengers to Purchase Additional Tickets' (2004) 69 *Journal of Air Law and Commerce* 803; MD O'Hara, 'Please Weight to Be Seated': Recognizing Obesity as a Disability to Prevent Discrimination in Public Accommodations' (1996) 17 *Whittier Law Review* 895.

this will be the case but the policy treats a large person the same as a large musical instrument. Northwest Airlines, American Airlines and Continental Airlines have similar policies—fat passengers must purchase a second seat at the same price as the first. Beyond seating, airplane bathrooms are tiny, making them difficult to use for people of size as well as people with disabilities.

In 2004, the Organization for Economic Cooperation and Development (OECD) ranked Britain's obesity problem as the worst in Europe and the third-worst in the world, behind Mexico and the USA. In 2015, the UK Chief Medical Officer Sally Davies warned that obesity threatens the health of women and babies[10] and stated that obesity should be a national priority, with action taken across society to prevent it. According to current figures, 61.9% of adults in England are overweight or obese.[11] Obesity is apparently also increasing in children: government figures from 2002[12] stated that almost 17% of children aged 2 to 15 years are obese;[13] this had risen to 28% in 2015.[14] We are repeatedly told that 'obesity' has now risen to epidemic proportions around the world at an alarming rate. US Surgeon General Richard Carmona described obesity as a worse 'terror within' than terrorist attacks.[15] Being fat is therefore regarded as a problem in the public mind and as something to be feared and avoided, especially if you are a woman. Should weight also be a protected ground in anti-discrimination law?

A. Applying the Anti-stigma Principle

i. Is the 'Mark' Arbitrary or Does It Have Some Meaning in and of Itself?

The BMI standards are supposedly objective but in fact can change—from 1980–2000, the upper limit for the overweight category was reduced, which meant that more people fell into the 'obese' category. This indicates the arbitrariness of standards for body size—body size per se has no inherent meaning and there is no universal explanation of why people are shaped as they are. Beyond this, size is also no guide to individual ability or skills—it has no meaning in and of itself although, as will be discussed below, society often imputes negative meanings to

[10] S Boseley, 'Obesity endangers health of women and babies, warns UK's chief medical officer' *The Guardian* (11 December 2015).

[11] Department of Health Policy Paper, '2010 to 2015 government policy: obesity and healthy eating' (updated 8 May 2015).

[12] Health Survey for England 2002.

[13] 'A 3-year old child dies from heart failure brought on because she was so overweight', *The Guardian* (27 May 2004) 13; 'Children will die before their parents'—warning by Commons Health Select Committee', *The Guardian* (27 May 2004) 7.

[14] Department of Health Policy Paper, '2010 to 2015 government policy: obesity and healthy eating' (updated 8 May 2015).

[15] A Kirkland, *Fat Rights: Dilemma of Difference and Personhood* (New York, NYU Press, 2008) ix.

being fat. In particular, size is not an indicator of fitness or health, although this is the main reason for the official interest in the overweight and the obese.

As far as the government is concerned, size reduces health and therefore increases costs; in particular, for the public purse and employers, weight is a risk. There is undeniably a correlation between certain conditions and corpulence: according to medical experts, fat people are more prone to heart disease, strokes, high blood pressure, diabetes, chronic depression and many other life threatening conditions. Yet this does not mean that every large person will inevitably suffer from any of these conditions.

The current fat epidemic is a complex phenomenon caused by more than excess energy intake and low energy expenditure. Consumption of too much food, too much rich food or too much fast food, in conjunction with a sedentary lifestyle—desk jobs and low-active leisure activities—is just one way to become fat. Research suggests that obesity arises from a complex interaction of non-behavioural reasons including environmental, genetic, psychological, physiological, metabolic, socioeconomic, lifestyle and cultural factors.[16]

Fatness can be the result of genetic or biological problems such as malfunctioning thyroid or pituitary glands. An example is Prader Willi syndrome, a rare genetic disorder where sufferers have a constant desire to eat and a lifelong battle to control their weight. About 70% inherit it from their father and 30% from the mother. It can go undiagnosed and left untreated sufferers can eat themselves to death—a 13-year-old Californian girl who died in 1997 weighing 49 stone was thought to be an undiagnosed Prader Willi case.[17] Also, medication can promote weight gain[18] as can sleep deprivation—tired bodies produce too little leptin, a hormone that regulates appetite, resulting in cravings for sweet and salty foods.[19]

Experts also suggest that a metabolism that is designed to cope with undernutrition cannot quickly adapt to normal levels of nutrition: studies have found that mothers who experienced starvation during pregnancy tend to have children metabolically predisposed to retain fat. Thus if the mother comes from a poor community but the child grows up in a culture where food is abundant, the food environment conflicts with the biological metabolism and results in weight gain. This may explain the predominance of obesity in some migrant communities.

The 'pain of poverty'[20] is both a cause and consequence of overweight and obesity. Poor families suffer from what is known as 'shantytown syndrome'—overeating as a response to uncertain patterns of labour and irregular income

[16] D Crawford and RW Jeffery (eds), *Obesity Prevention and Public Health* (Oxford, Oxford University Press, 2005).

[17] J Laurance, 'The boy who can't stop eating', *The Independent Review* (19 October 2004) 6.

[18] Weight gain is a side effect of some medication used to manage the menopause, for example.

[19] D Rapoport MD, director of the sleep program at New York University School of Medicine. Reported in *Health on Parade*, 28 August 2005), available at http://www.anred.com/obese.html.

[20] G Critser, *Fat Land: How Americans Became the Fattest People in the World* (New York, Houghton Mifflin, 2003) 111.

which make the source of tomorrow's meals unknown.[21] Added to which, the poor tend to live in neighbourhoods full of cheap food restaurants and devoid of safe places to play and exercise. Between 1965 and 1985, the average number of hours spent watching TV for Americans aged 18–64 went from 10.4 hrs per week to 15 hours per week.[22] A study by the Centre for Disease Control in 1994 discovered that the percentage of white girls who reported watching four or more hours of TV a day was 15.6; in comparison, the percentage of black girls was 43.1 and Mexican American girls was 28.3. Parental concerns about crime explained this—parents in minority neighbourhoods were 'twice as likely as white parents to report that their neighbourhoods were dangerous' and they regarded it as better for children to watch TV than get shot or molested.[23] In urban environments ravaged by drugs and violence, food acts as a safe shelter and the television a shield from dangerous streets. In particular, black men avoid running on the streets for fear of being mistaken for a criminal.[24] As Critser says, on one level success with weight loss is not just a triumph of will but a triumph of an 'economic and social class' which can afford regular visits to a physician, has access to safe streets and a safe park in which to jog and walk, has the support of friends who share values of thinness, can afford healthy home cooked food, and has access to books and medical journals about health.[25]

More generally, the 'nutrition transition' and the loss of 'nutritional self-determination' has contributed to growing waistlines. People are not necessarily eating more:[26] it is accepted that the level of fats and sugars in the everyday diet has risen. The 'nutrition transition' has led to lower consumption of fibre, complex carbohydrates, fruits and vegetables and an increase in the ingestion of fat, cholesterol, sugar and other refined carbohydrates. International food supplies now contain more fat[27] and added sweeteners, and we eat more animal-source foods (meat, fish and milk) than cereals and grains.[28] The addition of fats and sugars to the food supply, especially cheap sweeteners derived from corn (high fructose corn syrup or HFCS)[29], has been identified as a major contributor to the

[21] Critser, *Fat Land* (n 20) 130–31.

[22] LJ Harnack and KH Schmitz, 'The Role of Nutrition and Physical Activity in the Obesity Epidemic' in Crawford and Jeffrey, *Obesity Prevention* (n 16) 30.

[23] Critser, *Fat Land* (n 20) 73.

[24] DK Cassell and DH Gleaves, *The Encyclopaedia of Obesity and Eating Disorders*, Third Edition (New York, Infobase Publishing, 2009) 15.

[25] Critser, *Fat Land* (n 20) 2.

[26] K Fox, 'Underactivity or Over-Nutrition?' in L Voss and T Wilkin (eds), *Adult Obesity: A Paediatric Challenge* (London, Taylor and Francis, 2003) 14.

[27] From 1991–1996/7: global production of vegetable fats and oils (soybean, sunflower, rapeseed, palm, groundnut) rose from 60–71 million metric tons.

[28] BM Popkin, 'The Implications of the Nutrition Transition for Obesity in the Developing World' (2001) 131(3) *Journal of Nutrition* 8715.

[29] Critser, *Fat Land* (n 20) 11–12. The oil equivalent of HFCS is palm oil, also known as 'tree lard' or 'axle grease', which was transformed in mid 1970s to a viable commercial fat that could be used to fry chips and bake, as well as increase the shelf life of ready made foodstuffs. It was in plentiful supply and therefore cheap, but a highly saturated fat.

obesity epidemic.[30] HFCS is used in frozen foods, baked goods, products with a long shelf life (including those in vending machines) and sweet drinks: by the mid-1980s Coke and Pepsi were using 100% HFCS instead of the 50% sucrose / 50% fructose used previously.[31]

HFCS is popular because it is cheap to produce and six times sweeter than cane sugar. However, the economic advantages of HFCS—farmers have a market for their corn and consumers have cheap basic foodstuffs—need to be offset against the health costs. HFCS tricks the liver into releasing insulin into the blood stream, in preparation for cells to absorb the nutrients contained in natural cane sugar. When no nutrients are discovered, two things happen: first, the released insulin remains in the blood. Second, insulin resistance develops, because to avoid being 'tricked' by nutritionless corn sugar, cells lose their responsiveness to it, resulting in a surfeit of sugar in the blood. This is the scenario of type 2 diabetes: too much insulin in the body and too much sugar in the blood.[32] Diabetes can lead to other illnesses: high blood pressure, gallstones, coronary artery disease, hypertension and stroke.

Thus the true price of cheap 'value' meals is a dangerous nutritional transition. The pleasure of fat and sugar-loaded convenience foods also results in loss of 'nutritional self-determination', or the ability to control the amount of non-nutritional substances (fats and sugar) that we ingest.[33] Loss of nutritional control is an element of the 'obesogenic' environment in which we live—a world flooded with fat-ridden and sugar-laden foods, labour saving devices, motorised transport and sedentary work and leisure activities. Given this, it is unsurprising that more people are finding it hard to stay thin. Some profit from this, selling diet foods, running health centres and making television commercials. Heymbrand suggests that 'obesity is a tremendous economic engine … built into the very fabric of our economic system' which makes it 'an essentially irreversible state'.[34]

It seems therefore that our approach to obesity needs to 'acknowledge properly the influence of an obesogenic environment and not be based on a misconceived notion of will power'.[35] As argued by Dr Susan Jebb of the Medical Research Council, 'the notion of obesity simply being a product of personal over-indulgence has to be abandoned for good'.[36]

[30] RW Jeffery and JA Linde, 'Evolving Environmental Factors in the Obesity Epidemic' in D Crawford, RW Jeffery, K Ball and J Brug (eds) *Obesity Epidemiology: From Aetiology to Public Health* (Oxford, Oxford University Press, 2010).

[31] Critser, *Fat Land* (n 20) 18.

[32] Critser, *Fat Land* (n 20) 134–37; Wilkin in Voss and Wilkin, *Adult Obesity* (n 25) 39.

[33] Critser, *Fat Land* (n 20) 33.

[34] GA Bray, 'Coherent, Preventive and Management Strategies for Obesity' in Ciba Foundation Symposium, *The Origins and Consequences of Obesity* (Chicester, England, John Wiley and Sons, 1996) 253.

[35] Hill in Voss and Wilkin, *Adult Obesity* (n 26) 61.

[36] B Butland, S Jebb, PK McPherson, S Thomas, J Mardell and V Parry, *Tackling Obesities: Future Choices* (London, Government Office for Science, 2007), available at https://www.gov.uk/government/uploads/system/uploads/attachment_data/file/287937/07-1184x-tackling-obesities-future-choices-report.pdf and http://news.bbc.co.uk/1/hi/health/7047244.stm.

Governments have thus far done little to protect individuals from the nutritional transition and loss of nutritional autonomy: in Britain, £70m is spent on promoting foods that are high in fat, salt and sugar while the Department of Health has a total budget of £750,000;[37] in the USA the food industry spends about '\$50 per person per year to publicise food products whilst the USDA spends about \$1.50 per person per year for all types of nutritional education'.[38]

ii. Is the Mark Used as a Social Label?

Sadly, despite the obesogenic environment, the stigma associated with overweight and obesity is so intense that many people fear becoming fat. In one study, 25% of women and 17% of men said they would sacrifice three or more years of their lives to be thin. Some said they smoke cigarettes in an effort to remain thin or reject the advice that they quit smoking because they fear they will gain weight.[39] Children associate fatness with low intelligence, social alienation and unattractiveness; adults see the obese as undisciplined, inactive, unappealing and with emotional or psychological impairments. Research by Brylinsky and Moore found that by age 9–10 children have negative perceptions of the chubby body type and a favourable perception of the 'average' body.[40] One study found that people display more negative attitudes toward overweight employees than toward ex-felons or ex-mental illness patients.[41] Fat people are labelled sloppy, dirty, liars, stupid, lonely and of course, lazy.[42]

iii. Does this Label Have a Long History? How Embedded Is It in Society?

Fattism has an changing history. In Stone Age and Ancient Greek societies 'rotund' women were considered beautiful; during Christianity, gluttony was considered a sin; yet by the time of the Renaissance, largeness was again considered beautiful.[43] Magna Mater, the Earth Goddess had 'a short, round body, rolls of fat around her waist, and large, drooping breasts'.[44]

At the start of the twentieth century, corpulence was again fashionable for men and women. Byrd writes that 'buxom, sound and sensuous' Lillian Russell who weighed over 200 lbs, was the '*sine qua non* of prosperous, well-heeled American

[37] S Leather, 'Social Inequalities, Nutrition and Obesity' in Voss and Wilkin, *Adult Obesity* (n 26) 56.

[38] Jeffery and Linde, 'Evolving Environmental Factors' (n 30) 64.

[39] RM Puhl and KD Brownell, 'Psychosocial Origins of Obesity Stigma: Toward Changing a Powerful and Pervasive Bias' (2003) 4 *Obesity Review* 213.

[40] JA Brylinsky and JC Moore, 'The Identification of Body Build Stereotypes in Young Children' (1994) 28 *Journal Research in Personality* 170. See also J Wardle, C Volz and C Golding, 'Social Variation in Attitudes to Obesity in Children' (1995) 19 *International Journal of Obesity* 562.

[41] See http://www.obesity.org/discrimination/employment.shtml.

[42] SW Kirkpatrick, and DM Sanders, 'Body Image Stereotypes: A Developmental Comparison' (1978) 132 *Journal of Genetic Psychology* 87.

[43] O'Hara, 'Please Weight To Be Seated' (n 9).

[44] JC Chrisler, '"Why Can't You Control Yourself?" Fat Should Be a Feminist Issue' (2012) 66 *Sex Roles* 608.

beauty', admired as much for her robust appetite as her sparkling diamonds. The Statue of Liberty also demonstrates that there was a time when avoirdupois was a sign of health while thinness was seen as ugly—it represented poverty, frailty and ill health. Visible bone structure suggested the 'taint of both manual labor and low socio-economic class, two things the well-to-do American trencherman of the late nineteenth century wanted to be defined against'.[45] The 'orgy of excess' only ended with the start of World War II, when women's bodies in particular suddenly became the targets of the new cult of thinness. Fat became ugly, an indication of laziness, irresponsibility, sloppiness and a lack of self-control except, Byrd argues, in the case of black women; even in the twenty-first century, America retains vestiges of the 'mammy' Aunt Chloe, the ever nurturing, God-fearing full bodied black woman whom every child can trust.[46]

iv. Can the Label Be 'Wished Away'?

It is impossible to wish the label away: 'The notion that fat is bad is thus extended to the notion that fat is bad for you—and then, by further extension, that fat people themselves are bad.'[47] Fattism is so entrenched that it is easier for legislators to pass bills protecting food manufacturers rather than their often ill-informed consumers: by the end of 2004, few of the over 110 bills designed to tackle weight discrimination in America had become law; in contrast, by March 2005, 15 US states had passed laws banning obesity lawsuits[48] such as New Mexico's 'Right to Eat Enchiladas' Act.[49] Weight stigma has also been described as a vicious cycle: 'weight stigma begets weight gain'.[50]

v. Is the Label Used to Stereotype Those Possessing it?

There are many collective beliefs held about persons who are overweight and obese. The assumption is usually made that weight is always due to overeating and lack of exercise. This type of behavioural understanding of weight is encouraged by official campaigns that stress healthy eating and lifestyles.[51] The more obesity is attributed to individual behaviour, the greater anti-fat prejudice becomes.[52] Such campaigns implicitly condone public vilification of the overweight and discrimination on the

[45] S Byrd, 'Civil Rights and the "Twinkie" Tax: The 900-Pound Gorilla in the War on Obesity' (2004) 65 *Louisiana Law Review* 303.

[46] Byrd, 'Twinkie Tax' (n 45). The other black female stereotypes are the innocent, round-eyed vulnerable 'Topsy', the promiscous 'Peaches' and the emasculating matriarch 'Caldonia'.

[47] Chrisler, 'Why Can't You Control Yourself?' (n 44).

[48] Fried in Voss and Wilkin, *Adult Obesity* (n 26) 267 and 279.

[49] Senate Bill 291 introduced by Steve Komadina, 47th legislature, Session 1, 2005.

[50] AJ Tomiyama, 'Weight Stigma is Stressful. A Review of Evidence for the Cyclic Obesity/Weight-Based Stigma Model' (2014) 82 *Appetite* 8.

[51] See for example the British Health Department's three-year 'Change4Life' healthy eating campaign, available at http://news.bbc.co.uk/1/hi/health/7791820.stm.

[52] Hill in Voss and Wilkin, *Adult Obesity* (n 26) 70.

basis of size: if fat is a result of overeating and lack of exercise, then fat people are lazy and deserve neither legal assistance nor sympathy but retribution and punishment. Yet, as explained above, the behavioural focus must be reviewed: it is questionable that the obesity epidemic has arisen because people have 'deliberately decided to gain weight'.[53]

Stereotypes abound, especially for fat black women. Shaw[54] argues that in the USA, fatness and blackness have a similar and complex relationship with the female body, as the twenty-first century ideal of womanhood is not only slim but also white. Thus according to modern aesthetic standards, both size and skin colour undermine her viability to be accepted as a woman. Both characteristics (blackness and fatness) necessitate 'a degree of erasure' in order to render these women 'viable entities by Western aesthetic standards.'[55] Only the capacity for mothering restores the viability of the fat black woman in the western social imaginary—her big body 'represents an overabundance of maternal resources.'

vi. Does the Stereotype Reduce the Humanity of Those Who Are Its Targets? Does it evoke a punitive response?

People whose body size does not correspond to popular social norms of size are subjected to a number of stereotypes[56] and prejudices—'fattism' has been described as the 'last great acceptable prejudice'.[57] For example, in the workplace they must endure expectations of lower levels of performance: fat job applicants are evaluated as less capable, being viewed as lazy, lacking in social skills, unable to get along with customers and colleagues, and un-intelligent. Employers associate fat employees with higher costs (higher insurance premiums, greater absenteeism, costs of special accommodations, such as having to purchase new desks and chairs for their use). Employers may also discriminate in order to please others. Even medical professionals 'view obese patients as less self-disciplined, less compliant and more annoying than non-obese ones' and are likely to have less patience and desire to help them.[58] And there is no escape at home—family members are reportedly the most regular tormenters, with 47% of overweight girls and 34% of overweight boys reporting weight bias from families.[59] Almost every stereotype is negative: undisciplined, unmotivated, weak-willed, incompetent, emotional, unattractive

[53] Hill in Voss and Wilkin, *Adult Obesity* (n 26) 69.

[54] AE Shaw, *The Embodiment of Disobedience: Fat Black Women's Unruly Political Bodies* (Lanham, MD, Lexington Books, 2006).

[55] Shaw, *Embodiment of Disobedience* (n 54) 1.

[56] E Rothblum, C Miller, and B Garbutt, 'Stereotypes of Obese Female Job Applicants' (1988) 7 *International Journal of Eating Disorders* 277.

[57] R Pelling, 'Of course it's ok to call another woman a Hobnob-guzzling, lazy lard arse', *Independent on Sunday* (18 September 2005).

[58] S Flint, 'Obesity Stigma: Prevalence and Impact in Healthcare' (2015) 1 *British Journal of Obesity* 1.

[59] R Puhl, '*Bias, Discrimination, and Obesity: A Social Injustice and Public Health Priority*', available at http://www.phila.gov/health/pdfs/BiasDiscriminationandObesityASocialInjusticeandPublicHealth-Priority_4_16_11.pdf.

and unlikable.[60] The only positive stereotype imagines fat people to be funny and warm. This is ironic, as the social rejection encountered by many overweight people can lead to depression. Being a target of weight discrimination can also result in anxiety, self-neglect and thoughts of suicide.[61]

vii. *Do These Targets Have Low Social Power and Low Interpersonal Status?*

There are a number of fat celebrities and public figures—most are white men such as comedian James Cordon and Conservative MP Eric Pickles. Most fat people however endure everyday public disdain and are often the target of overt discrimination, open ridicule and public humiliation, even apparently being spat at on the street.[62] When a journalist donned a 'fat suit' she was not only treated differently, but also reported feeling different, because she took up more public space and sensed resentment for this.[63] 'Anti-fat' attitudes are prevalent in the home and society, even amongst stigmatised communities,[64] and permeate the workplace.[65] Size reduces work opportunities and life chances. Being overweight is bad for job prospects and career: society in general and employers in particular are 'fat phobic'. One study of over 10,000 people found that '[b]oth men and women who had been overweight were less likely to have married, had completed fewer years of education, and had lower household incomes, lower self-esteem, and higher rates of poverty that those who had not been overweight'.[66]

Fat black women are seen to represent a 'domestic caretaker', always ready and available in the 'ultimate state of subservience to whiteness' to nurture those who contribute to her economic oppression. Her fatness symbolises maternal strength and social weakness: 'an infinite reservoir of maternal dedication, suggesting an *inability* to be oppressed since their supply of strength, love, and other emotional resources can never be depleted'. Beyond this, Shaw asserts that the link between fat and motherhood 'implies an inclination, if not need, to serve as caretaker, which in turn implies a sadomasochistic element of desire and fulfilment in black womens experience of economic abuse and marginalisation, and mitigates moral responsibility on the part of her abusers'.[67]

[60] Chrisler, 'Why Can't You Control Yourself?' (n 44).

[61] JL Pomeranz and RM Puhl, 'New Developments in the Law for Obesity Discrimination Protection' (2013) 21(3) *Obesity* 469.

[62] Pelling, 'Hobnob-guzzling, lazy lard arse' (n 57).

[63] O'Hara, 'Please Weight To Be Seated' (n 9).

[64] J Whitesel, *Fat Gay Men: Girth, Mirth, and the Politics of Stigma* (New York, NYU Press, 2014).

[65] S Solovay, Tipping the Scales of Justice 2000; R Pool, *Fat: Fighting the Obesity Epidemic* (Oxford, Oxford University Press, 2001); JB Korn, 'Fat' (1997) 77(1) *Boston University Law Review* 27.

[66] SL Gortmaker, A Must, JM Perrin, AM Sobol and W Dietz, 'Social and Economic Consequences of Overweight in Adolescence and Young Adulthood' (1993) 329 *New England Journal of Medicine* 1008–12, 1036–37.

[67] Shaw, *Embodiment of Disobedience* (n 54) 21.

viii. Do These Targets Suffer Discrimination as a Result?

Obesity is a public health issue but 'fattism' also affects those who are just overweight. Weight discrimination[68] is prevalent—the general public, government and employers are fatphobic—and according to a 2015 study, thriving with impunity.[69] Negative meanings associated with weight influence decision making at many levels, leading to discrimination. Weight discrimination follows the same pattern as other prohibited forms: stereotype, stigma, prejudice and discrimination resulting in adverse outcomes.[70] For example, Jennifer Portnick who was 5'8" tall and weighed just over 17 stone (240 lbs) was rejected for training as an exercise teacher just because of her size. She had been doing high impact aerobics for 15 years and due to her impressive stamina was invited to audition to be a certified 'Jazzercise' instructor. However, the assessors focused on her weight rather than her fitness—they encouraged her to trim down, wanting her to look 'fit', that is, thin; fat looked unhealthy.[71]

Empirical studies indicate that there is a prevalence of weight discrimination in employment. Fat women are also refused jobs and promotion in roles that they have successfully demonstrated competence. For example, Bonnie Cook, who was 5'3" and weighed over 23 stone (329 lbs), was refused a contract to continue in her post because, despite her excellent employment record, her employer assumed that her weight would prevent her doing the job properly. Likewise, Mary Nedder, who was 5'6" and weighed 26 stone (375 lbs) was sacked as a teacher because the College President believed that her size reduced her ability to teach. Promotions are also sometimes withheld because of weight. Deborah Marks weighed 19 stone (270 lbs) and had been named 'Telemarketer of the Year' by her employer. Yet she was refused a client-facing role as a sales representative, and when she complained her supervisor told her to lose weight because presentation was extremely important.

Fat women can be refused employment in jobs for which they are otherwise qualified. Arazella Manuel applied for a job as a shuttle bus driver with Texas Bus Lines, taking visitors to Houston between hotels and the airports. She passed all qualifying tests and the physical exam. She was 5'7" tall and weighed 24 stone (345 lbs) with normal blood pressure and had no health problems. Nonetheless

[68] E Rothblum, P Brand, C Miller and H Oetien, 'The Relationship between Obesity, Employment Discrimination, and Employment-Related Victimization' (1990) 37(3) *Journal of Vocational Behavior* 251.

[69] JP Shinall, 'Occupational Characteristics and the Obesity Wage Penalty' (2015) Vanderbilt Law and Economics Research Paper No 16-12; Vanderbilt Public Law Research Paper No 16-23. See also http://www.xojane.com/issues/weight-discrimination-at-work.

[70] BM Wolfe, 'Presidential Address—Obesity Discrimination: What Can We Do?' (2012) 8 *Surgery for Obesity and Related Diseases* 495–500, 496.

[71] K Horner, 'A Growing Problem: Why The Federal Government Needs To Shoulder The Burden In Protecting Workers From Weight Discrimination' (2005) 54 *Catholic University Law Review* 589; O Poole, 'Victory for "too fat" fitness instructor', available at http://www.telegraph.co.uk/news/worldnews/northamerica/usa/1393682/Victory-for-too-fat-fitness-instructor.html.

the doctor refused to pass her because of her weight, as he was concerned that her size would prevent her from helping passengers in an emergency. Texas Buslines therefore withdrew its conditional offer of employment.[72]

Catherine McDermott, another large woman, applied to Xerox for a job as a business systems consultant. After her obligatory pre-employment medical examination, the Director of Health Services for Xerox advised her would-be manager that she posed a long-term financial risk to the company: he advised that over the long term she would have a high level of absenteeism, and would be a high user of disability benefits, medical care plans and life insurance.[73] Xerox therefore refused to hire her. Similarly, Joyce English, who was 5'8" and 24 stone (341 lbs), applied for a job as a Customer Service Representative at the Philadelphia Electric Company (PECO). She also passed all pre-employment tests but the examining physician refused to certify her for employment due to her size. Again, it was argued she was at risk of medical problems leading to high absenteeism, low productivity and other costs to the company.[74]

Studies demonstrate that overweight candidates are less likely to be hired even if equally competent on job related tests as non-fat candidates. In a poll conducted in 2005, nearly 80% of 300 senior leaders in major companies acknowledged that there was a prejudice against fat people in business: more than two thirds agreed that 'fat people were seen as lacking in self-discipline and self-control, energy and drive'.[75] Routine discrimination on the grounds of size was also discovered by *Personnel Today* during a survey conducted in 2005.[76] The survey reported that corporations openly and regularly discriminate against the overweight. 2000 human resource personnel were asked to choose between two equally qualified job applicants, one fat and the other a 'normal weight': 93% cent chose the latter, only 7% the former; 12% said they would not employ 'fat' people in client-facing roles; 30% agreed that 'obesity is a valid medical reason for not employing a person'; 47% thought that obesity impeded employee output; and 11% thought obesity was a fair ground for dismissal.

Studies published by the American Obesity Association suggest that discrimination based on weight is far more common than discrimination based on personal characteristics such as sex. A study found that applicant weight explained 34.6% of the variance in hiring decisions, whereas sex explained only 10.6% of the variance.[77] Researchers have also found that 'if hired, persons who are obese are often assigned to non-visible jobs, receive more disciplinary actions, have their performance

[72] *EEOC v Texas Bus Lines*, 923 F. Supp. 965 (S.D.TX 1996), 971.

[73] *McDermott v Xerox Corp*, 102 A.D.2d 543 (1984), 544.

[74] *PECO v Pennsylvania Human Relations Commission and Joyce A English*, 68 Pa. Commw. 212 (1982), 228.

[75] N Jackson, 'When bigger isn't always better'. *The Independent*, 11 February 2007.

[76] See 'Obesity research: Fattism is the last bastion of employee discrimination' *Personnel Today* (25 October 2005), available at http://www.personneltoday.com/hr/obesity-research-fattism-is-the-last-bastion-of-employee-discrimination/.

[77] See n 40 above.

evaluated more negatively'[78] and according to a recent study, earn less when compared to non-obese employees.[79] Furthermore, employers judge overweight job applicants more harshly than those with a conviction or a history of mental illness. Overweight individuals are rated less desirable as subordinates, co-workers and bosses. Studies show that weight discrimination is indeed 'a widespread phenomenon that has a significant negative impact on the lives of untold individuals'.[80] It is evident at every phase of the employment cycle including: career counselling, selection, placement, compensation, promotion, discipline and discharge. Being 'slightly overweight, extremely overweight, or obese are all generally viewed in various employment contexts as less desirable than being average or thin'.[81]

ix. Do the Targets Suffer Exclusion?

Overweight and obese individuals suffer exclusion in employment, education, healthcare, access to public accommodations, goods and services. Empirical evidence shows that the impact of excess avoirdupois is worse for girls and women. A 14-year analysis of schoolchildren and their eventual prospects found that obese girls were likely to be trapped in low-earning jobs by the time that they are age 30.[82] Research has found that overweight and obese young adult women in the US and UK earn significantly less than non-overweight women or those with other chronic health problems. There is a 'wage penalty' for being overweight: being 13 pounds overweight was found to lower income by $9,000 per year.[83] Shinall found that every pound reduces the opportunity to work in a higher paid, public-facing position with high pay; those who push themselves to get these jobs anyway will likely earn an average of 5% less than their thinner peers.[84]

Fat women suffer more exclusion than fat men—overweight women are evaluated more negatively than overweight men.[85] For example, in the airline industry women are subject to more stringent weight standards than men. United Airlines[86]

[78] RF Bento, LF White and SR Zacur, 'The Stigma of Obesity and Discrimination in Performance Appraisal: A Theoretical Model' (2012) 23(15) *The International Journal of Human Resource Management* 3196.

[79] JB Shinall, 'Why Obese Workers Earn Less: Occupational Sorting and Its Implications for the Legal System' (15 January 2014).

[80] MV Roehling, 'Weight Discrimination in the American Workplace: Ethical Issues and Analysis' (2002) 40(2) *Journal of Business Ethics* 177.

[81] MP Bell, ME McLaughlin and JM Sequeira, 'Age, disability, and obesity: Similarities, differences, and common threads', in MS Stockdale and FJ (eds) *The Psychology and Management of Workplace Diversity* (Malden, MA, Blackwell, 2003) 210.

[82] R Dobson and L Jones (2005) 'Overweight girls face a lifetime of discrimination and low pay'. *The Independent on Sunday*, 18 September,

[83] TA Judge and DM Cable 'When It Comes to Pay, Do the Thin Win? The Effect of Weight on Pay for Men and Women' (2011) 96(1) *Journal of Applied Psychology* 95.

[84] Shinall, 'Why Obese Workers Earn Less' (n 79).

[85] Roehling, 'Weight Discrimination' (n 80) 178.

[86] In *Frank v United Airlines* a group of female employees who had failed to comply with United's weight requirements for women, successfully challenged the airline's weight policy. United dropped its weight policy in 1993.

had a weight policy for flight attendants that discriminated on the basis of sex: the maximum weights for male flight attendants were based on weight tables for men with *large* body frames, while the maximum weights for female flight attendants were based on weight tables for females with *medium* body frames. The maximum weight for a 5'7", 30-year-old woman was 142 lbs, while a man of the same height and age could weigh up to 161 lbs. In *Gerdom*[87] Continental Airlines defended its more stringent weight restrictions for females as a genuine occupational qualification (GOQ): svelte, attractive stewardesses were part of its competitive strategy. In 2009, Air India fired 10 air hostesses whom it decided were 'too fat to fly'. The hostesses had failed to slim down to meet company weight restrictions, calculated according to height and age.[88] One hostess, 51-year-old Sheela Joshi, had worked with Air India for 25 years and was grounded when a spot weigh-in found that she was 1.9 kg over the prescribed limit for her height. The Indian High Court of Delhi upheld Air India's policy as constitutional.

Progress is also stunted: overweight women receive less desirable job assignments than overweight men and 'while even mildly obese women earn significantly less than their non-obese counterparts, there is not a similar wage penalty among mildly obese men'.[89] Young obese women also earn 12% less than non-obese women.[90] Studies have concluded that: overweight women earn less than non-overweight women, but overweight men did not earn less than slim men; overweight women are more segregated into lower paying occupations but overweight men are more dispersed in higher paying occupations; overweight women have less schooling, earn less annually, have 10% higher rates of poverty and are 20% less likely to be married than non-overweight women. This is especially problematic because women are more likely to be obese than men.[91]

Overweight black women are also more excluded than overweight white women. Weight discrimination is intersectional: corpulence has more consequences for black women in the labour market, even though women of colour are rarely the focus of or included in studies on size and eating habits. It has long been assumed that this cohort has a more positive approach to body size and does not have a problematic relationship with food. A study at the University of Arizona claimed that 70% of black girls were satisfied with their bodies compared to 90% of white girls who were *dissatisfied* with their size.[92] Media depictions also stereotype fat

[87] *Gerdom v Continental Airlines, Inc*, 692 F.2d 602, 605–06 (9th Cir. 1982). These arguments were rejected by the court, which held that customer preference was unrelated to the ability to do the job and could not justify a weight policy that discriminated against females. See Roehling, 'Weight Discrimination' (n 80) 179.

[88] *Sheela Joshi and Ors v Indian Airlines Ltd*, Writ Petition C Nos. 12875–83 (2006), 31 May 2007.

[89] Roehling, 'Weight Discrimination' (n 80) 186.

[90] Bell, McLaughlin and Sequeira (n 81) 202.

[91] MP Bell and ME McLaughlin, 'Outcomes of Appearance and Obesity in Organisations' in AM Konrad, P Prasad and J Pringle (eds), *Handbook of Workplace Diversity* (London, Sage, 2006) 455.

[92] Critser, *Fat Land* (n 20) 118; M Ingrassia, 'The Body of the Beholder Mind: White girls dislike their bodies, but black girls are proud of theirs, a new study shows. Why is fat to some fit to others?' 66 *Newsweek* (24 April 1995).

black women—the face of anorexia is a white girl who is a victim of a terrible illness, whereas obesity is a consequence of bad choices. This depiction sends a message about class. Eating disorders are viewed as a consequence of immorality for the poor but the result of illness amongst the wealthy.[93]

Shaw describes the 'triple fetishization' of the fat, black, female body which signifies 'the primal, the erotic and the exotic'.[94] An internalisation of this historical fetishisation may explain why black women are more accepting of their weight than white women. It may also be the case that amongst persistently impoverished black communities, fat retains the positive connotations of the pre-War period while thinness still equates to poverty. This could explain the higher prevalence of obesity amongst black women.

However, this should not lead to the conclusion that black women are not concerned about being fat.[95] It is gradually being acknowledged that black women also have complicated relationships with their bodies: a 10-year study on bulimia, based on data from over 2,300 school girls in California, Ohio and Washington, DC concluded that black girls are more likely to be bulimic than white girls.[96] Clinicians report that almost 8% of their visitors are African-American women who 'are just as likely to abuse laxatives as white women are'[97] to avoid weight gain. This trend may be related to acculturation and assimilation into dominant norms, with acceptance of fat declining as the level of education and income rises. Research into black college populations suggests that the more integrated and middle-class women of colour are, the more likely they are to display a problematic relationship to their body and food, and develop eating disorders.[98]

Some studies have argued that overweight white women are evaluated more harshly than black women.[99] This might be so: as more white women in the labour market have shattered the glass ceiling than black women, more white women in management roles may experience negative consequences due to their weight. It may also be true that black women find greater size acceptance within their communities than their white counterparts do within white communities. This cohort may have a broader definition of attractiveness—incorporating factors

[93] AC Saguy and K Gruys, 'Morality and Health: News Media Constructions of Overweight and Eating Disorders' (2010) 57(2) *Social Problems* 231.

[94] Shaw, *Embodiment of Disobedience* (n 54) 49.

[95] LKG Hsu, 'Are Eating Disorders Becoming More Common among Blacks?' (1987) *International Journal of Eating Disorders* 6, 113–24.

[96] University of Southern California. 'Black Girls are 50 Percent More Likely to Be Bulimic than White Girls.' *Science Daily*, 25 March 2009. See at http://www.sciencedaily.com/releases/2009/03/090318140532.htm. See also J Gray, K Ford and L Kelly (1988) 'The Prevalence of Bulimia in a Black College Population'. 7 *International Journal of Eating Disorders*, 733–40.

[97] M Fitzgibbon and M Stolley, 'Eating Disorders and Minorities', http://www.pbs.org/wgbh/nova/body/eating-disorders-minorities.html; M Fitzgibbon and M Stolley (2009) 'Minority Women: The Untold Story', available at: http://www.pbs.org/wgbh/nova/thin/minorities.html [accessed: 16 June 2009].

[98] Shaw, *Embodiment of Disobedience* (n 54) 78.

[99] A van Dusen, 'Is Weight Affecting Your Career?', available at http://style.uk.msn.com/wellbeing/healthyeating/article.aspx?cp-documentid=8457078.

such as style, personal grooming and posture—but remains vulnerable to eating disorders arising from the portrayal of the successful career woman as smart and thin. Oprah Winfrey is a perfect example of how pernicious this stereotype can be.[100] Paradoxically, the more positive approach to size within their communities may mean that black and Hispanic women with food management problems are unable to turn to their friends or family for support: while white girls and women discuss these problems, communities of colour may not.[101] Also, the higher acceptance of avoirdupois reduces the incentive to address weight problems, and ultimately leaves them more vulnerable to weight discrimination in the labour market.

x. *Is Their Access to Key Resources Blocked?*

People who are overweight or obese huddle together in low income population groups. The prevalence of overweight and obesity in the population varies not only by income and class but also by race and ethnicity. Among African Americans, 28.6% are classified as obese, compared with 21% of Hispanics and 18% of whites.[102] In the USA, about 40% of black Hispanic and Native American women are obese.[103] In households with an annual income of less than $10,000, 33% of blacks, 26% of Hispanics and 20% of whites were found to be obese. Black and single-parent (predominantly female) households tend to fall into this lower income bracket. In households with an annual income between $20–25,000, 27% of blacks, 18% of Hispanics and 20% of whites were found to be obese. In households with an income of $50,000 or more, 23% of blacks, 22% of Hispanics and 16% of whites were obese.[104]

The higher prevalence of overweight and obesity amongst women of colour has at least two implications. First, employer standards on size are likely to negatively affect more women of colour. This was the argument raised by an African American woman who was denied a hostess-trainee position because her hip measurements exceeded the maximum allowed by the employer's purportedly neutral height and weight chart. She raised a complaint of indirect discrimination arguing that due to genetic differences, the employer's hip measurement standard had a disproportionate impact on African American women.[105] Second, employer prejudices on size are likely to apply to more black women as they are less likely to be in hiring and firing positions.[106] There are, statistically speaking,

[100] E Tempesta and V Siebert, 'Fish Is Your Friend', available at http://www.dailymail.co.uk/femail/article-3497154/Fish-friend-Oprah-reveals-dieting-tips-flaunting-30lb-weight-loss-cover-O-Magazine.html (17 March 2016).

[101] L Adesioye. 'Black Girls Have Body Issues Too', *The Guardian*, 7 April 2009, available at https://www.theguardian.com/commentisfree/cifamerica/2009/apr/07/african-american-women-bulimia

[102] Bell, McLaughlin and Sequeira (n 81).

[103] Bell and McLaughlin, 'Outcomes of Appearance' (n 91).

[104] Critser, *Fat Land* (n 20) 110.

[105] Roehling, 'Weight Discrimination' (n 80).

[106] Bell and McLaughlin, 'Outcomes of Appearance' (n 91) 463.

more white male and female managers who are fat phobic and more black women workers who are fat.

III. Fat Phobia and Anti-discrimination Law

'Fattism' is therefore a significant problem, especially for women. However, anti-discrimination law rarely includes protection from weight discrimination. Weight discrimination is acceptable largely as a result of the widespread assumption that fat is mutable[107]—fat is seen as voluntary, therefore there is a low level of public sympathy for the overweight and obese.[108] Regulatory responses have included a suggestion that fat people be put in prison camps or a proposal that discrimination against fat people be legalised in insurance, work and education.[109] Organisations such as the National Association for the Advancement of Fat Acceptance (NAAFA) fighting for protection therefore have a difficult task.

Where there is a will to provide protection, it is a challenge to fit claims into the existing legal frameworks. The Equality Act 2010 is silent on this issue—there has never been legal protection against weight discrimination in the UK. The same applies to the federal level in the USA, where only one state, Michigan, explicitly bans weight discrimination. Attribution theory[110] can explain the narrow treatment of weight discrimination in anti-discrimination law: it only enjoys legal protection if it is an accident of disease or disability. The public is not responsible if the individual can be held to blame.

Statutes that focus on disability and/or appearance have been used with some success by individuals suffering from weight stigma. This section will explore the opportunities and limits of this approach to weight discrimination in the USA and Europe. It will be seen that the use of disability discrimination law in the USA has been replicated by the Court of Justice of the European Union (CJEU) in Luxembourg. However, as argued below, use of the anti-stigma principle will allow for a clearer and more consistent approach to tackling weight discrimination.

A. Tackling Weight Discrimination in Employment in the USA

In the USA, disability discrimination legislation has been used to challenge weight discrimination. The women mentioned previously—Cook, Manuel, McDermott

[107] JB Korn, '**Fat**' (1997) *Boston University Law Review* 77, 25–67.
[108] JE Oliver, and T Lee, 'Public Opinion and the Politics of America's Obesity Epidemic' (2005) 5 *Journal of Health, Politics and Policy* 923.
[109] S Byrd, 'Twinkie Tax' (n 45) 304.
[110] P Corrigan, FE Markowitz, A Watson, D Rowan and MA Kubiak, 'An Attribution Model of Public Discrimination towards Persons with Mental Illness' (2003) 44 *Journal of Health and Social Behaviour* 162, 163.

and Nedder—were able to use the Americans with Disabilities Act (ADA). Under the ADA, a disability is defined as:

> (A) a physical or mental impairment that substantially limits one or more of the major life activities of such individual; (B) a record of such an impairment; or (C) being regarded as having such an impairment.[111]

According to this definition, even if an obese person has difficulty performing the normal daily functions of living and working, he or she will not be considered disabled under the ADA unless the obesity 'substantially limits' a major life activity. 'Major life activities' has a broad interpretation and can include everything from 'caring for one's self, performing manual tasks, walking, seeing, hearing, speaking, breathing, learning, and [even] working'.[112] The disabling condition must be a certified medical condition, thus obesity per se does not meet the definition of a disability under the ADA.[113] An obese individual must be able to show that the obesity is the *result of* a physiological impairment in order to enjoy protection under the ADA. Bonnie Cook[114] was successful because she demonstrated a medical source to her weight problem—she won her case because she was able to demonstrate that her weight problems stemmed from a metabolic dysfunction and could thus be classified as a disability under the ADA.

Manuel and McDermott were successful because judges held that the employers had wrongly imputed a disability to them. The examining doctor said in court that he observed Ms Manuel 'literally waddling down the hall' and estimated that it took her about five times as long as it took somebody else. He felt that he 'owed the public and other people the right to have a driver that could give them some protection in case of an accident or fire or something like that'. Manuel won her case: it had already been held in *Francis*[115] that Section C covers cases where an employer discriminates against an employee because of a *perception* that the employee is morbidly obese, or suffers from a weight condition that is the symptom of a physiological disorder. Likewise, in *O'Connor*[116] Mr O'Connor had been

[111] Americans with Disabilities Act (ADA) 42 USC § 12102(2); see also *Francis v City of Meriden*, 129 F.3d 281, 286 (2d Cir. 1997).

[112] See *Hazeldine v Beverage Media, Inc*, 954 F. Supp. 697 (SDNY 1997) and *Bragdon v Abbott*, 524 US 624, 638–39 (1998).

[113] *Torcasio v Murray* 57 F.3d 1340, 1354 (4th Cir. 1995). Torcasio, who weighed 460 lbs and had a waist of 78", sued officials at Virginia's Department of Corrections claiming that he had been treated unfairly because of his size. The court found that size alone did not qualify as a disability under the ADA.

[114] *Cook v Rhode Island, Department of Health, Retardation, and Hospitals*, 10 F.3d 17, 23, 28 (1st Cir. 1993). See O'Hara (n 9) on attempts to extend this to public accommodations.

[115] *Francis v City of Meriden* 129 F.3d at 286. See also *Furst v State of New York Unified Court System*, 1999 US Dist. LEXIS 22588, 1999 WL 1021817.

[116] O'*Connor v McDonald's Restaurants*, No 3:02 CV 382 SRU, 2003 WL 1343259 (D. Conn. 19 March 2003). See also *Warner v Asplundh Tree Expert Co* (No Civ.A. 303CV1267JCH, 2003 WL 22937718 (D. Conn. 10 December 2003) 3d 17, 23, 28 (1st Cir. 1993). However in *Smaw v Virginia Department of State Police*, 862 F. Supp. 1469, 1475 (ED Va 1994) the ADA did not protect a state trooper demoted because of her weight.

promised a job at McDonald's but then not allowed to start working because with a waist size of 54" he was perceived to be morbidly obese. The Federal District Court in Connecticut allowed him protection under the ADA for three reasons: first, McDonald's regarded him as morbidly obese; second, morbid obesity may qualify as a physical disability under federal law and, third, McDonald's refused to hire him because it *perceived* him as substantially limited in the major life activity of working due to his morbid obesity.

As different treatment based on appearance alone is not protected by the ADA, Deborah Marks could not follow this route, as being 'unpresentable' does not equate to a disability.[117] Marks also could not use the Civil Rights Act 1965 because weight is not included in that statute. Similarly, Joyce English was unable to use the ADA. The Pennsylvania Human Relations Commission argued that she was morbidly obese and protected by the ADA. However, the doctor who examined her found her not to be disabled because she was not in any way limited in her functioning by health problems. The court defended the employers 'inherent right to discriminate among applicants for employment [based on risk of loss to the company] and to eliminate those who have a high potential for absenteeism and low productivity'.[118] Similarly in *Coleman*[119] the 11th circuit Court found no protection under the ADA. Mr Coleman was fired from his job of 23 years when he failed to meet the weight guidelines. He did not argue that his weight was related to a disability. The court stressed that the ADA was meant to protect people who are truly disabled, saying

> It is incumbent on the courts to faithfully adhere to the intended scope of the statute so that it does not become a 'catch-all cause of action for discrimination based on appearance, size, and any number of other things far removed from the reasons the statutes were passed.

State laws have provided some limited relief. Michigan is the only state with laws that specifically include height and weight as protected categories under anti-discrimination law: the Elliot Larsen Civil Rights Act bans discrimination in employment based on race, colour, religion, national origin, age sex, height, weight or marital status.[120] Cases decided under disability provisions in state laws have had different outcomes. For example, in *Cassista* obesity was held not to be a disability within the meaning of California's Fair Employment and Housing Act unless linked to a physiological condition or disorder affecting one or more of the body systems.[121] Likewise, obesity[122] and morbid obesity[123] are not seen

[117] *Marks v National Communications Association, Inc*, 72 F.Supp 2d (SDNY 1999), 322, 327.

[118] *PECO v Pennsylvania Human Relations Commission and Joyce A English* [68].

[119] *Coleman v Georgia Power Co*, 81 F. Supp 2d 1365 (ND Ga 2000) Pa Commw 212 (1982), 228.

[120] Mich Comp Laws Ann § 37.2102 (1985 & Supp 1993 3), Act 453 of 1976, Sec 209.

[121] *Cassista v Community Foods, Inc*, 856 P.2d 1143, 1144 (Cal. 1993). Discussed in E Kristen, 'Addressing the Problem of Weight Discrimination in Employment' (2002) 90 *California Law Review* 57.

[122] *Civil Service Commission of City of Pittsburgh v Commonwealth of Pennsylvania, Pennsylvania Human Relations Commission*, 591 A.2d 281, 283–84 (Pa. 1991).

[123] *Philadelphia Elec Co v Pennsylvania Human Relations Commission*, 448 A.2d 701, 707 (Pa. Commw. Ct. 1982).

as disabilities under the Pennsylvania Human Relations Act unless linked to a physiological disorder, cosmetic disfigurement or anatomical loss that affects the major body systems. A North Dakota court[124] decided that a woman weighing over 21 stone (300 lbs) failed to demonstrate that her weight was a disability so could not pursue an action for discrimination. A Missouri[125] court held that an obese woman with high blood pressure who took no action to manage her condition did not have a disability. The District of Columbia Human Rights Law does not mention weight but outlaws discrimination in employment based upon 'race, color, religion, national origin, sex, age, marital status, personal appearance, sexual orientation, family responsibilities, physical handicap, matriculation, or political affiliation'.[126] In *Greene*, a Washington court decided that obesity was not even covered by law as it was not an immutable condition.[127]

Some cities have enacted their own legal prohibitions of weight and appearance discrimination. San Francisco[128] bars weight and personal appearance discrimination—Jennifer Portnick won her case invoking this statute against the refusal by Jazzercise to provide her with the training necessary to open a franchise. She challenged the assumption that fitness equated to size in a case before the San Francisco Human Rights Commission. The case was settled in May 2002 when Jazzercise Inc. agreed to remove the need to look 'fit' from company policy.[129] Santa Cruz law defines unlawful discrimination as 'differential treatment as a result of that person's race, color, creed, religion, national origin, ancestry, disability, marital status, sex gender, sexual orientation, height, weight, or physical characteristic'.[130]

The New Jersey Law Against Discrimination helped Mr Gimello[131] when he was sacked by his employer, Agency Rent-a-Car for his weight, despite excellent work reviews. He won back pay, legal costs, and $10,000 for pain and suffering. The New York Human Rights Law (NYHRL) also recognises clinically diagnosed morbid obesity as a disability.[132] The Court held that employers have no right to refuse employment, because of their weight, to persons who can do a job. Diagnosis is key: in *Delta Air Lines v New York*, where a number of women challenged Delta's weight and appearance requirements for flight attendants under the NYHRL, they lost because they did not establish that they were 'medically incapable' of meeting

[124] *Krein v Marian Manor Nursing Home*, 415 N.W.2d 793, 796 (N.D. 1987).

[125] *Missouri Comm'n on Human Rights v Southwestern Bell Tel Co*, 699 S.W 2d 75, 79 (Mo. Ct. App. 1985).

[126] DC Code Ann § 1-2501 (1987 & Supp 1993, Subchapter II, Sec. 1-2512.

[127] *Greene v Union Pac RR Co*, 548 F. Supp 3, 5 (WD Wash. 1981).

[128] San Francisco Administrative Code Chapters 12A, 12B and 12C; San Francisco Municipal Code/Police Code Article 33.

[129] O'Poole, n 71.

[130] Santa Cruz Municipal Code, Chapter 9.83. Discussed by R Post 'Prejudicial Appearances: The Logic of American Antidiscrimination Law' (2000) 88 *California Law Review* 1.

[131] *Gimello v Agency Rent-A-Car Sys Inc*, 594 A.2d 264 (NJ Super Ct. App. Div. 1991).

[132] *State Div of Human Rights v Xerox Corp*, 480 N.E.2d 695, 698 (NY 1985).

Delta's weight requirements due to a diagnosed medical condition.[133] Likewise in another case, a New York Appeals Board[134] held that the complainant had suffered discrimination not due to her weight but due to low job performance caused by her weight.

B. Tackling Weight Discrimination in Employment in the UK

The DDA 1995 and the subsequent Equality Act 2010 do not prohibit perceived disability, but the disability discrimination approach taken in the USA could also be applied in the UK. Disability in the UK Equality Act 2010 is defined in very similar terms: 'a person has a disability … if he has a physical or mental impairment which has a substantial and long term adverse effect on his ability to carry out normal day to day activities'. Thus being obese can be a disability where, for example, difficulties are related to weight either directly (joint/muscle strain or shortness of breath) or indirectly (as a consequence of reduced cardiac output, the risk of stroke or diabetes). Depending on the consequences for everyday mobility, this can fall under disability—for example, walking can become difficult because of knee strain due to prolonged excess weight on the joint. The employer must then make reasonable changes to accommodate the needs of the claimant. This can mean re-organisation of work duties, adjustment of the workspace (providing a more comfortable chair and desk) or an allowance for business rather than economy class travel.

However, Irish equality law does include perceptions of disability. Section 6(1) of the Irish Employment Equality Act (EEA) covers discrimination on the grounds of disability, including actual and potential difficulties. In particular, section 6(2)(e) defines disability as

> a condition, illness or disease which affects a person's thought processes, perception of reality, emotions or judgment or which results in disturbed behaviour, and shall be taken to include a disability which exists at present, or which previously existed but no longer exists, or which may exist in the future or which is imputed to a person.

It was used in a case where a care attendant was denied a post as staff nurse with the Health Service Executive (HSE), because the HSE presumed her obesity was a disability.[135]

The first successful claim of weight discrimination in the UK only happened following a case in the EU, *Kaltoft*,[136] which confirmed that weight discrimination is protected as a disability under EU anti-discrimination law. EU law does

[133] *Delta Air Lines v New York State Div. of Human Rights*, 91 N.Y.2d 65, 73, 689 N.E.2d 898, 666 N.Y.S. 2d 1004 (1997).

[134] *Thomas J Lipton, Inc v New York State Human Rights Appeal Bd*, 413 N.Y.S.2d 2 233 (1979).

[135] *Health Service Employee v The Health Service Executive*, December E2006-013.

[136] *FOA, acting on behalf of Karsten Kaltoft v Billund Kommune* [2015] IRLR 146, ECJ.

not formally prohibit weight discrimination—like other public health issues, this remains within the competence of the Member States[137]—but in the first case of its kind, the Court of Justice of the European Union (CJEU) decided that discrimination on the grounds of obesity can fall within the disability strand of the Equal Treatment Directive 2000/78. This was stated in answer to questions arising before a Danish court during a case concerning the weight of a childminder.

Mr Kaltoft was hired by the municipality of Billund in 1998 on a permanent contract as a childminder. He was obese at the time of his initial employment and, despite periods of weight loss, remained such throughout his 15 years in this post. From March 2010, he appeared to be under informal review, being visited by his boss and asked about his weight. During 2010, when the number of children in Billund reduced, he was given fewer children to look after. That same year, he was selected for dismissal. When Kaltoft asked why he was the only childminder to be dismissed, he was told it was due to his decreased workload. Kaltoft was convinced that it had something to do with his weight.

His trade union brought an action before the District Court seeking compensation for him, arguing that he had been subjected to weight discrimination. The Danish court stayed proceedings in the national court to ask the CJEU four questions, of which only the first and fourth were answered: whether it is contrary to EU law (for example Article 6 TEU on fundamental rights) for a public-sector employer to discriminate on grounds of obesity in the labour market, and whether obesity could be deemed to be a disability covered by Directive 2000/78/EC.

The first question was easily answered: citing *Chacon Navas*[138] and *Coleman*,[139] the Fourth Chamber of the Court of Justice declared that 'EU law must be interpreted as not laying down a general principle of non-discrimination on grounds of obesity as such'.[140] The Fourth Chamber then considered whether obesity is a disability. Its reasoning began from the purpose of Directive 2000/78: it noted that this Directive was introduced to set out a 'general framework for combating discrimination, as regards employment and occupation, on any of the grounds referred to in that article, which include disability'. The meaning of direct discrimination in the Directive and its scope of application was then highlighted—as per Article 3(1)(c) it covers all persons in the public and private sectors, and all phases of employment including dismissals. It also cited *HK Danmark*[141] and *Glatzel*,[142] where the CJEU

[137] The Commission has in the past funded public health projects, eg, the Ensemble Prévenons l'Obésité des Enfants ('let's work together to prevent childhood obesity'), a nutrition education programme in France.

[138] C-13/05 *Chacón Navas v Eurest Colectividades SA*.

[139] C-303/06 *Coleman v Attridge Law*.

[140] *Kaltoft* (n 136) [40].

[141] C 335 & 337/11 *HK Danmark, acting on behalf of Jette Ring v Dansk almennyttigt Boligselskab* (C-335/11) and *HK Danmark, acting on behalf of Lone Skouboe Werge v Dansk Arbejdsgiverforening acting on behalf of Pro Display A/S* (C-337/11).

[142] C-356/12 *Wolfgang Glatzel v Freistaat Bayern*.

took inspiration from the EU ratification of the United Nations Convention on the Rights of Persons with Disabilities, which states that

> 53 … the concept of 'disability' must be understood as referring to a limitation which results in particular from long-term physical, mental or psychological impairments which in interaction with various barriers may hinder the full and effective participation of the person concerned in professional life on an equal basis with other workers.

The Chamber thus concluded that in order to be compatible with Directive 2000/78, the concept of 'disability', first, 'must be understood as referring not only to the impossibility of exercising a professional activity, but also to a *hindrance* to the exercise of such an activity' and, second, that the concept had to be open-ended in relation to the 'origin of the disability'. It was not dependent upon 'the extent to which the person may or may not have contributed to the onset of his disability'.[143] Thus while obesity itself is not a 'disability' within the meaning of Directive 2000/78, the Chamber decided that obesity could be covered by the concept of 'disability' in that Directive where

> 59 'the obesity of the worker concerned entails a limitation which results in particular from physical, mental or psychological impairments that in interaction with various barriers may hinder the full and effective participation of that person in professional life on an equal basis with other workers, and the limitation is a long-term one, obesity can be covered by the concept of 'disability' within the meaning of Directive 2000/78.
>
> 60 Such would be the case, in particular, if the obesity of the worker hindered his full and effective participation in professional life on an equal basis with other workers on account of reduced mobility or the onset, in that person, of medical conditions preventing him from carrying out his work or causing discomfort when carrying out his professional activity.[144]

It was left for the Danish court to decide whether, despite the fact that he was able to work effectively for 15 years as a childminder, his obesity nonetheless limited Kaltoft during his term of employment in the way envisaged by the EU concept of 'disability'. He would then have to prove that his dismissal was because of his obesity. Specifically dismissed was the idea of culpability for the disability.

An employment tribunal in Northern Ireland has since applied the three basic principles set out in *Kaltoft* to a disability harassment case: *Bickerstaff v Butcher*.[145] Morbidly obese, with a BMI of 48.5, as a result of his weight Mr Bickerstaff suffered from sleep apnoea and gout. He worked at Randox Laboratories where he claimed that because of his weight he experienced harassment by colleagues. The worst offender was a Mr Butcher, who had made inappropriate comments that Bickerstaff was 'so fat he could hardly walk' and that he was 'so fat he would hardly feel a knife being stuck into him'. The Tribunal unanimously agreed that

[143] *Kaltoft* (n 135) [54]–[56].
[144] *Kaltoft* (n 135) [59]–[60].
[145] *Bickerstaff v Butcher* NIIT/92/14; *Bickerstaff v Butcher* [2015] 92/14 FET.

Bickerstaff was disabled and upheld his claim of harassment. The judge was satisfied that Bickerstaff had been 'harassed for a reason which related to his disability'. As in *Kaltoft*, the decision did not consider the reason for Butcher's size—the consequence was important, not the cause. The Tribunal focused on the impact of his weight on his activities at work rather than why he was obese.

Obesity can indeed be a disability rights issue. However, this approach to protection is problematic: weight is per se not a disability and entrenching protection from obesity in disability law would establish above-average weight as an aberrant departure from a 'normal' body. This is precisely the stereotype and stigma that courts need to address if fat people are to be protected from discrimination. As shown by Jennifer Portnick, fat is not a disability and should not have to be treated as such. Also there is no clear guidance on when weight is 'normal'—the medical definitions of 'overweight' and 'obesity' are guidelines only and can vary based on height.

The response to weight discrimination in anti-discrimination law suggests that although it has long moved away from immutability, vestiges of attribution theory remain. The anti-stigma principle would disrupt such ideas and at the same time provide a clear and effective logic to extend anti-discrimination law to prohibit discrimination on the basis of weight. As discrimination against the overweight and obese is likely to continue, the sooner it is used provide reliable and effective protection to these persons from discrimination, the better. The American Society for Metabolic and Bariatric Surgery (ASMBS) has called for the US government to reduce obesity discrimination as it addresses the obesity epidemic through education and outreach to improve awareness of nutrition as well as identification and reduction of weight stigma.[146]

IV. Conclusion

The rise in the number of people who are overweight and obese should perhaps not be surprising: the more we earn, the more our pattern of consumption changes. The combination of lower food prices with faster yet more sedentary lifestyles encourage us to pay less attention to what we eat. Put together with mass media promoting a new mode of consumption, and technological development which encourages reduced household and leisure effort, the rise in body size of the general population should have been expected.[147] It is clear that we need to abandon the idea that being overweight and obesity are simple consequences of personal over-indulgence.

There is good reason to be concerned about the discriminatory treatment suffered by corpulent members of society. Size is not a general determinant of

[146] Wolfe, 'Obesity Discrimination: What Can We Do?' (n 70) 495, 498.
[147] Popkin, 'The Nutrition Transition' (n 28).

aptitude, ability or performance yet overweight and obese individuals are subjected to discrimination in multiple areas of everyday life including education, health care, public accommodation and the workplace.[148] Overweight and obese persons are explicitly unprotected by anti-discrimination law, even though studies show that weight discrimination is a widespread phenomenon, evident at every phase of the employment cycle. There is, however implicit protection created by the extension of existing disability discrimination law—this may help the obese to some extent by providing much needed protection—demeaning treatment and derogatory comments relating to weight may constitute disability discrimination harassment.

This chapter has illustrated how the anti-stigma principle can provide more effective protection without further stigmatising the overweight and obese. Weight discrimination would satisfy all 10 'threshold' questions posed by the anti-stigma principle. It is therefore a strong contender for the position of the 10th protected characteristic. The question then arises as to how far the anti-stigma principle can take anti-discrimination law; this will be discussed in the following chapter.

[148] Pomeranz and Puhl, 'Developments in the Law for Obesity' (n 61).

8

Tattoos—Beyond Anti-discrimination Law?

The previous chapter considered who should benefit from legal protection against discrimination under the anti-stigma principle. An equally important question is: which groups would not enjoy protection? It is clear that protection from discrimination has over the years expanded, creating a need to clarify why it is not provided. The anti-stigma principle is useful in this task. It can explain the boundaries of anti-discrimination law.

A good example of an area that is increasingly considered an omission from anti-discrimination law is protection of persons with tattoos. There is evidence that persons with tattoos—a growing proportion of the workforce—are subjected to 'ink-ism' at work. Employers remain concerned about the appearance of their employees and are very averse to tattoos. Studies show that even a small tattoo can have a negative impact on a career. Ink-ism is nowhere explicitly protected, and rules on 'appearance' rarely cover it. As yet there has not been a successful prosecution for this and there is some support for it to be explicitly prohibited in anti-discrimination law.

Should this concern be translated into legal protection for persons with tattoos? This question may well be answered in the affirmative when compared with other attributes: a tattoo may be as fundamental to a person's identity as their sexuality. However, analysis under the anti-stigma principle may lead to a different response. Such an analysis will be conducted in this chapter and, as will be seen, ink-ism would not be a protected characteristic according to the anti-stigma principle: although persons with tattoos are treated negatively in some workplaces, this does not extend to punitive treatment across multiple spheres. The anti-stigma principle reserves the protection of anti-discrimination law to those whose experience of powerlessness is punitive and widespread.

This chapter begins with examples of appearance discrimination in general before discussing tattoos in particular. Employers have long imposed dress norms upon their employees, usually with a great deal of success as their business rationale has been accepted by courts. Thus men with long hair, women who want to wear trousers or refuse to wear hats have lost their cases. The same has applied thus far with tattoos. The second section will then examine where tattoo discrimination has occurred and how it has been dealt with in anti-discrimination law—this has usually been through the use of rules on appearance. Throughout the chapter examples will be drawn from multiple jurisdictions. The final section will conduct an analysis using the anti-stigma principle to demonstrate why tattoos should not be brought within the scope of anti-discrimination law. It concludes that where the tattoo is part of a religion or a cultural practice of identity and belonging, as amongst the Maori people of New Zealand or Polynesia, this should be tackled as indirect discrimination on the grounds of religion or race.

I. Appearance at Work

Beauty matters. It is not only in the USA that physical attractiveness is a 'prized possession'.[1] According to economist Daniel Hammermesh, attractive employees earn $230,000 more than their 'unattractive' peers.[2] Companies such as Gap, Benetton or Abercrombie and Fitch apparently pride themselves on hiring the most attractive young people from every background. However, the idea of beauty in society has changed. For many, it now includes having at least one tattoo. Women are slightly more likely than men to have a tattoo.[3] Tattoos have been described as a 'benign rite of passage for many Americans' especially women even though these can have a significant effect on their appearance, and a negative impact on their careers.

Tattoos are increasingly common across all classes and in all contexts—Samantha Cameron, wife to former UK Prime Minister David, has an image of a dolphin tattooed on her ankle. The wife of former German President Christian Wulff sported a larger and more visible tribal tattoo on her arm.[4] The last five to 10 years have seen a significant increase in the popularity of tattoos, and beyond this a huge surge in 'sleeves', which are tattoos that cover the whole arm or lower leg. Some go so far as to tattoo their whole body.[5] Previously confined to bikers or sailors, circus-people, prisoners and gang members, tattoos have now become so popular that one in five Britons today has a tattoo. It has been estimated that 60% of university students have a tattoo.[6] A 2013 Harris Poll[7] estimated that one in five

[1] FJ Cavico, SC Muffler and BG Mujtaba, 'Appearance Discrimination, "Lookism" and "Lookphobia" in the workplace' (2012) 28(5) *Journal of Applied Business Research* 791.

[2] Cavico, Muffler and Mujtaba, 'Lookism and Look-phobia' (n 1).

[3] 'Ink blots', *The Economist* (2 August 2014), available at http://www.economist.com/news/united-states/21610334-body-art-growing-more-popular-though-few-employers-are-keen-ink-blots.

[4] D Scally, 'The former first lady with the prominent tattoo' *The Irish Times* (20 September 2012) http://www.irishtimes.com/news/the-former-first-lady-with-the-prominent-tattoo-1.534124.

[5] http://rickgenest.com; 'Britain's most tattooed man turned away from polling station', available at http://www.itv.com/news/central/2015-05-08/britains-most-tattooed-man-turned-away-from-polling-station/.

[6] P Drazewski, 'Tattoo Stigma and Job Discrimination' (manuscript on file with author). See also AD Arndt and M Glassman, 'What Tattoos Tell Customers about Salespeople: The Role of Gender Norms' (2012) *Marketing Management Journal*; JW Totten, TJ Lipscomb and MA Jones, 'Attitudes Toward and Stereotypes of Persons with Body Art: Implications for Marketing Management' (2009) 13(2) *Academy of Marketing Studies Journal* 77.

[7] 'One in five US adults now has a tattoo' (23 February 2012), available at http://www.theharrispoll.com/health-and-life/One_in_Five_U_S__Adults_Now_Has_a_Tattoo.html.

US adults has at least one tattoo (21%)—up from 16% in 2003 and 14% in 2008. Tattoos are most common amongst adults aged 30–39 (38%); 30% of those 25–29 have tattoos; 27% of those 40–49; and 22% of those 18–24. Older persons are less likely to be tattooed: just 11% of those 50–64 and 5% of those 65 and older.

Their impact can be negative because appearance still matters very much in the workplace.[8] Most employers seek to promote a particular image of themselves through their employees. From the employer perspective, the employee is a reflection of the organisation. Dress standards exist with precise stipulations such as:

> Hair must be clean, neatly combed and arranged in a traditional style (Men: no longer than mid-collar in the back, to the earlobe on the side), and natural in color. Extreme looks such as unnatural hair color, extreme ornamentation for hair or shaved-in designs are unacceptable.[9]

Others state that women may not wear trousers,[10] or must wear hats,[11] skirts and make up.[12] However, it is not all about long hair or make up, and body markings and piercings increasingly challenge these corporate dress codes. As these become more popular, so that to have a tattoo or a nose stud is no longer seen as extraordinary in society, company dress codes are giving rise to more conflict between management and staff. In some cases the employer wants to 'harness' the personality of the employee as part of the image of the company.[13] This can result in the employer demanding control over the appearance of the worker to the extent that a worker with tattoos may be asked to cover them up so that they are not visible when dealing with customers. A business reason is often given: customers will not like it.

Cloutier is an example of where workplace grooming codes clashed with general cultural norms. Kimberly Cloutier[14] began working for Costco in West Springfield, Massachusetts, in July 1997. At the start of her employment she had four tattoos on her upper arm and 11 earrings. These attracted no attention until 1998 when she began to work at the delicatessen department at Costco, just as Costco introduced a new dress code banning workers in this section from wearing any form of facial jewellery. Cloutier refused to remove her earrings and requested a transfer to a part of the store where the no-jewellery rule did not apply. Costco

[8] J Fowler-Hermes, 'The Beauty and the Beast in the Workplace: Appearance-based Discrimination Claims Under EEO Laws' (2001) 75(4) *The Florida Bar Journal* 32, available at https://www.floridabar.org/divcom/jn/jnjournal01.nsf/c0d731e03de9828d852574580042ae7a/3c84f1732a06780f85256b1100573d1b!OpenDocument&Highlight=0,*.

[9] *Rivera v Trump Plaza Hotel*, 702 A.2d 1359 (NJ Super Ct App Div 1997) where two men were fired after wearing ponytails to work, or in the UK *Smith v Safeway* [1995] IRLR 132 and *Dansie v The Commissioner of Police for the Metropolis* [2009] UKEAT 0234_09_2010.

[10] *Seabrook v City of New York*, 80 FEP Cases (BNA) 1453 (SDNY 1999), *aff'd*, 210 F.3d 355 (2000) where female employees of the US Prison Service (Department of Corrections) brought a class action against the DOC dress code that required all employees to wear trousers.

[11] *Burret v West Birmingham Health Authority* [1994] IRLR 7 (EAT); 3 March 1994 (CA).

[12] *Jespersen v Harrah's Operating Co*, 280 F.Supp.2d 1189, 1192–93 (D.Nev. 2002).

[13] P Fleming, *Resisting Work: The Corporatization of Life and its Discontents* (Philadelphia, Temple University Press, 2014).

[14] *Cloutier v Costco*, 390 F.3d 126 (1st Cir. 2004).

approved this transfer and soon thereafter promoted Kimberly to cashier. Cloutier proceeded to pierce her eyebrows without her employer raising any objections. In March 2001, Costco revised its dress code again to introduce a store-wide ban on any facial jewellery except earrings. In June 2001, Cloutier and a coworker, Jennifer Theriaque, were told to remove their facial piercings.

II. Legal Responses to Corporate Appearance Policies and Rules

Courts tend to be sympathetic to these employer demands. Judges recognise and defer to the employer assertion that controlling personal appearance standards is vital to their 'public image'. Dress codes are seen as minimally intrusive, and if the employee is unable to reach a compromise, judges find it reasonable for the worker to leave the organisation to take a job elsewhere.[15] However, exit is not always an option.

Thus under most anti-discrimination law, it remains lawful to treat somebody differently based upon their appearance. Thus, in order to seek a remedy, complainants must be creative. Appearance discrimination can be a proxy for other forms of discrimination, such as race or sex, thus a remedy can be found by linking appearance rules to a prohibited ground such as race, sex or even religion.

A. Race and Sex Discrimination

Using this approach, the Equal Employment Opportunity Commission (EEOC) in the USA brought a successful case against clothing retailer Abercrombie and Fitch. The EEOC linked the company preference for 'preppy' employees to race, arguing that 'preppy' was a euphemism for white and middle class, which discriminated against black and minority ethnic applicants. Likewise, in *Hollins*[16] an African-American woman argued that her employer's unwritten policy that hairstyles could not be 'eye-catching' applied only to her dreadlocks, commonly worn by black women. She lost before the district court but won upon appeal to the Sixth Circuit after demonstrating that white women were not subject to the 'eye-catching' requirement.

[15] This is also presented as a solution for religious discrimination.

[16] *Hollins v Atlantic*, 188 F.3d 652 (6th Cir. 1999). See also *McManus v MCI*, 82 FEP Cases (BNA) 1063 (DDC 2000). Also *Fitzpatrick v City of Atlanta*, 2 F.3d 1112 (11th Cir 1993) where a group of African-American firefighters claimed a ban on beards was indirectly discriminatory.

However, this approach does not always work. In *Jespersen* it was unsuccessfully argued that the obligation to wear make-up was in fact sex discrimination. *Kleinsorge*[17] also failed—in this case a male employee was fired for wearing an earring to work, in violation of the employer's dress code. However, earrings were not per se banned, as women could wear them. Kleinsorge complained that these different standards for women and men constituted sex discrimination. His arguments were rejected by the district court, which found that although the details of the dress standards were different, it was not the case that the application or enforcement of the standards differed between the women and men. The court held that 'minor differences in personal appearance regulations that reflect customary modes of grooming do not constitute sex discrimination within the meaning of [Title VII]'.[18]

B. Religious Belief Discrimination

In other cases, individuals have asserted a religion or belief to defend their dress habits, with varied levels of success. For example, in *Seabrook* the female complainants argued that it was contrary to their religion to wear trousers. However, their employer—the Department of Corrections—argued that this was essentially a genuine occupational requirement, a defence that was accepted by the court. In *Swartzentruber*, the complainant wore a tattoo of a hooded man and a burning cross. It was common knowledge that he was a member of the Klu Klux Klan and management feared that the tattoo would cause racial offence to his colleagues, who were both black and white. As a result he was instructed to cover the tattoo, which he agreed to do but monitoring showed that he did not. Due to the monitoring, he complained of harassment, presenting the unlikely argument that the tattoo was an expression of religious belief and the employer request thus offended his 'religious beliefs'. The court swiftly found that Swartzentruber had no genuine religious belief that called for him to display such a tattoo.[19]

Kimberley Cloutier initially had more success claiming a religious belief. She[20] and Theriaque responded that they were members of a new religion—the Church of Body Modification (CBM)[21]—of which eyebrow piercing was a ritual. The Church had been founded in 1999 and had over 1,000 members, who were sent out into the world to be 'confident role models' in learning, teaching, and displaying body modifications. On this basis, Theriaque found a way to compromise with

[17] *Kleinsorge v.Island Corp.*, 81 FEP Cases (BNA) 1601 (ED Pa 2000).

[18] Fowler-Hermes, 'The Beauty and the Beast' (n 8). See also *Knott v Missouri Pac Ry Co*, 527 F.2d 1249 (8th Cir. 1975).

[19] Discussed in JJ MacDonald Jnr, 'Civil Rights for the Aesthetically Challenged' (2003) 29 *Employee Relations Law Journal* 2.

[20] *Cloutier v Costco* (2004) US App LEXIS 24763 (1 December 2004).

[21] See http://www.uscobm.com.

Costco; she requested and was granted permission to wear plastic retainers instead of her jewellery to prevent the piercings from closing. Cloutier made an alternative suggestion. She requested permission to cover her eyebrow piercing with a flesh-coloured plaster, as she had been doing with her tattoos. This was rejected by the manager and she was sent home. Just over two weeks later she was dismissed for 'unexcused absences resulting from noncompliance with the dress code'.

Cloutier then registered a complaint for discrimination on grounds of religion with the EEOC. She asserted that CBM teaching required her to be a constant, confident role model for body modification at all times, thus requiring her eyebrow piercings to remain visible. At mediation with the EEOC, Costco then agreed to allow her return to work if either she wore a plastic retainer (like Theriaque) or covered her jewellery with a plaster (as she had suggested). Cloutier however rejected both suggestions—she would only accept a total exemption from Costco's no-facial-jewellery policy as any other solution would undermine her religious convictions.

The EEOC found in favour of Cloutier and she then sought damages of $2,000,000 in court—and lost. The District court found for Costco on the ground that its offer at the EEOC mediation session was a reasonable accommodation. The First Circuit (Boston) court upheld the District court judgment on the grounds that Cloutier had been unreasonable, because the only accommodation she would accept, it held, would impose an 'undue hardship' on Costco. Title VII also provides protection to employers in these type of cases. Unlike the ADA, an employer can demonstrate 'undue hardship' to overcome a religious objection by simply showing that the employee's proposed accommodation imposes more than a *de minimis* cost. 'Cost' includes non-economic costs such as compromising the integrity of a seniority system. The First Circuit held that the insistence on a personal blanket exemption would indeed compromise the integrity of Costco policy. It stated that

> It is axiomatic that, for better or for worse, employees reflect on employers. This is particularly true of employees who regularly interact with customers as [Kimberly] did in her cashier position. Even if [Kimberly] did not regularly receive any complaints about her appearance, her facial jewellery influenced Costco's public image and, in Costco's calculation, detracted from its professionalism [...] We are faced with the similar situation of an employee who will accept no accommodation short of an outright exemption from a neutral dress code. Granting such an exemption would be an undue hardship because it would adversely affect the employer's public image. Costco has made a determination that facial piercings, aside from earrings, detract from the 'neat, clean, and professional image' that it aims to cultivate. Such a business determination is within its discretion.[22]

Only one state in the USA explicitly prohibits appearance discrimination in law. Michigan's Elliot Larsen Act mentions two specific aspects: height and weight. Municipal laws go further—as well as Washington, DC, cities such as Urbana,

[22] *Cloutier v Costco Wholesale Corp*. 390 F.3d 126 C.A.1 (Mass.), 2004.

Illinois or Madison, Wisconsin and Santa Cruz, California have introduced explicit appearance protection. The bill proposed in Santa Cruz sparked a heated debate about whether this was an appropriate use of anti-discrimination law or a move towards a 'moral imperialism' that would undermine the logic of the anti-discrimination principle.[23] Would tattoos fare otherwise under the anti-stigma principle?

III. The Anti-stigma Principle and Tattoos

A. Applying the 10 Questions

i. Is the 'Mark' Arbitrary or Does It Have Some Meaning in and of Itself?

Tattoos always have meaning, especially to the wearer. According to Thompson, '[h]owever rudimentary, tattoos often symbolize something that the wearer has a strong emotional attachment to, be it a pop cultural reference, a hobby, a relationship, a life event, or a material item'.[24] The design of the tattoo is specially determined accordingly—to demonstrate allegiance and loyalty, admiration and/or devotion, commemoration, or identity and individuality.[25] People may have tattoos for many different reasons—perhaps to rebel against society or to show love for an admired or dear departed one. Tattoos can also be instrumental, for example, one tattoo artist specializes in inking over mastectomy scars.[26] This form of body modification is, therefore, rarely arbitrary. For some persons with tattoos, there is little difference between tattoos and plastic surgery—both are ways of changing appearance.[27] Yet body modifications such as breast enlargements, nose jobs and weight loss are all fully socially acceptable. This may be because tattoos occupy a different ontology of beauty than large breasts or a small nose. Arguably, while the design of every tattoo has meaning, the tattoo itself is no indication of ability to do a job.

ii. Is the Mark Used as a Social Label?

Tattoos have always had a dual meaning, even—as now—within the same society. Those who have tattoos see them differently to non-tattooed persons. For the

[23] R Post, 1998–99 Brennan Center Symposium Lecture: 'Prejudicial Appearances: The Logic of American Antidiscrimination Law', (2000) *Calif Law Rev* 88(1), 1.

[24] BY Thompson, *Covered in Ink: Tattoos, Women and the Politics of the Body* (New York, New York University Press, 2015).

[25] M Tiggemann and LA Hopkins, 'Tattoos and Piercings: Bodily Expressions of Uniqueness?' (2011) 8(3) *Body Image* 245.

[26] Thompson, *Covered in Ink* (n 24) 13.

[27] BBC News Online, 'Tattoo cover-up "discriminates"' (19 June 2006), available at http://news.bbc.co.uk/1/hi/5079470.stm.

former they can be a symbol of loyalty and devotion, of commemoration or of personal expression. For non-tattooed persons, tattoos are ugly and indicate deviance and disruption[28]—criminality for men and sexual promiscuity/criminality for women.[29] Tattooed people are continually negatively perceived. Readers of an article on tattoos in *The Economist*—a progressive liberal conservative news magazine with an engaged and educated readership—made the following comments about tattoos:

> Personally I put the tattoo thing into the same group of concerns about someone in the office who dresses in revealing or sloppy clothing, or has excessive jewelry, BO, perfume, makeup etc.
>
> People with tattoos are associated with deviance and disruption. They belong to the category of persons who look as if they cannot take care of themselves, and thus cannot take care of another person's business.[30]

Indeed, according to a 2013 Harris Poll, at least two in five say that people with tattoos are less attractive (45%) or sexy (39%); 27% say that people with tattoos are less intelligent, healthy (25%) and spiritual (25%). According to 82% a tattoo was no indicator of strength and athleticism; yet 50% of those who are non-tattooed said that a tattoo indicates rebelliousness.[31]

iii. Does this Label Have a Long History? How Embedded Is It in Society?

Tattooing is a historical form of body modification that exists in many parts of the world. In the culture of Polynesia it was initially seen as a positive practice perverted by outsiders; yet on the other side of the Pacific in Japan, it has always been perceived as negative. It has also always been seen as negative in the cultures of the Atlantic until the current period. The negative history of tattoos in Europe, America and Japan have dominated the general public perception.

Tattooing has been a practice in Polynesia for almost 2000 years and is an ancient art in the countries of the Pacific such as Fiji, Samoa and Tonga. In these cultures, tattooing was traditionally a symbol of strength and courage—there were no sophisticated tools used and the healing process was long and painful. In Fiji, women were the expert tattooists. The tattoos could only be drawn by a 'Master', who was a highly trained individual well respected in society. The Master had authority to decide who could be tattooed, when and what design could be used. Tattoos were drawn as part of a ritual, and the tattooing was preceded by fasting

[28] P Drazewski, 'Tattoo Stigma and Job Discrimination' (n 6). AJ Towler and DJ Schneider, 'Distinctions among stigmatized groups' (2005) 35(1) *Journal of Applied Social Psychology* 1.

[29] Thompson, *Covered in Ink* (n 24); L Leblanc, *Pretty in Punk—Girls Gender Resistance in a Boys SubCulture* (New Brunswick, Rutgers University Press, 1999).

[30] Bradshsi, 2 August 2014, 15:51.

[31] 'One in Five US Adults now has a tattoo' (23 February 2012), available at http://www.theharrispoll.com/health-and-life/One_in_Five_U_S__Adults_Now_Has_a_Tattoo.html.

or dieting. In Samoa, male tattooing was the counterpart to female childbirth: both were proof of 'pain tolerance' and a sign of maturity.[32] Tattoos were an art form, never seen as a taint until the arrival of missionaries from Europe.[33] Under religious conversion and colonialism, the tattooed became targets for violent suppression.

It is also an ancient art in Japan, where tattooing goes back to at least 5,000 bc. Japanese culture also had a particular place for tattoos but here is was negative: during the seventh and eighth centuries tattooing was used as a form of punishment for criminals. Today tattoos remain linked to the Yakuza, or Japanese mafia. Yakuza members are tattooed all over their body; these 'tattoo suits' are only visible when naked. The association has endured, and it is this historic connection with the world of crime that remains the strongest.[34] The same attitude towards tattoos also prevails in mainstream culture in other parts of Asia.

In the USA, Native Americans used tattoos to indicate their tribal affinity as in Polynesia. Yet in white society their tattoos made them 'oddities' and they were displayed in circuses that travelled the country entertaining the settlers. Thus only those outside of mainstream society voluntarily wore tattoos—circus people, servicemen and prison inmates—yet the purpose of the tattoo was to mark their belonging to another family, such as the navy, the military or a gang. Persons with tattoos were also stereotyped in theory: criminologists described tattoos as a 'secondary characteristic' of criminality and medical professionals used them as indicators of mental illness. Tattoos were also linked to disease due to the unsanitary conditions in the parlours: when a jaundice and hepatitis B epidemic broke out in New York City in 1961, all tattoo parlours were banned until 1997,[35] even though lack of attention to public hygiene was endemic throughout society at that time. Some states in the USA—Cleveland, Rhode Island and Massachusetts for example—continue to ban tattooing.

By the late twentieth century this stigma had declined—many popstars, musicians, actors and even some politician's wives wear tattoos. Some lawyers and other professionals also have tattoos. The link to deviance has reduced as they are no longer associated solely with the poor working class but have become a middle-class phenomenon. In Denmark, tattoos are both commonplace and accepted, in society and in the workplace, whether this be the more conservative environment of a university or the more relaxed context of information technology. Even the smallest Danish towns have two or three tattoo studios, and they must be as sanitary as any hospital.

[32] Thompson, *Covered in Ink* (n 24) 21.

[33] See http://www.pbs.org/skinstories/culture/index.html.

[34] J Kelly, 'Should anti-tattoo discrimination be illegal?' BBC News Magazine (18 August 2014), available at http://www.bbc.co.uk/news/magazine-28758900.

[35] Thompson, *Covered in Ink* (n 24) 27–31.

iv. Can the Label Be 'Wished Away'?

It is difficult for tattoos to lose their negative label completely. As recently as 2012 the Mayor of Osaka in Japan imposed a ban on tattooed public sector workers, stating that they would have to go to work in the private sector. Tattoos are also banned in other public places such as gyms and parks.[36] To some extent this negative label is age specific: what many older persons find repugnant and distasteful, may be viewed as artful and an expression of identity by the younger generation. Many see tattoos as an art form, with the body being the canvas for a technical skill requiring years of training.[37] Tattoos are just another form of body modification, like plastic surgery.[38]

Yet the label is not all encompassing. The stigma of a tattoo matters predominantly in relation to employment—this is where almost all problems arise—but there may be no stigma at all. Some workplaces specifically identify themselves as tattoo-friendly: IKEA, Whole Foods, Borders Books, Petco, Barnes and Noble, Forever 21, Staples and Lowes are some companies listed by Thompson.[39] This also applies to prisons: during his survey a prison services manager told Timming that having tattoos made it easier to bond with inmates. Timming also found that firms with a younger clientele were less averse to tattoos. The more conservative the work environment, the more ink-phobic the workplace is likely to be, as employers think primarily about the reaction of their customers. However, the type of tattoo and its location makes a difference and, where possible, covering tends to be allowed. Timming also concluded that as the aversion to tattoos is declining, the label is undergoing significant change. Also, as mentioned above, even permanent tattoos can now be removed. Thus the label can be removed and the stigma attached to it is also declining.

v. Is the Label Used to Stereotype Those Possessing It?

The label undeniably gives rise to a series of negative stereotypes, as illustrated by readers of *The Economist*. One comment reads:

> Hard to imagine hiring anyone with tattoos, as any visible tattoos indicate that (a) the person has no aesthetic taste and is responding eagerly to fully commercialized mass culture with no ability to be skeptical, (b) the person actually thinks there is something original about having a tattoo when exactly the opposite applies—more evidence of an inability to think critically, (c) the person is unable to picture the future when this fad will have fully expired—evidence of an inability to think ahead, and (d) the

[36] See n 33 above.

[37] CR Sanders, *Customizing the Body: The Art and Culture of Tattooing* (Philadelphia, Temple University Press, 1989).

[38] Drazewski (n 28).

[39] Thompson, *Covered in Ink* (n 24) 103.

> person denigrates (or simply doesn't consider) the reactions of others, showing lack of thoughtfulness. It's notable that there is absolutely nothing positive about tattoos.[40]

Another wrote that:

> If there was a rule saying that tattoos actually had to say verbally the reason/attribute the person got it, what would they say? My candidates: 'Poor Impulse Control' (credit: Neil Stephenson); 'Seeks Attention'; 'Illiterate' (we've all seen this one 'spelled' out); 'Ignorant'; 'Needy'; 'Insecure'; 'Hoping This Tattoo Convinces You I'm A {Badass/Rebel}'; 'Pathetic'. Who would want to hire a person who has permanently marked themselves into a condition where they cannot stop making these statements?[41]

vi. Does the Stereotype Reduce the Humanity of Those Who Are Its Targets?

There is a large amount of intolerance and dismissal of the tattooed—they are subject to disparagement, such as: 'If you have a visible tattoo then you are stupid. Which is why employers should avoid them.'[42] Tattooed women are subjected to sexually derogatory comments—a tattoo at the base of a woman's spine is sometimes referred to as a 'slag tag' or 'tramp stamp'.[43] There is no similar equivalent for tattooed men.

vii. Do These Targets Have Low Social Power and Low Interpersonal Status?

Society perceives the tattooed differently, and for many decades conspicuous tattoos led to a loss of social status. However, as tattoos have been 'repackaged'[44] by the middle class, this is no longer the case. Tattooed persons do not per se have low social power or interpersonal status in or beyond the workplace. In fact, given their prevalence amongst celebrities, tattooed persons can have significant amounts of social power and status. A tattoo fully covering the back can be easily covered to satisfy the dress code in a bank or a law firm. Yet, there may be a race and gender lens to this question: according to Thompson, black men and poor whites are subjected to profiling by the authorities, white women who transgress femininity with their tattoos endure public interpersonal sanctions and tattooed black women are criminalised. It seems that the tattoo itself does not determine loss of social status; rather the general status of the tattooed person determines this.

[40] glnz 3 August 2014, 22:32.
[41] Jake Swenson 3 August 2014, 16:52.
[42] Subscre_E 2 August 2014, 10:24.
[43] APenNameAndThatA 2 August 2014, 04:42.
[44] Margo DeMello, *Bodies of Inscription: A Cultural History of the Modern Tattoo Community* (Durham, Duke University Press, 2000).

viii. Do These Targets Suffer Discrimination as a Result?

Discrimination in employment may explain why tattoo removal has increased 440% in the last 10 years.[45] Many firms claim that maximising profits calls for pandering to customer expectations,[46] an argument used many years ago in relation to race. Given the social label associated with tattoos, they discriminate against applicants and employees with tattoos. Many have explicit anti-tattoo policies, such as HMV: in 2012 the music store introduced a new policy banning its staff from wearing prominent tattoos. Its updated dress code stated an expectation of a 'high level of personal grooming'. It instructed staff to cover up or remove tattoos and 'extreme body art'. Discrete tattoos or piercings could be worn. These guidelines were apparently designed to balance the expression of personality with customer expectations.[47]

Dismissal and refusal to hire or promote is common in white and blue collar jobs across the UK. For example, in 2012, a female procurement consultant in Milton Keynes had her contract terminated because of a visible 4 cm image of a butterfly on her foot which contravened the no-visible-inking policy of her employer. A 39-year-old mother-of-three from Yorkshire with a tattoo on her arm stating that 'Everything happens for a reason' was, in 2013, fired as a waitress when customers complained. An employee working at retail giant Next was fired because his managers disliked his 80 tattoos.[48] A bus-girl in a restaurant was refused her promised promotion after she had a 'half-sleeve' tattoo painted on her arm—she was told that it was better for her to wash dishes in the kitchen than serve tables front-of-house.

Tattoos have also stunted the careers of persons working with children. In 2014, a school assistant with tattoos on her arms and facial piercings resigned after she was told that these body modifications were not setting a good example and should be covered. A childminder was also warned that her body modifications (piercing and tattoos) could lose potential clients to the business.[49]

ix. Do the Targets Suffer Exclusion?

Research by Andrew Timming amongst service-sector managers has shown that tattooed applicants consistently rank lower as job candidates, despite being as qualified as people without tattoos. Many managers across the sector are wary of placing applicants with very visible tattoos in customer-facing roles. He concluded that visible tattoos were a 'turn-off' for hiring managers. His research has revealed

[45] See n 3 above.

[46] Post, 'Prejudicial Appearances' (n 23).

[47] S Joseph, 'HMV bans staff tattoos to boost customer experience' (24 October 2012), available at http://www.marketingweek.com/2012/10/24/hmv-bans-staff-tattoos-to-boost-customer-experience/.

[48] J Kelly, 'Should anti-tattoo discrimination be illegal?', BBC News Magazine (18 August 2014), available at http://www.bbc.co.uk/news/magazine-28758900.

[49] 'I lost a job because of my tattoos', http://www.bbc.co.uk/news/magazine-29211526

that if a person with visible tattoos was hired, managers think clients would associate the company with words like 'untidy', 'repugnant' and 'unsavoury'. Enforcement agencies are tattoo-averse: the Metropolitan Police, for example, bans tattoos on the face, neck and hands, above the collar line as well as tattoos anywhere on the body that are 'discriminatory, violent or intimidating'.[50] A recent court case confirmed that the national police in Germany can reject a job application if the candidate has visible tattoos because the German state cannot be represented by tattooed persons.[51] Decisions mirror those taken by courts in the USA.[52]

However, there is variance between and within sectors, depending on the expectations of the clientele. In the airline industry policies differ from one company to another. Some have a very strict ban, and go to significant lengths to uphold it. Singapore Airlines, for example, apparently checks its female flight attendants for tattoos by having them appear in swimsuits. Monarch Airlines does not subject staff to a quasi-beauty parade but does question cabin crews about visible as well as hidden tattoos. Ryanair also forbid visible tattoos—only those that can be covered by the uniform are allowed.[53] Emirates and Easyjet appear most flexible. Emirates asks specifically about any tattoos that might be visible in uniform, and employees are required to sign a statement confirming the absence of tattoos on 'unacceptable' areas: lower arms, legs mid-calf down, and the neck. Easyjet is even more flexible, and the company will apparently issue long sleeved shirts if the employee has tattoos on the arms and wrist.[54]

Requests to cover are also made by airlines in countries where tattoos belong to traditional culture. In such circumstances this could potentially be indirect race discrimination. In New Zealand, where tattooing is integral to Maori culture, Air New Zealand found itself in trouble when it insisted that a Maori applicant for a cabin position cover her '*ta moko*', a traditional Maori tattoo symbolising identity and reflecting history.[55] The *ta moko* is often on the face but Claire Nathan wore hers on her forearm. Nathan had been asked to complete a form containing a question on visible tattoos, and she wrote that she had a *ta moko* on her left arm, depicting her children and heritage. Her interview was stopped immediately this came to light. She was told by the airline that because she was applying for a customer-facing role, tattoos that could not be covered by the uniform were unacceptable. The airline dress code banned visible tattoos to accommodate customer

[50] 'No tattoo if you want the job!', available at http://rt.com/uk/190572-tattoo-convention-jobs-fired/ (3 October 2014).

[51] 'Urteil in Darmstadt: Bundespolizei darf Bewerberin wegen Tätowierung ablehnen' *Der Spiegel Online*, available at http://www.spiegel.de/panorama/justiz/bundespolizei-darf-bewerberin-wege.

[52] *Riggs v City of Fort Worth* 229 F.Supp.2d 572 (ND Tex 2002); *Inturri v City of Hartford* 305-2114, 165 Fed Appx 66, 2006 US App Lexis 2538 (2d Cir., 31 January 2006).

[53] See http://www.cabincrew.com.

[54] 'The Trouble with Tattoos' (11 June 2013), available at http://www.cabincrew.com/lifestyle/the-trouble-with-tattoos/1116.

[55] Jim Roberts and Michael O'Brien, 'A Lot of Ink Gets Used on Tattoos' (4 July 2013), available from http://www.heskethhenry.co.nz/Articles.html.

preference: Air New Zealand said the policy was intended to make customers comfortable as apparently many came from cultures where tattoos were considered to be frightening or intimidating.

The public response to this ban was surprise and skepticism, on three fronts. First, Air New Zealand uses a Maori image, the *koru*,[56] in its logo. Second, it regularly uses heavily tattooed celebrities, such as pop singer Gin Wigmore and the All Blacks national rugby team, in advertising campaigns. Third, other airlines in New Zealand have more flexibility towards cultural tattoos. Jetstar, for example, requires all tattoos to be covered while on duty but the dress code makes allowances for cultural tattoos. Virgin Airlines and Qantas are as 'brand sensitive' as Air New Zealand, requiring all tattoos to be covered, which is not always possible with cultural tattoos such as the *ta moko* especially if worn on the face as per tradition.

x. *Is Their Access to Key Resources Blocked?*

A tattoo is a risk in some areas of employment, especially work in the services sector that is client facing. Even in office jobs where most work is conducted on the phone, managers often force inked persons to cover up their body art, even in summer and even if this is a detriment to their health.[57] However, as discussed earlier, some workplaces are tattoo friendly. Also, beyond employment there are few examples of the type of blanket exclusion seen in relation to other characteristics. For example, it is unlikely that a tattooed person would be excluded from a club in central London, as a black woman was for being 'too dark' and 'too fat'.[58] Public spaces remain open to persons with tattoos, and tattooed persons are not profiled by the police or subjected to hate-based violence—there are too many famous people with tattoos for that to happen. There are tattooed persons in advertisements and on television, and there are television shows about tattooed persons. The aversion to tattoos at work does not result in total societal rejection and punishment. Unlike being overweight or obese, having a tattoo does not affect multiple areas of everyday life—there is no difficulty with access to public spaces or healthcare and hospitals, educational institutions or other goods and services. Thus while there may be financial consequences, the experience of tattoo discrimination is unlikely to lead to depression, anxiety, self-harm or suicide. The only exception to this may be where the tattoo is an ancestral form of identity such as the *ta moko*.

[56] In Maori design, the koru is commonly used as a symbol of creation because of its fluid circular shape. Based on the unfurling fern frond of the native New Zealand silver fern, the circular shape of the koru conveys the idea of perpetual movement, while its inner coil, the corm with rolled up inner leaflets, suggests a return to the point of origin. In the larger scheme, this is a metaphor for the way in which life both changes and stays the same. See http://www.mountainjade.co.nz/blog/the-koru-meaning-new-life-harmony/.

[57] Drazewski (n 28).

[58] J Elgot, 'Dstrkt nightclub denies ban on dark and overweight women', *The Guardian* (1 October 2015), available at http://www.theguardian.com/uk-news/2015/oct/01/dstrkt-nightclub-denies-ban-dark-overweight-women-west-end-london.

IV. Legal Protection Against Ink-ism

Around the world, the law tends not to protect tattooed employees: in Germany and the USA[59] courts have held that public employees—in particular the police—can be asked to cover their tattoos or be banned from having them. The UK Equality Act 2010 offers no protection—secondary legislation was specifically introduced to clarify that tattoos and piercings were excluded. The Equality Act 2010 (Disability) Regulations 2010[60] updated the previous statutory instrument setting out per se exclusions from the definition of a disability. As of 2010, tattoos and body piercings were included in this list, thus they are not seen as severe disfigurements that have a substantial adverse effect on the ability of a person to carry out normal day-to-day activities. They rank alongside hay fever, exhibitionism, voyeurism and some mental health conditions (a tendency to set fires, steal, or physically or sexually abuse other persons) which are also expressly excluded.

It cannot be denied that people with tattoos experience differential treatment because of their tattoos; however, in most cases it is hard to equate this with the discrimination associated with many other protected characteristics. While there is clearly intolerance and negative treatment in the workplace, beyond this sphere it is neither as intense nor punitive. The difficulties at work do not spill over into life in general such that tattooed people suffer comprehensive everyday subjugation and dehumanisation. The only exception to this may be where the tattoo is part of racial or religious identity: in these cases, however, protection would be provided under the characteristics of race or religion.

It may be that tattoos should be treated under race or religion in the same way as addiction under disability. Usually an addiction to any substance does not amount to a disability under the Equality Act 2010 unless it is rooted in a medical condition, which means that addictions that are the result of former medically prescribed drugs or medical procedures are included. Likewise, tattoo discrimination should be prohibited when it is linked to a racial or ethnic identity, or religious belief. This approach would protect the peoples of America, New Zealand and Australia whose cultural traditions of tattooing have been disparaged by white European imperialists, thus protecting Native American tribes, Aboriginal peoples and members of the Maori tribes. This approach has already been proposed in Australia.

[59] J Gorner, 3 July 2015, 'Chicago Police officers sue over tattoo cover up rule' http://www.chicagotribune.com/news/local/breaking/ct-chicago-police-tattoo-lawsuit-met-20150702-story.html

[60] Equality Act 2010 (Disability) Regulations 2010 (SI 2010/2128), on the definition of disability in the Equality Act 2010 (entering into force on 1 October 2010), replacing the Disability Discrimination (Meaning of Disability) Regulations 1996 (SI 1996/1455).

A. Race, Ethnic or National Origin

Ottley and Sowden suggest that requests to cover up a tattoo can be indirect discrimination if

> the wearing of a tattoo is common to a particular race (for example it is part of their culture), there may be room for arguing that requiring a person of that race to comply with a condition (such as covering up tattoos) is discriminatory, on the basis that the condition or requirement is one which a substantially higher proportion of people not of that race, comply or are able to comply.[61]

As discussed in Chapter 2, Australia has anti-discrimination law at national and state level. The Racial Discrimination Act 1975 prohibits discrimination on the basis of race, colour, nationality or ethnic origin. It may therefore provide protection to persons wearing culturally specific tattoos as an expression of their race or ethnic origin, unless the organisational requirement to be non-tattooed or cover it up could be justified. The employer would need to be able to demonstrate the existence of compelling business reasons to support the dress code. In the absence of this, the prohibition could constitute a requirement which has the effect of nullifying or impairing that expression. The employee's reasons for wearing the tattoo would therefore be very important to the case. However, as can be seen in *Haupini*, this approach is not always successful.

In 2010 the New Zealand Human Rights Commission participated in its first case concerning tattoos. The case revolved around the *ta moko*. Ms Haupini[62] worked for a catering and food service company owned by SRCC. She wore a *ta moko* on her forearm and was instructed by her employer to cover it up, as it was considered to look unprofessional. Haupini brought a claim of race discrimination, asserting that she had been afforded less favourable conditions at work and subjected to a detriment on the basis of her race, ethnic or national origins constituting direct discrimination contrary to the New Zealand Human Rights Act. This was denied by the employer, who nevertheless asserted the right to impose a dress code which prohibited visible tattoos. This was an important case because it was the first of its kind to go to a hearing—previous cases had settled. Thus it enabled the Human Rights Tribunal to hear evidence and oral submissions.[63]

The Tribunal found for the employer. It held there was no discrimination on the basis of race for a number of reasons. First, the company norm was not to

[61] R Ottley and L Sowden, 'Can an employer ban tattoos in the workplace? 15 December 2012, available at http://www.mondaq.com/australia/x/211352/employee+rights+labour+relations/Can+an+employer+ban+tattoos+in+the+workplace.

[62] *Haupini v SRCC Holdings Ltd* (2011) 9 NZCLC 93, 952; [2011] NZHRRT 20; *Haupini v SRCC Holdings Ltd* HRRT 27/2010.

[63] Annual Report 2011, Human Rights Commission Te Kahui Tika Tangata and the Office of Human Rights Proceedings Te Tari Whakatau Take Tika Tangata, p 38, available at http://www.parliament.nz/resource/mi-nz/50DBHOH_PAP22323_1/d56e1be0f81c78d1f8573884d657df38ebde9716.

ask Maoris to cover their tattoos—the instruction had been given in relation to a specific client function. Thus there was a reasonable business-related reason for the request. Second, given this reason, no discriminatory intent was found. Third, the request was held to be a reasonable option as it was temporary. Fourth, Nathan did not inform her employer that she objected to the request, giving no chance for its retraction. The tribunal concluded that it would be wrong to force what it felt was really a claim for direct discrimination on the basis of culture into concepts of race and/or national or ethnic origin.[64] The request to cover up was not closely enough related to her race or ethnicity to constitute an act of direct (or even indirect) discrimination. Yet, it went on to say that even as a claim based on culture, it would hesitate to accept the argument that every Māori would consider an organisational 'no tattoos' policy to be 'disrespectful of their whakapapa, cultural tradition and custom'[65] in the absence of strong supporting evidence.

B. Culture

Culture is not a prohibited ground of discrimination under the New Zealand Human Rights Act 1973, but it is prohibited by the New Zealand Bill of Rights Act[66] (NZBORA) which specifically protects minority rights to the enjoyment of culture. The protection from discrimination in section 19 of NZBOA is limited to the grounds set out in the Human Rights Act 1993[67] but section 20 is broader—it deals with the rights of minorities and states:

> A person who belongs to an ethnic, religious, or linguistic minority in New Zealand shall not be denied the right, in community with other members of that minority, to enjoy the culture, to profess and practice the religion, or to use the language, of that minority.

Section 3 of NZBORA limits application of this Act to actions of the government and public authorities but this could be interpreted to extend it to the acts of others.[68] In order to succeed under section 20, it would therefore have to be

[64] *Haupini* [2011] (n 62) [53]. See also M Chen, 'SuperDiversity Stocktake: Implications for Business, Government and New Zealand' (New Zealand, SuperDiversity Centre for Law, Policy and Business, 2015).

[65] *Haupini* [2011] (n 62) [62.b].

[66] New Zealand Bill of Rights Act 1990—Public Act 1990 No. 109. Date of Assent: 28 August 1990.

[67] Section 19 Freedom from discrimination: '(1) Everyone has the right to freedom from discrimination on the grounds of discrimination in the Human Rights Act 1993. (2) Measures taken in good faith for the purpose of assisting or advancing persons or groups of persons disadvantaged because of discrimination that is unlawful by virtue of Part 2 of the Human Rights Act 1993 do not constitute discrimination.'

[68] Chen considers that this may not be an obstacle as the United Nations Human Rights Committee has stated in its General Comment on the interpretation of Art 27 of the ICCPR (the equivalent of section 20), that it requires the state to take positive steps to prevent the denial of the right by third parties: UNHRC *General Comment 18—Non-discrimination* UN Doc HRI/GEN/1/Rev 1(1994). A similar conclusion has been reached, for example, in respect of the right to life and the right to freedom from

established that a sufficient proportion of Maori would agree that a no tattoos policy denies their right to enjoy culture. However, denials can be justified under section 5 which states:

> subject to Section 4, the rights and freedoms contained in this Bill of Rights may be subject only to such reasonable limits prescribed by law as can be demonstrably justified in a free and democratic society.

The Tribunal in *Haupini* did not say explicitly that the employer had a good reason for the request. It only noted that there was scope for such a policy to be reasonable.[69]

C. Physical Features

The Equal Opportunity Act 2010 in the state of Victoria, Australia includes a prohibition of discrimination on the basis of 'physical features'. This prohibition is unique—Victoria is the only Australian jurisdiction to provide legal protection on this basis. The definition of 'physical features' includes height, weight, size or other bodily characteristics. The phrase 'bodily characteristics' has been interpreted widely to include tattoos as well as the styling, colour and location of hair.[70] However, it excludes personal hygiene (such as body odour), not wearing underwear, overeating as well as transsexualism.[71]

A refusal to employ or decision to terminate employment on this ground therefore constitutes discrimination. However, there are three exceptions—this does not apply if the position is for work in the employer's home (for example as a home help) or work in a dramatic or an artistic performance, photographic or modelling work or any similar employment. It also does not apply where the discrimination is reasonably necessary to protect the health, safety or property of any person (including the person discriminated against).[72]

There has been just one case—*Jamieson*[73]—which suggests that tattoos can be considered to constitute a *physical feature*. However, in this case the Tribunal came to its decision without explicitly holding that tattoos are physical features. Nonetheless, Jamieson can be interpreted to provide individuals in Victoria with specific protection from discrimination on account of their tattoos.

torture, both of which oblige the state to also take action to prevent threats to these rights by private persons or entities.

[69] *Haupini* [2011] (n 62) [68].

[70] See *Fratas v Drake International Ltd t/as Drake Jobseek* (1998) EOC 93-038 VCAT.

[71] However, this has been held to constitute an impairment—see *Menzies v Waycott & Anor* [2001] VCAT 415.

[72] *Hill v Canterbury Road Lodge Pty Ltd* [2004] VCAT 1365.

[73] *Jamieson v Benalla Golf Club Inc* (2000) VCAT 1849 (30 September 2000).

D. Free Speech

There has been one case in California, where the process of tattooing—rather than tattoos themselves—has been protected by law. In *Anderson*,[74] the Californian Federal Court was asked to consider whether a municipal ban on tattoo shops violated the First Amendment on free speech. The question arose when Mr Anderson sought to open a tattoo parlour in the city of Hermosa Beach but could not as these shops were banned by the Hermosa Beach Municipal Code.[75] He argued that this was unconstitutional under the First (free speech) and Fourteenth (citizenship rights and equal protection of the laws) Amendments.

Many other courts had already been asked this question on free speech and had decided that such a ban was compatible with the First Amendment.[76] The Federal Court in *Anderson* disagreed, recognising the act of tattooing as constituting 'speech' and therefore as protected by the first amendment right of free speech:

> We hold that tattooing is purely expressive activity fully protected by the First Amendment, and that a total ban on such activity is not a reasonable 'time, place, or manner' restriction.[77]

The ban was therefore unconstitutional, and thus employees in California who claim discrimination based on their tattoos may be successful if the tattoo depicts political speech or religious expression.

V. Conclusion

Chapter 7 explored the potential of the anti-stigma principle to expand the scope of anti-discrimination; this chapter has considered how effective it can be to determine the outer limits of anti-discrimination law, using tattoos as an example. Many social and labour shifts have occurred in the last decades. From the idea of a job for life, we now have a labour market characterised as 'precarious'.[78] Young people entering and moving up or through the labour market face different challenges and have different expectations of their jobs and employers. While

[74] *Anderson v City of Hermosa Beach* 621 F.3d 1051 (9th Cir 2010).

[75] Code § 17.06.070.

[76] *Hold Fast Tattoo, LLC v City of North Chicago*, 580 F.Supp.2d 656, 659–61 (N.D.Ill. 2008); *Yurkew v Sinclair*, 495 F.Supp. 1248, 1253–55 (D.Minn. 1980); *State v Brady*, 492 N.E.2d 34, 39 (Ind. Ct. App. 1986); *People v O'Sullivan*, 96 Misc.2d 52, 409 N.Y.S.2d 332, 333 (1978); *State v White*, 348 S.C. 532, 560 S.E.2d 420, 423–24 (2002); *Blue Horseshoe Tattoo, V, Ltd v City of Norfolk*, 72 Va. Cir. 388, 390 (Cir. Ct. 2007).

[77] *Anderson v City of Hermosa Beach* 621 F.3d 1051 (9th Cir 2010).

[78] J Fudge and R Owens, 'Precarious Work, Women and the New Economy: The Challenge to Legal Norms' in J Fudge and R Owens, *Precarious Work, Women and the New Economy: The Challenge to Legal Norms* (Oxford, Hart Publishing, 2006) 3.

they may not expect a job for life, they may have a higher expectation of respect for their individuality and diversity. They are thus less accepting of organisational rules relating to their personal appearance and will turn to law to defend these rights. They have been disappointed thus far: employers may lawfully refuse to hire someone because they have a tattoo, lawfully ask employees to cover up any visible tattoos while at work, and lawfully dismiss an employee for getting a tattoo.[79] This may help to explain why tattoo removal has increased dramatically in the last 10 years.[80]

It is questionable that in the twentieth century, courts should allow customer preferences to influence employer conduct. These same arguments were used to justify race discrimination in the UK and elsewhere in the 1960s and 1970s, when workplaces were more segregated. Employers can no longer lawfully respond to customer preferences to work only with white employees or men. Why do courts thus allow employers to lawfully impose vague ideas that customers prefer non-tattooed employees? If the law were to say no to this justification, courts would have to do the same. However, on the contrary, the UK Equality Act specifically excludes tattoos.

There seems to be strong evidence that persons with tattoos are unfairly excluded from the labour market. Yet the evidence also shows that much depends upon the nature of the organisation's business, its culture and perhaps even the whim of a specific manager. Thus it remains debateable whether anti-discrimination law should provide specific protection.

Tattoos can be seen as a choice with consequences. These consequences are not always exclusionary. Even in the workplace it is often *visible* tattoos that are banned not tattoos per se: there are even tattoo-friendly workplaces.[81] Treatment is (sometimes) negative rather than punitive. Employers are already willing to accommodate tattoos in a way that is not always extended to individuals with other protected characteristics. Finally, it is very likely that the march of time is on the side of the tattooed. Attitudes are changing quickly as tattooing becomes a more normalised and white middle-class phenomenon. According to Timming:

> Tattooed applicants can take comfort in the fact that the stigma associated with body art appears to be on the wane and that, as a corollary, there will likely be an increase in the number of potentially sympathetic tattooed hiring managers.[82]

A tipping point will appear when there are enough tattooed managers to make this less of an issue at work. Attitudes will also change irreversibly due to the numbers

[79] 'No tattoo if you want the job!' (3 October 2014), available at http://rt.com/uk/190572-tattoo-convention-jobs-fired/.

[80] See n 3 above.

[81] Thompson, *Covered in Ink* (n 24) 119.

[82] AR Timming, D Nickson, D Re and DI Perrett, 'What Do You Think of My Ink? Assessing the Effects of Body Art on Employment Chances' (2015) *Human Resource Management*. http://www.britsoc.co.uk/media/57046/Tattoos_reduce_chances_of_getting_a_job_new_research_says_2_PR030913.pdf.

of younger well-educated people with tattoos entering the labour market. Attitudes will thus change irrespective of the law as employers—especially those seeking specialist skills—come to realise that they cannot afford to exclude talent. This is already visible in the military where, faced with flagging recruitment figures, the British Army is considering a relaxation of its rules to permit tattoos on the face, neck and hands. The US Army has also amended its code to permit tattoos, but content and location are strictly set out. Tattoos may not be of images that are extremist, indecent, sexist or racist or on the face; sleeve and band tattoos are forbidden below the elbow or knee, as are more than four tattoos in these locations.[83]

Thus in the near future it may be more the size and place of a tattoo that makes the difference rather than the tattoo per se. Timming argues that design will also be key: racist symbols and depictions of drugs, violence, crime, football or death are likely to remain problematic—in other words any depiction that can be associated with something negative. Even now many employers accept small inoffensive, gender appropriate[84] tattoos that can be covered.

Bearing this in mind, the anti-stigma principle would not lead to the introduction of specific legal protection from tattoo discrimination. It would preserve the protection of anti-discrimination law for stigmatised groups whose 'experiences of relative powerlessness occur frequently and across multiple contexts and are not balanced or somehow offset by high power experiences'.[85] While the treatment is undoubtedly unfair, tattoo prohibitions at work do not satisfy the procedural test of the anti-stigma principle. A tattoo is always a symbol of something, however basic that may be. Not only do the tattooed choose when to be tattooed, but also where to have the tattoo and the design of the tattoo. There is therefore nothing arbitrary about a tattoo—it always has a very personal meaning. In addition, for many a tattoo is a mark that can be discarded, since even permanent tattoos can now be removed.[86] Persons like Claire Nathan or Haupini who wear a tattoo that is a mark of belonging—either to a particular tribe as in maori culture or a religion, like the *ta moko*—would be protected under the anti-stigma principle, as this would be indirect discrimination due to race and/or religion.

[83] Army Regulation 670-1 'wear and appearance of army uniforms and insignia'.

[84] Thompson, *Covered in Ink* (n 24).

[85] LS Richmann and MR Lattanner 'Self-regulatory Processes Underlying Structural Stigma and Health', (2014) 103 *Social Science and Medicine*, 95.

[86] 'Tattoos are no longer permanent but removal can be a long and costly business' *The Telegraph* (12 January 2015), available at http://www.telegraph.co.uk/news/health/11330641/Tattoos-are-no-longer-permanent-but-removal-can-be-a-long-and-costly-business.html.

Conclusion

The aim of this book was to develop a theory of anti-discrimination law that would enable the reconstruction of what, how and who this law 'sees'. My aim was to create a law to prevent and protect from discrimination by tackling the social as well as interpersonal and institutional acts of discrimination. I attempted to do by using the idea of stigma to create an anti-stigma principle that highlights the social sphere and power. I illustrated that stigma is a concept used in litigation in both national and international courts—from South Africa and Australia to the European Union. It is also used across a range of disciplines from development studies to zoology. The anti-stigma principle is therefore inter-disciplinary, as it is built using insights on stigma from critical social psychological, criminology, sociology and public health.

My starting point was that stigma is the source of all discrimination. Stigmatised groups are like faces at the bottom of a well[1]—we do not see them and if we do, we pay no attention to them. As Loury argues in relation to racial discrimination, stigma desensitises society to the suffering of groups and so plays a significant role in the perpetuation of discrimination. Current laws designed to combat discrimination do little to tackle stigma and social understanding.[2] Anti-discrimination law based upon the anti-stigma principle would, however, do so.

Desensitisation skews social understanding of discrimination, as do narratives of colour blindness which have been used to support discrimination as well as oppose it. For example, it supported Jim Crow voting restrictions, literacy tests and other facially race neutral rules that disadvantaged black people.[3] The social consciousness of the anti-stigma principle takes the opposite approach to 'blindness': if anti-discrimination law is to promote blindness, it should be to social meaning not the attribute itself. As Andrews points out, just because difference was used as an indice for domination and oppression does not make difference per se wrong.[4] In promoting 'blindness' public policy makers fall into the trap

[1] D. Bell, Faces at the Bottom of the Well: the Permanence of Racism (New York, Basic Books, 1992).

[2] G Loury, 'Racial Stigma: Toward a New Paradigm for Discrimination Theory'. Essay drawn upon a paper, 'Racial Justice: The Superficial Morality of Colour-Blindness in the United States', prepared for the United Nations Research Institute for Social Development, and delivered at the World Conference Against Racism, Durban, South Africa, September 2001.

[3] FC Harris and RC Lieberman (eds), *Beyond Discrimination: Racist Equality in a Postracist Era* (Russell Sage Foundation, 2013) 18.

[4] K Andrews, 'The Problem of Political Blackness: Lessons from the Black Suplementary School Movement' (2016) *Ethnic and Racial Studies* 1466.

of problematising difference rather than the social attitudes that make forms of difference negative.

The anti-stigma principle broadens the focus of anti-discrimination law, as it emphasises that it is the social meaning that we need to be blind to not the characteristic itself. Identification of stigma as the source of discrimination is akin to the 'social model'[5] of disability, which also emphasises that the problem of discrimination lies not in the attribute but 'results from the structures, practices and attitudes that prevent the person from exercising his or her capabilities'.[6] Stigma highlights that the problems of 'legislating disability'[7] apply to some extent to anti-discrimination law as a whole. In effect, current anti-discrimination law adopts the medical model of disability: it looks at the attribute of a person as an 'impairment' rather than regarding the response to that attribute as the problem.

The anti-stigma principle therefore takes the social model from being the norm of disability discrimination law to being the norm for anti-discrimination law as a whole. In so doing it institutionalises within anti-discrimination law the fact that the burden of stigma is asymmetric: it is borne by the targets, who must become adept at managing responses of perceivers to the stigma on an everyday basis. It makes anti-discrimination law sensitive to the 'informational signals' attached to attributes, statuses and conditions as well as the behaviours evoked in response to these signals. Identification, investigation and correction of such 'signals' therefore becomes as key to effectively challenging discrimination as litigation. Recognition of the modes of transmission of these signals also becomes important.

Starting with Goffman's study of stigma, I highlighted that his work focused on interpersonal—or 'face to face'—interaction in 'mixed' settings, where stigmatised persons interact with those who are not stigmatised. His interest was to observe what happened in these settings between 'normals', 'discredited' and 'discreditable' individuals. He did not consider the background or contexts of his subjects, just how they behaved with each other. His approach to stigma continues to inform much work in the behavioural sciences.

However, critical scholars addressed the a-contextual setting of his work by prioritising the environment and emphasising the role of power in stigma. The factors identified by Link and Phelan not only explain the process of stigmatisation but also how it contributes to discrimination, because powerful groups use their power to label and stereotype less powerful groups, and utilise a range of mechanisms for discriminatory outcomes.[8] Hannem and Bruckert use the work

[5] C Barnes and G Mercer (eds), *The Social Model of Disability: Europe and the Majority World* (The Disability Press 2005).

[6] K Wells, 'The Impact of the Framework Employment Directive on UK Disability Discrimination Law' 2003 32 *Industrial Law Journal* 253.

[7] F Kumari Campbell, 'Legislating Disability: Negative Ontologies and the Government of Legal Identities' in S Tremain (ed), *Foucault and the Government of Disability* (Ann Arbor, University of Michigan Press, 2005).

[8] BG Link and JC Phelan, 'Conceptualizing Stigma' (2001) 27 *Annual Review of Sociology* 378.

of Foucault to create a concept that is both interpersonal and institutional, highlighting that stigma is about low social power *and* low interpersonal status. They developed a theoretical perspective recognising stigma as multi-level, 'symbolically realised in individual interactions and structurally embedded in the cultural values, practices and institutions of a society'.[9] They define structural stigma as a process that occurs 'when stigmatic assumptions become embedded in social policies and practices'. The process results in a contamination of certain attributes and a dehumanisation of those with these attributes.

A critical understanding of stigma therefore recognises that stigma and stigmatisation are social practices. Stigma is a process not just of what people do to each other (interpersonal power) but also of what society entertains and allows people to do to each other (institutional power). Stigmatisation is an inescapable 'persistent predicament',[10] that is, a general pattern of disadvantage that is connected to processes of labeling, stereotyping, status loss, and discrimination. The process of stigmatisation begins with identification of an arbitrary attribute or condition. A stigma is first and foremost not something *in the person* but a designation or tag that others affix to the person because of an arbitrary 'mark'. That marked attribute or condition is then given a meaning and used as a label to demean and treat in a dehumanised way.

This definition recognises stigma as a social practice engaged in by individuals and institutions, in both private and public spheres where both support the other.[11] The power imbalance is played out between individuals but is rooted in larger social practices, such as media portrayals or even welfare policies. Stigma may be, but does not need to be, embedded in policy. It can just be 'common sense' that provides the context for individuals to dehumanise others. A white vigilante can shoot and kill a young black male like Trayvon Martin with impunity because of the existence of a social common sense: 'everybody knows' that young black boys are dangerous and the high incarceration rates exists to prove it. An employer who harasses a young woman like Rachael Bayliss Flannery in the workplace feels free to do so because 'everybody knows' young black women are promiscuous and the images of young black women in film, media, literature and music exist to prove it.

Models of stigma based upon this more critical definition are multi-factoral, multi-layered and dynamic. They incorporate multiple spheres: Pryor and Reeder use the idea that there are four types of stigma—public stigma, self-stigma, stigma by association and structural stigma—occurring on three levels—societal,

[9] S Hannem and C Bruckert (eds), *Stigma Re-visited: Re-examining the Mark* (University of Ottowa Press, 2012), 10.

[10] 'Conceptualising Stigma' (n 8) 378.

[11] JE Pachankis, ML Hatzenbuehler and TJ Starks, 'The influence of structural stigma and rejection sensitivity on young sexual minority men's daily tobacco and alcohol use' (2014) 103 *Social Science & Medicine* 67.

interpersonal and individual.[12] Public stigma, as the root of all stigma, is at the centre of their model. Likewise, the 'Stigma Mechanisms in Health Disparities' model centres public stigma. Public stigma can be defined as a collective negative reaction to a stigma that confers lower social status and power to those who possess the stigmatized attribute. It 'initiates a cascade of processes that ultimately lead to disparate outcomes among stigmatized and non-stigmatized individuals'.

Pryor and Reeder introduce a new language to anti-discrimination law—instead of 'victims' and 'perpetrators' it is possible to speak of 'targets' and 'perceivers'. A 'target' is the person with the stigmatised attributes and the 'perceiver' is the person who stigmatises. This language highlights that stigmatisation is a deliberate action: perceivers use stigma as a justification to treat targets of stigma as if they should *never* have any expectation to enjoy full and equal participation in social, political and economic life. As shown in Chapters 7 and 8, the anti-stigma principle would not require anti-discrimination law to protect all stigma, only those which satisfy certain conditions. While weight discrimination would be protected according to the anti-stigma principle, tattoo discrimination would not—wearing tattoos cannot be seen as a 'persistent predicament'. Other laws can be created where necessary, such as the Part Time Workers Regulation 2000.[13]

The anti-stigma principle can inform the reconstruction of anti-discrimination law, which would refer to 'stigmatised characteristics' instead of 'protected characteristics'. The principle can correct the vision of anti-discrimination law to see both social practices and individual behaviour. It recognises the *dynamic* nature of stigma, its *embeddedness* in society and its *arbitrary* nature. It can also recognise multiple stigma. It can be summarised as 'stigma-plus': Goffman's understanding of stigma, plus a structural and an environmental perspective. It is the understanding of the role of stigma in interpersonal relations within the context of social relations—it frames human interaction within broader practices.

This multi-level view of stigma recognises it as a process within a context. It sets the individual—both stigmatised and stigmatiser—within a social environment which enables and facilitates this process. This context includes but is not limited to the built environment: as disability campaigners have pointed out, the absence of elevators or presence of stairs in public buildings can subtly stigmatise those with impaired mobility, and portraits of austere white men in august clothing displayed on the walls of public institutions can subtly inform women of colour that they do not belong to a specific tradition. It therefore allocates both individual and social responsibility for stigma.

Prioritisation of social norms in discrimination explicitly acknowledges that there is another point of responsibility for these acts: as well as the individual who is responsible for their actions, there is the society that is responsible for creation and

[12] ER Bos, JB Pryor, GD Reeder and S Stutterheim, 'Stigma Advances in Theory and Research' (2013) 35 *Basic and Applied Social Psychology* 1.

[13] Part Time Workers (Prevention of Less Favourable Treatment) Regulations 2000 (SI 2000/1551) (see *MoJ v Burton* 2015 UKEAT/0210/15/LA, 27 November 2015).

maintenance of discrimination-supporting norms, or stigma. The idea of social responsibility for discrimination does not remove responsibility from individuals, but recognises the role of the social context of discriminatory acts. Individuals that are devalued inside a normative framework will be devalued in everyday relations. Anti-discrimination law therefore needs to address stigma at the public or social level as well as at the individual face-to-face level.

The 'anti-stigma principle' in anti-discrimination law remains ocularcentric but adopts a broader vision. Foregrounding process throws attention upon context and the patterns by which differences have been constructed as such. To speak of patterns is to invoke historicity, a continued process of differentiation, and also to acknowledge the constituent forces of stigmatisation. These may change from place to place. However, the anti-stigma principle does not lose sight of the individual; rather, it sets individual actions within the context of 'common sense', systems and structures. An anti-discrimination law that recognises social practices addresses not only individual responsibility but also social responsibility. A logic of discrimination informed by the anti-stigma principle would by definition highlight individual (micro) and social (macro) practices, with both as important as the other.

Application of the anti-stigma principle has the potential to move the design of anti-discrimination law from a quasi-biological to a socio-relational basis. It takes social interaction as the starting point instead of immutability and individual attributes alone. In so doing, it steps beyond identity to address—as demanded by intersectionality—interlocking systems of oppression. It recognises that stigma(s) cannot be examined 'in isolation from the economic and social structure of a given society';[14] they widen the spotlight of discrimination law to society. They are by definition contextual: they are socially determined and maintained, thus to focus on them is to prioritise social meanings[15] and the background role of society in everyday discrimination. Restoration of the link between discrimination and society is necessary because discrimination law separated from society can lose its legitimacy if seen solely as a manifestation of identity politics.

Thus the anti-stigma principle restores the social in the framework of anti-discrimination law: society is complicit in discrimination—social mores are a repository of stigma providing justifications for everyday discriminatory actions and decision making. The anti-stigma principle disrupts the prevailing analysis of discrimination, making it multi-level and pluralist.

Discrimination in the social environment is perhaps the hardest sphere to tackle. Stigma at this level is diffuse, subtle and invisible. It is therefore at its most powerful. Yet there is very little in current anti-discrimination law that focuses on this important level, which is the source of stigma and thus the source of discrimination. So even if an immigration judge is forced to resign after making

[14] E Goffman, *Stigma: Notes on a Spoiled Identity* (London, Penguin, 1990) 1.
[15] R Page, *Stigma* (London, Routledge, 1984).

a racist comment[16] nothing is done about the stigma upon which this comment is based. It remains untouched and available to be drawn upon by another individual at another time and place.

Under the anti-stigma principle, tools to address this type of stigma become the norm rather than the exception of antidiscrimination law. The first generation of anti-discrimination law using the anti-stigma principle will mainstream social responsibility by focusing on collective action to tackle discrimination, alongside tools to tackle interpersonal discrimination. Legal action to tackle discrimination will need an approach as all encompassing and decisive as action to tackle public health viruses such as Ebola. In order to demonstrate the value of approaching discrimination as a virus, I compared the public action taken to combat the Ebola virus with the positive action envisaged as a collective mechanism in the Equality Act 2010. I suggested that positive action would arguably find stronger public support as a public health issue than an equality issue and proposed that instead of calling such measures 'positive action', initiatives at this level would be described as 'public action'. Instead of disconnected initiatives, public action would include more education and training, more communication at all levels, more public campaigns, and more conversation.

Finally, as the principle focuses on stigmatisation as a process rather than pre-formed categories it creates an anti-discrimination law that can tackle discrimination without having to worry about whether it is single dimensional or intersectional—the anti-stigma principle assumes complexity as its norm. It complements the single dimension approach and facilitates a multiple and intersectional vision.

The anti-stigma principle therefore reconstructs the vision of anti-discrimination law—it improves not only what it sees but also how it sees. By embedding anti-discrimination law in society rather than in the campaigns of resourceful interest groups, the anti-stigma principle makes it less susceptible to capture by powerful groups. It makes the rationale for anti-discrimination law transparent, clarifying why some attributes are included but not others. It sets a standard that operates as a flexible boundary. Any new claim for protection would need to demonstrate a social salience similar to existing attributes in order to qualify. The 'entry criteria' would include the factors set out in Chapter 7: arbitrariness, a history of oppression, inescapability, reduction of humanity, exclusion and purposeful discrimination as well as the absence of political power to obtain redress. Social data alone would not be enough to warrant protection under anti-discrimination law. Finally, as it is sensitive to context, the anti-stigma principle does not demand uniformity—as a principle that travels well, it could be used as a foundational principle of anti-discrimination law in the EU.

[16] N Bunyan, 'Judge resigns after making racist remark about victim' *The Guardian* (7 December 2014), available at http://www.theguardian.com/law/2014/dec/07/judge-resigns-racist-remark-about-victim-richard-hollingworth.

INDEX

Introductory Note

References such as '178–9' indicate (not necessarily continuous) discussion of a topic across a range of pages. Because the whole of this work is about 'stigma' and 'discrimination', use of these terms (and certain others which occur throughout) as entry points has been restricted. Please look under the appropriate detailed entries. Wherever possible in the case of topics with many references, these have either been divided into sub-topics or only the most significant discussions of the topic are listed.

www.ingramcontent.com/pod-product-compliance
Ingram Content Group UK Ltd.
Pitfield, Milton Keynes, MK11 3LW, UK
UKHW020138290926
15471UKWH00003B/566

9 781509 929825